Here's What Business Leaders and Travelers Say About This Book:

"Driving With No Brakes is a fascinating, inspiring, and enlightening look at the interwoven development of Grand Circle and the lives of Alan and Harriet Lewis. The use of stories, and the review of learning from mistakes, keeps the book at a very human and personal level and allows the reader to draw learning and inspiration from the Lewises' experience. Driving With No Brakes is not only worthwhile but a delight to read."

— Michael Brimm, Emeritus Professor of Organizational Behavior and Management, INSEAD

"Alan and Harriet have made a significant contribution—to companies for how they engage their employees at levels unseen even among the Fortune 100, to the concept of 'shared value,' where they combined their travelers' experience with social impact, and to the field for such a heartfelt rendering of their journey from big hearts to catalytic philanthropists."

— Kyle Peterson, Managing Director, FSG Social Impact Advisors

"Grand Circle's compassionate and sensible approach to philanthropy offers a wonderful model for other international organizations working to change the world. It's inspiring to witness how a simple concept, to help improve lives, has evolved into a worldwide effort involving hundreds if not thousands of people."

— Nancy Dunnan, Publisher, *TravelSmart*

"I like the humor, the full disclosure of mistakes, the playfulness, and the daring of this lively little volume. And I admire just how quickly Grand Circle's leaders learn from experience and put that learning to use by moving in new directions."

— Roland S. Barth, Education Consultant, Author, and Founding Director of Harvard Principals' Center

"For customers, Grand Circle is committed to being the best travel company for older Americans who want to experience peoples and places all over the world in ways that will change their lives. For employees, the objective is to provide a workplace that is stimulating, fulfilling, and meaningful. For the world at large, Grand Circle is determined to be a global citizen—helping people in local, national, and global communities—to create a better world for everybody."

— Oivind Mathisen, Editor, *Cruise Industry News*

"The authors speak to the reader as one would talk to friends sharing a glass of wine after a wonderful meal together. It is a story about the birth of a leading travel company, as well as a journal of unique travel experiences. The writing, though sprinkled with humor, is sincere, with special emphasis put on the importance of having a vision: of dreaming, of camaraderie, and of global philanthropy. Alan and Harriet Lewis have opened themselves in revealing every step of their journey, their successes as well as their failures, and the hard work it has taken to make their company 'the best travel company in the world.'"

— Susan M. Giaccotto, 5-time traveler, Farmington, Connecticut

"Be prepared for a rip-roaring page turner. Alan and Harriet Lewis have written a book that will inspire and surprise the reader. It is full of funny and revealing stories about how and why they built this company into a world-class success. I have been traveling with the company for years and until now had little idea of the impact that they make in the lives of the people in the countries we visit."

— Mary Seal, 8-time traveler, Tucson, Arizona

"This book explains it all. Now we know why OAT is a perfect fit for us. OAT is better than doing it yourself … and we know because we did it for years. Only four companies have earned our brand loyalty: Lexus, Apple, Olympus, and OAT!"

— Diane & James Craig, 11-time travelers, Burnet, Texas

"Don't miss this opportunity to learn the difference between being a tourist and being a participant in other cultures. The Lewises share their amazing journey with Grand Circle and make you want to be part of their global trek and global awareness-building."

— Dan Jones, 23-time traveler, Greensboro, North Carolina

"After well over a dozen wonderful trips with Grand Circle companies, we finally discovered the secrets that made them so meaningful and informative. The Lewises have the vision and ability to really listen and learn from their associates and travelers, and then change and improve the operation. Their many stories of successes and failures make this an interesting read."

— Jan Verville, 18-time traveler, Manchester, New Hampshire

"Driving With No Brakes is somewhat of a misleading title, because Grand Circle is a very well thought-out company. The company's unconventional attitude has served it very well, not just financially, but more importantly, in immersing its loyal travelers in different cultures and helping to change people's lives. If more successful companies practiced giving back to the local and global communities, imagine the impact they could make on the health, education, and well-being of the world's people. I'm sure they would also realize that they could do very well by doing good."

— Anne Marie Healey, 2-time traveler, Randolph, Massachusetts

"This book tells the story of how one lone couple had a vision to not only transform a failing travel company into the most successful one in the world, but at the same time, create a charitable foundation that enriches people's lives in so many countries around the world."

— Marion Gianino, 18-time traveler, Melrose, Massachusetts

"Alan and Harriet Lewis prove that striving and succeeding have no parameters. Follow them on their incredible journey via some bumps on the road as they evolve their neonate company into the best traveling institution in the world!"

— Edna M. Tobias, 28-time traveler, Hermosa Beach, California

"Not just another self-serving, vainglorious book. There is a real message of interest to business people of every stripe, MBA students, travelers, and other travel companies. Sprinkled with personal anecdotes and humor throughout, this book is a good read."

— William Drake, 9-time traveler, Readfield, Maine

"Things I never knew about why I was having such a good time with Grand Circle. Now I know why I had such a great trip!"

— Christine Pava, 7-time traveler, Windsor, California

Driving With No Brakes

How a bunch of hooligans built the best travel company in the world

by Alan and Harriet Lewis
Co-Founders of Grand Circle Corporation

GRAND CIRCLE GCC CORPORATION

Library of Congress Control Number: 2010930353

ISBN: 978-0-615-37782-7

This book is printed on 10% post-recycled waste paper.

Printed in the United States of America

Jefferson City, Missouri

August 2010

Table of Contents

Acknowledgments

by Alan and Harriet Lewis

Our lives are blessed by so many people who have coached, guided and helped us along the way. Our children Edward and Charlotte have taught us much—especially to laugh often and love unconditionally.

We are grateful for our associates who share our dream and show up every day all around the world to help change people's lives. We are inspired by our travelers who entrust us with their dreams. This is a privilege we accept and never take for granted. There are too many to thank individually for their help on our journey, but they are in our hearts.

Several people have worked to bring this book to life and to print. Jim Best, our friend and advisor for many years, sat with us and endured hours of stories and recollections and our hashing out what was important to say. He gave shape and structure to our thoughts and stories.

Nancy Zerbey edited the book with care and humor. During the course of the book writing she became a part of Grand Circle, always championing the reader, and gently scolding us when we became too close to the subject.

Mark Frevert and Martha Prybylo, longtime and trusted leaders in the company, read, reread, and edited the book. They added memories and stories to the pot that help make the book lively and complete. They also gathered feedback from our travelers early on, to help us tell a story our travelers would really like to read.

Diane Rooney was a zealot on the timeline and production schedule. She kept a bunch of mavericks in line and on schedule. Without her this book would continue to linger and never make it to print.

To each and every associate, traveler, coach, and friend we are humbled by your trust in us and grateful for your support. So, as we often ask our travelers, "Where to next?"

Foreword

by Lady June Hillary

Ed and I have had a long and satisfying relationship with Grand Circle Foundation and with Alan and Harriet. They have become good friends and good supporters of Ed's Himalayan Trust. Ed was an original member of the board of advisors, and actively supported the Foundation all of his life, frequently acting as a spokesperson for the organization. I'm exceptionally proud that Overseas Adventure Travel has named its frequent traveler program the Sir Edmund Hillary Club.

I feel that the philosophy that Grand Circle Foundation follows is similar to my husband's. A philosophy of asking what is wanted, a wish list even, and working with local people to do it—build a school, fix a path, replace a roof, subsidize a teacher, or pay a doctor and most importantly, to follow up over the years with interest in the work. When the project is complete, then it belongs to the community. A very satisfying and effective way to go.

I remember one visit to Boston after a very pleasant day with very pleasant people. We walked toward the office and as we approached the door Harriet asked, "How much money would you need for your teacher training program?" As I went through I said "$50,000," and when I arrived on the other side, I added, "Please" … and our teacher training project was under way. The Himalayan Trust will celebrate its 50th birthday in May 2011 in Kathmandu and we'll always be grateful for the relaxed efficiency and continued support that Grand Circle Foundation has given us over nearly 20 years.

I hope you enjoy reading this story about a marvelous company. We've enjoyed working with it over the years and will be eternally grateful for Alan and Harriet's leadership and generosity.

Introduction

by Alan Lewis

This book has been an eye-opener for me. It's brought back many memories, and made me think about things I had pushed to the back of my mind. In my 25 years with Grand Circle, I've experienced much joy, but also many moments of sadness. Harriet and I have built a great company, but the journey has occasionally been bumpy. When I look back, I realize that we've accomplished a great deal, but not without making some huge mistakes.

This is not a self-congratulatory book. We've tried to tell the Grand Circle story as it really happened—warts and all. We want to share what has worked for us, what hasn't, and show how philanthropy has helped to propel our success. We strongly believe good works and social entrepreneurship can benefit business. In fact, we've seen it work. Grand Circle has done very well by doing good, and we hope our company's story will influence others to take the same path.

Harriet and I bought Grand Circle Travel in 1985, when it had just 16,000 customers. Though it had $27 million in sales, it was losing $2 million a year. Today, Grand Circle is one of the most respected travel companies in the world and the leader in providing international travel, adventure, and discovery to Americans over 50. Grand Circle has taken more than 1.5 million travelers overseas, owns or charters more than 60 ships, and has been profitable every year since 1987. Though 2009 saw an international financial crisis and worldwide recession, it was the third-best year in company history, and 2010 is shaping up to be even better, with more than $600 million in sales and $60 million in profit. This is a remarkable achievement, hard-won by a great group of people. We're even prouder of the work of Grand Circle Foundation, which is now helping villages and schools in 90 countries and has donated or pledged $50 million to help change people's lives all around the world.

Harriet and I have strived to build a different kind of company—a company that offers authentic travel experiences, builds philanthropy into everyday business, and creates a workplace where associates all over the world work with a sense of urgency, speak up and take risks, constantly improve our trips, and thrive in change. The company has a strong culture driven by these values and encourages leadership by every associate, no matter where they stand in the organization.

As Harriet and I wrote these stories and sorted through hundreds of photographs, I found the life lessons that really stuck with me had come from my mistakes—and from my father. My father was a successful man, an authority on life and, above all, people-smart. My parents divorced when I was a young child, and I saw my father only on occasion, but each encounter left an indelible imprint. One of those occasions even changed my life.

Growing up, I moved constantly within inner-city Boston—12 times in seven years, in fact. I was rebellious and ran with some rough company, and I got into trouble at every turn. After high school, I tried college, but I completed only one year before growing too restless to sit at a desk any longer. I wanted new experiences, so I moved to Florida and got a job as a beach lifeguard. One day, I saved a man's life and the story made the newspapers. My father visited me shortly afterward, while I was still puffed up with my new hero status. We got into a huge argument over the direction of my life. Actually, it was over its *lack* of direction. Was I going to be a lifeguard for the rest of my life? Did I like being called a hero so much that I wouldn't return to college? What was I going to do? It was distressing: the proudest moment of my life, and my father came to criticize, not praise.

He also came with an offer. He was a principal of a small travel company called United Travel Service in Boston, and if I would return north with him, he would get me a job so I could learn about the travel industry. Anger kept me from making a decision for a few days, but I finally agreed, and it was back to Boston.

In my new job, I flew overseas to Majorca. The island brought my senses alive. I had never experienced a different people with an entirely different history than ours, people who ate differently, talked differently, and lived in houses that looked nothing like Boston's. I loved it, and I instantly knew that the world would become my classroom.

By 1970, I was working as a trip leader. I got to go on cruises, and I visited Switzerland, England, Mexico, and the Mediterranean. It was all pretty exciting for a 21-year-old, and my passion for travel has never abated, not even to this day. In 1973 I founded my own company, Trans National Travel (TNT) with a partner, offering group-travel vacations all over the world. My life had been changed by travel. It had given gave me purpose and direction, and a whole new perspective on the world. After ten years at TNT I was ready to move on, to build something truly great, a travel company that would change other people's lives, too. This book tells the rest of the story—the story of Grand Circle. Every day, I marvel at how many people's lives have been changed by traveling with Grand Circle, working for our dynamic company, or sharing in the work of Grand Circle Foundation.

Whenever we meet travelers, new associates, business people, and young leaders, they all want to know how we did it. How did the company grow so fast over the years? How did we overcome all the global challenges? How did our unique corporate culture get started and how did we become a model for global philanthropy? We hear these questions every day.

So Harriet and I decided to write this book to tell our story—to share some lessons we've learned over the years and some mistakes we've made along the way. We hope sharing our experiences will help business leaders, social entrepreneurs, and young people just starting out, and we hope our travelers enjoy taking a peek inside their travel company. We have shared so many wonderful experiences with people all over the world. Now we are pleased to share our story and our company with you.

Edward, Alan, Harriet and Charlotte
at home in Boston, Christmas 1985.

CHAPTER 1

In Pursuit of a Dream

It seems strange that this whole crazy adventure began on a quiet little beach in Florida. But that's what happened.

It was 1985. Alan and I had recently sold our interest in a Boston company called Trans National Travel, or TNT. The company had been very successful and we had multiplied our original investment many times over. After working like crazy for 15 years, we were looking forward to traveling, spending time with our two young children, and figuring out where life might take us next.

People ask how Alan and I first got together. We're asked so often, we must seem like an odd couple. I guess maybe we are. We both grew up around Boston, but there the similarity ends. I was raised in a traditional New England family with my eyes set on college. Alan was a street-savvy kid with big dreams and a colorful past. You can see the attraction. After a few rocky dates in high school, we went our separate ways, but after graduation, we met again, and this time we connected. Still an odd couple—I was a special education teacher and Alan was an entrepreneur—but we found that we shared a passion for world travel and a strong desire to help other people.

By 1985, we had been together for 13 years and married for six. In that time, we'd developed the habit of taking long walks together whenever we needed to make a big decision. We walk in the city, on the beach, through the woods, anywhere and everywhere. We're famous for it. And that's how we came to be walking on the beach on Captiva Island, watching the dolphins play, about to make the most momentous decision of our lives.

I was still savoring the prospect of a month-long seaside vacation when Alan broke the news. Grand Circle Travel was for up for sale, and he wanted to buy it. So much for our leisurely semi-retirement! But that's Alan—restless, driving, always looking for the next big challenge. It didn't even surprise me that we had to make a decision right away—another company was expected to sign a contract for Grand Circle the very next day.

I was torn, but the decision was actually easy. Travel has always been our passion. It has changed and enriched our lives in countless wonderful ways. We have seen astonishing things, made friends all over the world, and had great fun. We have found common cause with people of other cultures, and discovered that no matter where you go in the world, people are pretty much alike. They cherish and provide for their families, seek better education for their children, socialize with friends and neighbors, celebrate joyous events, and long for a peaceful life.

As Alan and I walked that deserted beach, we talked about our dreams. We wanted to give other Americans the opportunity to experience travel the way we had experienced it: up-close, personal, and with a deep human connection. We also wanted to build a company where associates looked forward to coming to work, where they could grow into leadership roles and enrich their personal lives. The more we walked, the clearer the dream became. By the time we turned around to head home, we had our goal. We wanted nothing less than to help change people's lives in our company, in our community, and in the world.

Grand Circle was the path to our dream. With butterflies in our stomachs, we decided to go for it. Alan pulled on a polo shirt, some golf shorts and a pair of argyle socks, and caught the next plane to New York.

—*Harriet Lewis*

In 1985, Grand Circle Travel was a small travel company that had fallen a bit on hard times. It had long operated profitably as the travel service for the American Association of Retired Persons (AARP) under the management of AARP's insurance provider, Colonial Penn. But recently it had run into trouble. Though it had sales of $27 million and a good list of former AARP travelers, Grand Circle was losing more than $2 million a year, and Colonial Penn was looking to unload it. They had a buyer all lined up—Saga Holidays, a big British travel company that had just opened operations on our home turf, Boston.

On the plane north from Florida, Alan figured he was in for a fight. When he got to New York, he literally barged into negotiations between Colonial Penn and Saga. Saga couldn't believe it. They were very eager to buy Grand Circle, hoping to turn that list of AARP travelers into brand-new Saga customers. They had fire in their bellies and dollar signs in their eyes. Then along comes this gatecrasher, brashly shaking hands and waving a checkbook.

Alan was maybe a little less confident than he looked, for he had to make an on-the-spot calculation. If we really wanted Grand Circle, we'd need to bid higher than Saga. But how much higher? What was the company worth to us? We already had enough money to live comfortably and travel for the rest of our lives. Was it worth risking it all?

There was a legal risk, too. The sale of our interest in our old company, Trans National Travel (TNT), included a non-compete agreement that barred us from certain travel ventures. Was Grand Circle one of them? We didn't know. Risking our life's savings gave us pause, but spending months penned up with lawyers wasn't something we wanted to do *at all.* Above all, we valued our freedom to get up and go whenever and wherever we wanted.

These are things we had talked about on the beach, and we had come to some conclusions. We knew our dream was ambitious. We wanted to offer people wonderful travel experiences, build a really great company, and change people's lives at home, work, and abroad. We also wanted to have some fun while we were at it. This was no idle daydream, but a dream worth fighting for. There were obstacles, of course, but they weren't insurmountable. So long as we could keep our family whole and tight, we thought we'd be alright. We felt our dream was worth the risk.

People say, "Don't sweat the small stuff." We believe that. But we believe this even more: Never compromise on the dream stuff. The dream is what makes life worthwhile.

Alan Makes His Move

In that split-second moment of decision, Alan wagered big. He offered Colonial Penn $9 million for Grand Circle, several million more than the company was worth on paper. Why? Because we saw the company's potential. It had a recognized brand, global reach, and loyal travelers in the retired American market. We had become acquainted with many of the people at Grand Circle over the years and knew they were capable and experienced. We were confident we could move the company forward quickly and profitably.

We also saw what *wasn't* on paper. Every mergers-and-acquisitions team knows that the value of a company includes more than its assets and bottom line. Value also lies in the opportunity the company offers to the buyer, the opportunity to achieve its own goals. All Saga wanted was

Twenty years from now you will be more disappointed by the things you didn't do than by the ones you did do. So throw off the bowlines. Sail away from safe harbor. Catch the trade winds in your sails. Explore. Dream. Discover.

—Mark Twain

Grand Circle's list of travelers, but *we* wanted to make Grand Circle the leading travel company for retired Americans. Our dream was bigger, and this made Grand Circle more valuable to us than to Saga. Nine million dollars was the down payment on our dream, and we were ready to foot the bill.

Of course, Colonial Penn wondered if they could trust us to come up with $9 million. We were strangers to them, and solo venturers; Saga was a major European company with an official corporate presence in Boston. Saga looked like a safe bet; Alan looked like—God knows what. Dressed in their Armani suits and silk ties, these buttoned-up New Yorkers looked across the table and saw a cheeky, sunburned guy in an ill-pressed suit (at least he'd changed out of the shorts). Our unsolicited offer disquieted them. Sensing reluctance, Alan upped the ante. He wrote a $1 million check as a gesture of good faith and pushed it across the table. The offer was too good for Colonial Penn to pass up. Grand Circle was ours.

Except for that pesky non-compete agreement with TNT. We thought it didn't apply to our purchase of Grand Circle, but TNT thought differently, and we spent a little time debating the point in our lawyers' offices. We could have fought it in court, but we had bigger fish to fry. We needed to focus on getting Grand Circle profitable, so we negotiated a settlement, wrote another big check, and closed the door on the old days.

Postscript: How We Got Our Reputation

About a year later, we ran into some Saga executives in London. They drew us aside and tried to buy Grand Circle back from us. In fact, they offered us a fast million-dollar profit if we would sell the company then and there. But we had made good progress over the last year and we knew the company was on the verge of turning profitable, so we declined.

The Saga guys became even more insistent. Evidently they still smarted from losing the bidding contest the year before. When they wouldn't relent and let us get on with our business, Alan responded in typical Alan style: He offered to buy Saga, instead. We really didn't have enough money to make good on the offer, but Alan was riled

We have to have dreams
to make dreams come true.

—Kay Stewart,
   6-time traveler
   San Francisco, California

that Saga wouldn't take "no" for an answer. The audaciousness of our response enraged them. In fact, one of the Saga executives said that there was no way "a bunch of hooligans from Boston" could run a worldwide travel business. We eventually escaped the room, but our reputation was made, and many years of intense competition between the two companies ensued.

Trouble from the Get-Go

We had big dreams for Grand Circle in that first year, but we weren't wearing rose-colored glasses. We knew that problems—even crises—are the norm for the travel industry. You can't just design some itineraries, pick some hotels, book some passengers, and then sit back and relax. That's not how it works, because in the travel business something is always going wrong. Airline workers go on strike, travelers get sick, hotel reservations mysteriously disappear. Beyond these difficulties, real calamities are always happening in some part of the world.

In fact, things started getting dicey for us very quickly. We signed the purchase agreement with Colonial Penn on March 31, 1985. Almost before the ink was dry on the contract, terrorists fired a rocket at a Jordanian airliner in Athens. Two months later, a TWA flight was hijacked en route to Rome and an Air India flight was blown up in Irish airspace, killing 329 people. In October, the cruise ship *Achille Lauro* was hijacked in the Mediterranean and an American was murdered on deck. In December, Arab terrorists attacked airports in Rome and Vienna.

These developments constituted a real threat to the business. In fact, we could have walked away from the deal with Colonial Penn early on, invoking the material damages clause of the purchase agreement. But we didn't. We believed we could move forward with Grand Circle and do well, so we stayed the course—and negotiated a lower price for the company.

But things didn't get any better with the new year. On April 26, 1986, the United States launched an airstrike against Libya; suddenly Americans were unwelcome in many parts of the world. Eleven days

After my mother passed away 17 years ago, I cleaned out the desk I had used as a child. Tucked away in a drawer were stacks of old travel brochures that I'd been collecting since I was 9 years old. I remembered how I used to fantasize about going to Africa to see the see the lions and elephants, or to London to see the bridges falling down. There I was, 45 years old, realizing I'd been interested in travel from a very young age.

—Harriet Lewis

later, a nuclear reactor melted down in Chernobyl, and travel bookings fell all over Europe. These were serious developments for us because Europe and the Mediterranean were Grand Circle's bread-and-butter destinations. Our travelers were nervous, and we were, too.

Driving With No Brakes

On an offsite in Costa Rica with our board of directors in 1994, Alan and I were driving in a van that had seen better days. The trip had gone badly. The group had been raucous and quarrelsome. We got lost. The roads were steep, hard-scrabble, and dusty. As we made our way down a hill, Alan leaned over from the driver's seat and whispered, "We've lost the brakes."

I thought he was speaking metaphorically, referring to our inability to control the offsite. As our speed picked up, I realized he meant the van's brakes had literally failed. It got pretty dicey, but Alan managed to drive the van up an incline on the side of the road, banging against the curb along the way, until the vehicle finally stopped.

We got out and stood ashen-faced looking under the hood. I congratulated Alan on his driving skills. He said, "I have experience driving with no brakes. I feel like I've been doing it for years with Grand Circle."

—Jim O'Brien, Vice Chair
   Chairman, Kensington Investment Company

Grand Circle has seen countless world crises, and over the years we've become very adept at dealing with them. Today we have a protocol for responding to any world crisis, and we have a set of what we call "Extreme Competitive Advantages" that propel us through difficulties and position us to come out ahead. But in those early days, we flew a lot by the seat of our pants, relying on guts, instinct, and the advice of the good people we gathered around us.

Alan's Promise to Charlie

In our early years in the travel business, we had become friends or professionally associated with some of the best talent in the travel industry. Soon after we acquired Grand Circle, we gathered together an exceptional board of advisors and engaged leading industry consultants. We also brought in people from Trans National Travel, including Charlie Ritter, an old friend who'd been around the travel business for a while.

Charlie knew the score: The travel business was exciting, but it was also difficult and often a pain in the neck. Back in the 1980s, the industry was split between independent travel agents—22,000 of them— and a handful of large, direct-marketing companies like Saga and Olsen Travel World, based in Los Angeles. The big companies were hierarchical in organization and highly corporate in management style, filled with drones at the bottom of the ladder and "yes men" at the top. Leadership in those companies was largely a matter of issuing orders and not taking no for an answer. Backstabbing and office politicking were common, making the workplace unpleasant and unproductive. So when Alan asked Charlie to come work at Grand Circle, Charlie was dubious.

"Why should I come to work for you?" he asked.

"Because I'm going to build a different kind of company," Alan told him.

Charlie shook his head. "I'm tired of all this corporate B.S.," he said. "How do I know Grand Circle will be different?"

Alan explained our dream to build a company where leadership opportunities would be available to everyone who worked there. We wanted our associates to become as great as they could be—to lead from wherever they were, take risks, and always speak the truth without fear of reprisal. We wanted to create excellent trips and an empowering company culture.

"We can do this," Alan said. "I promise."

That was enough for Charlie. He jumped ship and soon got to work setting up the company's innovative computer system, fondly called GERT (Grand Circle Enters Revolutionary Technology). Other new hires came aboard at the same time: Bruce Epstein, Jan Hobbs-Bailey, Bruce Washburn, and Mark Frevert—mavericks all. Like Charlie, they came with years of experience and lots of big ideas, attracted by the opportunity to take leadership roles every day.

There were some tough times those first few months—times when I questioned whether the company was going to make it. I was in the lobby of our New York office on a cold winter day when an elderly couple approached holding an empty Grand Circle gift bag. They had come in from Long Island on the train to return it. The couple planned to go on one of our trips but the gentleman had to have major surgery, so they'd had to cancel. They had made the long trek into the city because they felt they shouldn't keep the bag after their money had been refunded. The gentleman's parting words were, "That's OK[ ] get another one."

At that point, I k[new] travelers wou[ld]hard times[.]

—Char[lie]
L[ ]

How We Became Addicted to Speed

We needed those big ideas right away. Besides facing worldwide crises, Grand Circle was losing money—more than $5,000 a day. We wanted to build a different kind of company, but first we needed to stop the red ink. We had already committed our life's savings to the company, so speed was of the essence. We had to work fast before the money ran out.

We were ruthless. Our first action was to get rid of the worst-performing trips—more than 300 of them—so we could focus on Grand Circle's best products. We continued marketing directly to the list of former AARP travelers, bypassing the travel agents, and made sure we stayed focused on our prime market: Americans over 50.

These actions increased our profit margin, but we never lost sight of our main goal: to build a company that would attract travelers, not tourists. We stopped hustling our customers from place to place, slowing the trips down so the travelers could better appreciate the people and cultures in our destinations. We also gave our customers more value for their money by cutting prices, eliminating middlemen overseas, and adding new features to the best trips.

Over the course of 12 months, we completely reinvented Grand Circle Travel. It was a wild ride, and we made mistakes. For instance, we closed the company's office in Long Beach, California, as a cost-cutting measure. Unfortunately, the associates who worked there were the ones with knowledge of the Far East and the American market west of the Rockies—knowledge we would need later, when the European theater was rattled by terrorist attacks and growing unrest in the Middle East. We couldn't have predicted those developments, of course, but had we ... lowly, we would not have faced that predicament.

g slowly isn't something we do at Grand Circle. In fact, ke that we are "addicted to speed." The compulsion to keep tly personal, partly strategic. Alan is restless and hard-ature, and Harriet likes to see practical results right away. ks in those days and weren't interested in bank financing, a fast return on our investment. But the prime reason for i to speed is the fast-changing nature of the group travel ject to international crises, fluctuating currencies, and petition, travel companies have to be fast and nimble. Speed mportant to every new venture. Other businesses can maybe view and slow course, but travel is a race run by rabbits.

A Moment of Truth

Worst was the commuting. Every Monday morning for six months, Alan and his Boston-based crew would catch the 5 a.m. commuter flight to New York, not returning until the end of the week. Harriet stayed at home in Boston.

This wasn't getting us closer to realizing our dream. We had two small children who deserved the attention of both parents. We knew what it was like to grow up in broken families. Harriet's father died when she was 13; Alan's parents divorced when he was young. We had always insisted that our children, Edward and Charlotte, would enjoy a close family life. Besides, we wanted to be together, to work as a couple. Ours was a shared dream, and we knew that our strengths and weaknesses balanced each other's. We felt that the business would benefit from the commitment and resolve of both of us. The decision was obvious: Either we had to move the family to New York City, or we had to move the company to Boston.

Harriet's First Trip

The first time I traveled out of the country was in 1970, when I was 21, just after I graduated from Kent State. I went to Europe with three girlfriends. We were truly footloose and fancy-free. I bought a backpack from the Army Navy store and packed two rolls of toilet paper and a copy of *Europe on $5 a Day*. We rented a VW Beetle, sang Judy Collins songs, and slept in hostels. Once, in Copenhagen, we slept in a bar. It was crazy.

Looking back, what strikes me is that everything seemed so brand-new. Travel was so freeing and so much fun. I talked politics with a bunch of Jordanian Communists in Bulgaria, and listened to a *muezzin* calling the faithful to prayer in Turkey. Alan sent me a letter and I picked it up at the American Express office. There were chickens in my train compartment. I was just constantly surprised. I knew right then that travel was going to be a big part of my life.

—Harriet Lewis

I've visited more than 100 countries over the years, and I still fantasize about so many others. For me, travel is addictive; I get a physical thrill when I add pages to my passport. And as my passport grows, so do I—both emotionally and spiritually. By meeting new people and seeing how they live their lives, I see how alike we all are, and I'm reminded that this truly is one world. Alan says that I come alive when I travel—that my whole body smiles and my eyes shine.

—Harriet Lewis

It was the week we moved in to Congress Street. As I stepped off the elevator into the wall-less sea of mismatched desks, I saw two men trying to rotate a desk. A woman was sitting on top of it, laughing her head off. People were rushing around like they had a plane to catch—and some of them did, as they were commuting between Boston and New York. Through the skylights, hordes of seagulls squawked and fought and did the nasty thing—all day and all night. Phones were constantly ringing, there were boxes everywhere, unusual characters coming and going. It was your basic madhouse.

—Karen Hansen,
25-year associate
Director, Corporate Marketing

Every advisor—business, legal, and personal—told us to leave the company in New York for at least a year. Business schools teach the same thing: After a corporate takeover, stay put and go slow; let the dust settle before making any big changes. But Boston was a vital part of our lives. We grew up in and around the city, our friends and family were there, and we were both ardent Red Sox fans. Could we live in the land of the hated Yankees? We hadn't gotten this far by doing things the way people told us to do them. We reminded ourselves: Never compromise on the dream stuff. Besides, we knew we'd be lost in New York. And so the decision was made. Grand Circle Travel would move to Boston.

From Madison Avenue to South Boston

Shortly before our first anniversary, we moved Grand Circle Travel from a skyscraper on New York's Madison Avenue to a crumbling warehouse in a deserted part of South Boston. Although it is a robust and picturesque district today, at the time, the neighborhood was separated from downtown by a polluted canal and piles of construction rubble. Nevertheless, our new home at 347 Congress Street had advantages. It was big, cheap, and had a genuine Boston feel. Easy access to South Station made it convenient for commuting associates, and street parking was plentiful (not so today!). It was also close by our house in Boston. Now we could both work on building a great company and be home for Charlotte and Edward when they got home from school.

The commuting wasn't over, of course, it just went the other way. After the move, our New York associates had to commute to Boston until they could relocate. It was hectic few months and few of us would have guessed that we'd come to call these the *good ol' days*.

In fact, our new South Boston home was a great fit for the "different kind of company" we were building. We wanted to promote open minds and open communication, to create a space where everyone saw themself as a leader and contributor. Traditional corporate architecture—big offices, fancy conference rooms, closed doors, and cubicles—is designed to do the opposite, to keep people in their place.

Our six-story building was nothing like that. Furnished with castoff furniture and covered in century-old brick dust, it wouldn't let us take ourselves too seriously. Our open plan encouraged people to speak up and feel safe in challenging others, including us. Our casual new digs in this funky part of town helped us create a freewheeling culture committed to doing something great.

A Big Mistake

When we decided to move the office from New York to Boston, we selected the 28 top-performing people in New York and planned to offer them a great package if they would transfer to Boston. We knew that New Yorkers are not always fond of Boston, and were worried about how they would take the news. So we delayed telling them. It didn't occur to us that New Yorkers might read the Sunday *Boston Globe*. When we arrived in New York Monday morning, we were greeted by associates wearing pig snouts.

This was our first big mistake, but it taught us a crucial lesson. If we wanted a different kind of company, we had to be forthright and honest with associates. It's sometimes painful, and we've stumbled occasionally, but since that day, we've delivered bad news as quickly and directly as possible. For example, when the terrorist attacks of 9/11 brought travel to a standstill, we had to lay off 250 associates. We informed everyone several days in advance of the impending layoffs, and told them exactly how it would be done. It was awful, but at least it was open and above board.

—Alan Lewis

Off to the White Mountains

We also established an important Grand Circle practice in those early days: offsite problem-solving. In the summer of 1986, at the height of the international terrorist attacks, when our European trips were floundering, Alan took his new leadership team to the White Mountains in New Hampshire to figure out what to do. Alan has always been a hands-on, experiential learner. He has served as a board member for the Hurricane Island Chapter of Outward Bound, and has long seen the value of taking difficult company issues outdoors, to offsites in unusual locations where participants could resolve top business issues and develop leadership skills. Offsites had been exceptionally successful at Trans National Travel and we wanted to instill them into the culture of our new company.

Lots of companies were doing offsites in those days, but they weren't getting much in the way of results. Too often, the staff would get out of the office, do a few icebreakers, maybe conduct a trust exercise and share a picnic at a hotel—only to find that the spirit of collaboration, invention, and motivation evaporated on the way home in the car. We couldn't afford that kind of offsite. We had a crisis on our hands. The phones were ringing off the hook in Boston, but they weren't travelers making reservations. They were travelers canceling trips.

What we needed was an action plan that could be executed the moment we returned to the office. As we hiked the steep, rocky trails and shivered in Greenleaf Hut, our primitive cabin, we agreed we needed to cut prices and run new promotions to generate sales down the road. But we needed sales now. Where would we get them?

Someone got the bright idea to re-book all the cancelled travelers to new destinations. After all, those customers had already told us they were eager to travel. All we needed to do was persuade them to go somewhere else. We put together a list of our best sales associates so we could form a SWAT team on Monday morning. We also designed a contest for the team, developed a script for the calls, set sales incentives, and decided on prizes for the associates who rebooked the most travelers. Ever since that hike into the White Mountains, our associates know to expect immediate action on Monday morning after an offsite.

When we came down from the mountains we had a plan, a newfound camaraderie, tired legs, and aching muscles. In fact, the vice president of sales had to be carried down the trail by his teammates. We were exhausted, but we knew we had turned a corner. Grand Circle would make it to the end of its first year.

The Dream Unfolds

In 1985 and 1986 we didn't have a two-inch-thick strategy book for Grand Circle; we were pretty much flying by the seat of our pants. But we did have a dream. We were determined to build a different kind of travel company. Initially, this meant four things to us. First, the new company had to fulfill us personally, reflecting our values and providing a foundation for our family. Second, it had to make money; without profits, all of our good intentions would come to naught. Third, we wanted to give our customers a genuine travel experience at an incredible value. Finally, we wanted to create a company culture that truly honored and empowered our hard-working associates.

By the end of that first year, we had made a lot of progress. We had purchased the company, moved it to Boston, hired new associates, eliminated the worst trips, improved the others, instituted offsites, and stared down a series of international crises. Grand Circle was still losing money, but not as much.

We were pleased with how far we had come, but we knew we weren't there yet. There was a fifth piece of our dream—to give back to our local and overseas communities through philanthropy—but that goal would have to wait until we had our feet more firmly beneath us. We weren't worried. We'd get there.

And, indeed we have. Since that fateful walk on a Florida beach, sales have grown to more than $600 million a year. The company has taken more than 1.5 million travelers overseas, and we've expanded our offerings to include small group adventures with Overseas Adventure Travel (OAT) as well as our own line of River Cruises. Today, our worldwide organization spans the globe with 38 offices, and we operate 60 ships.

In 1993, we formalized our commitment to philanthropy by launching Grand Circle Foundation. Since its founding, Grand Circle Foundation has donated or pledged more than $50 million to 163 projects worldwide. At the same time, our associates have engaged in countless hours of community service and given more than $750,000 to charities from their own pockets. The company has won many industry awards for social responsibility, and our travelers have honored us by donating more than $1 million through the Foundation to help people all over the world.

Life constantly tries to prick our dreams. If you have a dream that you want to make happen, you have to hold it tight and persevere. At times, we were lucky, but, in truth, we were mostly just stubborn. We refused to let go. We decided to write this book because we wanted to share the Grand Circle story with our travelers. We also wanted to give other entrepreneurs with big dreams a glimpse of what has worked for us. We consider this a midterm report card because we're definitely not done building our dream.

In 1985 Alan promised Charlie Ritter that Grand Circle was going to be a different kind of company. Charlie passed away some years back and we miss him. We're glad to have been able to keep that promise.

Grand Circle is different … and we're proud to say so.

It's been really exciting, and really fast. I remember running a marathon once and thinking, "This is like life." That's what Grand Circle's been like, too. There are great ups and great downs and lots of in-betweens, great joys and great heartbreaks and crisis. It turned out to be a great decision. We've never looked back.

—Harriet Lewis

Grand Circle's first Executive Team looks happy and cohesive as they prepare to head down the Salmon River in Idaho.

CHAPTER 2

Scrambling

About 15 years ago, I had an interesting conversation with Jim Best, who was consulting with Grand Circle on some leadership issues. Jim had consulted with a lot of other companies, so I asked him what he thought was different about Grand Circle.

"The way people have incorporated the company's vision, mission, and values into daily operations," Jim answered.

His answer puzzled me. "Isn't that the same for all companies?" I asked.

"None that I've ever encountered," Jim said. "Their mission and values are just inspirational words hanging on wall plaques in offices. Nobody pays any attention to them."

"But that's foolish," I said.

"To tell you the truth, I never thought so until I came to Grand Circle and saw how powerful they can be. I don't think I've been in a single meeting here without some element of mission or values being raised to frame a decision. That's unbelievable. How did you do it?"

I didn't answer him right away. He'd gotten me thinking about a piece of company history, and I was playing it back in my mind. Finally, I said, "We worked hard on our vision, mission, and values—too hard to let them become empty words. We fought about them. People lost their jobs over them. It goes back to the early days of the company. Harriet and I had a dream and we needed to express it in a way that people could grasp, so they could either move forward with us or move on to other employment."

"But I've never seen the vision, mission, or values on a plaque anywhere in the building," Jim said. "How did you ingrain them so deeply?"

"Can you recite them?" I asked.

"Pretty close."

"Well, how did you learn them?"

"They're printed in the front of every meeting handbook."

"That's because we want all our decisions to reflect our values. Harriet and I bring them up at every opportunity. It's important that the company remain focused on who we really are. Sure, we're here to make money, but more important, we're here to help change people's lives."

—Alan Lewis

By 1986, we had moved Grand Circle to Boston and had issued our first Boston-generated brochure. It was titled *Faraway Places* and we were very proud of it. The brochure had a picture of the Taj Mahal on the cover and the caption "Leadership in travel for active mature Americans." Unlike other travel brochures of that era, the photograph didn't display smiling tourists; it showed pilgrims approaching the temple.

The cover reflected our entire business model at the moment. In a kind of distilled simplicity, it defined our product and our target market. Our travelers would be Americans; we would design our trips for active seniors; we'd go to faraway places; and we'd provide opportunities for our travelers to engage with the people and cultures at our destinations. This first brochure cover was a crude vision statement.

Getting this much clarity hadn't been easy. The trips we had inherited from Colonial Penn were a crazy jumble of sightseeing excursions, countryside vacations, tours of foreign capitals, extended stays in apartment hotels, and mad-dash "passport-stampers." The company had only 16,000 customers, and yet it offered nearly 500 different trips, many of them special-order itineraries that might never be offered again.

Much of the work of the first two years was to get those trips under control. Our first action was to eliminate the worst-performing products—more than 300 trips in all. With the stinkers out of the way, we could focus the entire organization on the trips that were popular, profitable, and of really high quality. At the same time, we stopped using travel agents to market our trips, instead marketing directly to the AARP list, saving our customers the cost of the agents' commissions.

We were merciless, really, and the instinct to cut our losses and put our money on the sure thing when we are under pressure has stayed with us over the years. So when terrorists took down the World Trade Center on 9/11, we knew just what to do. We cut our product line by 20 percent, to focus attention on the trips that would really reward the customers who continued to travel. Today, we consider our relentless attention to unsurpassed value and excellence to be one of our Extreme Competitive Advantages, i.e., one of six unique strengths that keep us three to five years ahead of our competition.

Next, we slowed down the pacing of the trips that remained. Nobody likes pre-dawn wakeup calls or being marched from one famous site to another. Well, some do. Some tourists are competitive sightseers. They want to punch their ticket for as many sights as possible, even if the bus stops only momentarily, but we wanted to attract a different type of traveler. We wanted our travelers to have time to enjoy the people and cultures in our destinations, maybe explore a back-alley bazaar or linger over tea at a country inn. That couldn't happen if they were cooped up in a big bus most of the time, or if the tour guide held a stopwatch every time they got off.

Another early action was to give travelers more for their money. Sometimes we did this by cutting prices and squeezing our profit margin, but another way was to work directly with overseas travel suppliers. Honey Streit-Reyes, our European buyer, first proposed this strategy for our trips in Austria and Germany, the countries she knew best. Before she showed us the way, we had done what every other American travel company did: We partnered with European ground operators, who provided us with hotels, buses, meals, and tour guides in return for a piece of the action. By cutting out these middlemen, Honey negotiated better rates, and we passed those savings on to our travelers. Buying direct gave us better control over the trip experience, too, so we were able to improve the quality of those trips. It was a win-win strategy for us, though we were pretty unpopular with the ground operators in Europe for the better part of a decade.

We scrambled to make these trip changes happen, living by the slogan: "Fast, Flexible, and Time-Competitive!" We pushed forward with the changes, partly because we needed to cut our losses and partly because we were cocky. We believed we could radically reduce our trip offerings but still keep our customers. We thought our new lineup of well-paced, engaging, value-priced trips was that good. It turns out we were right.

A Bunch of Mavericks

Not everyone agreed with the new product strategy—we'll get to the naysayers in a moment—but the product changes helped save our $9 million investment. By the middle of 1987, Grand Circle was showing a profit. But our business and personal lives didn't settle down much. Everything was go, go, go.

To a great extent, Grand Circle was being driven by an energized group of young people who didn't quite grasp that what they were doing

I knew it wasn't an ordinary company when …

I knew it wasn't an ordinary company on the first day, because when I met Alan, we got into a fight—not physical, but intensely verbal. He offered me a job on a 30-day basis. How insulting! I blew up and told him exactly what I thought of a trial employment.

Two weeks later, I got called for a second interview. Rushing on foot across a busy street, I was hit by a truck. When I staggered into the meeting, late and bleeding, Alan asked, "What happened to you?" I told him I had been hit by a truck.

"Oh," was his only response. He thought I had just made some lame excuse, and went ahead with the interview. That 30-day job turned into 25 years and counting, making me the associate with the longest tenure in the company.

—Mark Frevert,
25-year associate
Executive Vice President/
Chief Architect

was difficult. Those were fun times. The staff was creative, rambunctious, and almost always irreverent toward the norms of business protocol and etiquette. They laughed a lot and played games, competed openly with each other, and ignored rank. We had organization charts, but few knew what they looked like on any particular day. People just went directly to whomever could help. Everybody spoke up and openly challenged people in authority, including us. It was wonderful: youthful, energetic, and bold.

Most of this early culture came naturally from our own personalities. We were young ourselves, in our mid-30s, casual in dress and lifestyle. We loved challenges, hated sycophants, and both of us loved to compete. This was exactly the "different kind of company" we had hoped to build. We wanted to attract independent-minded, high-performing people, put them to work in an open, demanding, and fun environment, and watch them grow into leaders. We had succeeded beyond our wildest dreams.

Our biggest fear was that we might lose our maverick style. We worried that as we prospered and grew, we'd become structured, complacent, and ordinary. That we'd become just like everyone else. We couldn't let that happen. While some young companies look forward to joining the staid ranks of Corporate America, we believed maintaining our irreverent, hard-charging culture was the key to building a truly great organization.

How could we channel all this energy and independence in a productive way? How could make our "different company" extraordinary, and keep our maverick spirit alive?

Building Something Special—The Grand Circle Culture

We needed more than a brochure and a slogan to give direction to our fledgling company. We didn't want to impose a structure or publish a rulebook, but somehow we had to make our company culture explicit. As travelers and veterans of the travel industry, we already knew a lot about culture. Culture is the spirit that differentiates one group of people from another—Christians from Hindus, Thais from Cambodians, Boy Scouts from Hell's Angels, Hatfields from McCoys. It's also the set of shared values that holds a group together, the expectations that govern its behavior. Different cultures make travel endlessly interesting, and different cultures are what make some people and organizations more successful than others. Culture is that powerful.

Not every organization talks about its culture, but every organization has one, and it's worth figuring out what it is before some crisis ignites a culture war. In the late 1980s, visioning exercises and mission statements were just beginning to make waves in business management circles. Many companies dismissed the effort as idealistic, irrelevant, "dreamy," or a craze, and it was around that time that President George H.W. Bush made light of the "vision thing."

Even those companies that embraced the idea of corporate culture had trouble putting it into play. Some arrived at their vision and mission by accident, treating some offhand remarks by the company president as commandments. Others tried to impose culture from the top down, drafting some empty words and executing them in curlicue script. We knew better. We believed that a well-considered culture would give us a blueprint for all our future actions; it could actually lead the business strategy. The vision, mission, and values had to capture our founding dream for the company, but they also had to be consensual, inspiring, directional, and specific.

There was serious work to do—so in typical Grand Circle style, we went on an offsite. That's part of our culture, too.

Turbulence on the Salmon River

In June of 1988, the leadership of Grand Circle went on a six-day Outward Bound-facilitated offsite down the Salmon River in Idaho. The Salmon River is also called The River of No Return, and we thought that was thrilling. We were young, adventurous, and eager to challenge ourselves. We intended to have fun, but the business goal was to define our future.

The white-water rafting *was* fun. Defining a vision for our future was not. Almost immediately, we got in a wrangle about the new product strategy. The group quickly split into two warring factions. One group wanted to sell high-volume, low-cost trips that covered a lot of territory in a short time. If you've seen the movie *If It's Tuesday, This Must Be Belgium,* you know the kind of drive-by, mass-market trip they had in

---

I knew it wasn't an ordinary company when . . .

Was it the time we had champagne at 9 o'clock in the morning when Desert Storm was over? Was it the time I dressed up as a southern belle to introduce our new *Delta Queen* river cruises? Was it the time Michael Aufhauser bought dry jeans from our caterer up at Pinnacle Leadership Center, and put his wet jeans on the grill to dry? Was it the time a couple of Maasai warriors came with us to Brown's Clam Shack, walking in like they were locals? The unusual has now become ordinary in my life.

—Linda Richardson,
22-year associate
Pinnacle Leadership Center

mind. Instead of whirlwind tours that left people exhausted, the other group wanted to offer unforgettable experiences at unsurpassed value that have a lasting impact on people's lives.

It got very ugly. Michael Shaw, one of our earliest hires, characterized the mass-market camp as wanting to sell "cheap and nasty holidays." They were, in fact, very good at selling that kind of trip, and they had contributed to our dramatic company turnaround. But that wasn't the kind of travel experience we really wanted to offer. This conflict was the 200-pound gorilla that had followed us from Congress Street to the Salmon River, and before long it began snarling.

To make matters worse, the rafting got scary. River safety expert Les Bechtel, who guided the group, was thrown from the raft into the rapids for the first time in his 12-year career. Jan Hobbs Bailey, one of our pioneering associates, was also tossed out of the raft—and sucked into a whirlpool. During an intense evening debriefing, an emotionally drained Charlie Ritter picked up a burning log from the campfire and threatened our facilitator, Bob Gordon, a leadership expert from Outward Bound.

The ambitious agenda and the raging river had created a perfect storm. Suddenly all the tough issues we'd been tiptoeing around came torpedoing up to the surface. Seeing that we did not have alignment on our goals, Alan pushed harder for a vision statement to define our product strategy. There was disagreement. The discussion became boisterous, then unruly. It was a real crisis moment for the company, but with crisis comes opportunity.

Departure of the Cheap and Nasties

By the end of the trip, we had clarified Grand Circle's company direction. Rejecting "cheap and nasty" vacations, the group committed to a high-value, high-excellence model that could provide authentic travel experiences at an affordable price without sacrificing quality. We also committed to the vision that our trips would help change people's lives.

Perhaps the entire group wasn't truly committed. Shortly after we returned to Boston, both the company president and the vice president for product development left the company. Like many travel executives of that era, they believed our vision was too idealistic and that the product strategy would fail. We think time has proven them wrong.

Big Mistakes

Over the years, my biggest mistakes have been staying with people too long because they were high-performers, even when I knew they didn't really share our values. The Salmon River offsite should have taught me better, but the lure of the big-shot high-producer is strong.

We once hired a former Disney executive to serve as our COO; you'd think he'd be good under pressure, but he completely fell apart on 9/11. Then there was this big guy we hired to be CFO—around 6' 7" and 270 pounds—but he couldn't handle the offsites; a tiny bit of drizzle sent him packing. From this, we learned that we shouldn't hire people so much on their skills and past performance, but rather on their commitment to our values.

If you have vision and mission you believe in, you must evaluate your people against them all the time, no matter how much you admire their energy or reputation, and no matter how much money they are bringing in. If you don't, you will live to regret it.

—Alan Lewis

Great Products Are the Key to a Great Company

The Salmon River offsite defined our product strategy, but we needed to take action to make this strategy a reality. As soon as we got back to Boston, we took another look at our trip offerings, this time with an eye to weeding out the "cheap and nasty" vacations and identifying the trips that could offer really meaningful experiences.

That meant more cuts, and this time it was harder. Our associates had been running the trips for more than three years, and they had become invested in them. Over the years, we have learned that people get attached to what they know; they'd rather fix what's broken than move on to something new. Someone always seems to step forward to defend a floundering product, giving reason after reason why it's a good idea to give the product a little more time.

We believe great companies do a few things exceptionally well. And we have found that the easiest way to focus attention on the exceptional products is to get rid of the bad ones.

—Alan Lewis

But this is not the way to build a strong company. Profitability depends on delivering unsurpassed value, and value depends on constantly improving the *best* products. If the destination is not popular, or the trip quality is poor, or the program does not align with your vision for the company, then it is best to cut the product; if you don't, it will soon take time and attention away from your best products.

So we cut and we built, eliminating the last of the Colonial Penn products that didn't suit our new product strategy, and consolidating the best features of some legacy programs like our Extended Vacations. Extended Vacations took travelers on two- or three-week tours that allowed them to stay a week or more in each destination; on some itineraries, travelers could add one or more weeks for less than $100 a week, and on Spain's Costa del Sol, they could stay half a year.

Extended Vacations met our criteria for slower pacing and discovery, and we rolled them out to new destinations: Interlaken, Lucerne, Gstaad, Guadalajara, the Amalfi Coast, London, Paris—even Yugoslavia, a country Americans seldom visited in those days. When the Yugoslavia trip became a bestseller, we knew we were on the right track. The vision and mission that caused such a fight on the Salmon River were fast delivering results.

Our Vision

Our vision defines what we hope to become: the best travel company for older Americans who want to experience people and places all over the world in ways that will change their lives. The vision has three key components: We will serve American travelers only; our travelers will be 50 years and older; and we will offer discovery-filled international trips (no domestic tours). Being clear about these three components allows us to design trips that can really help change our travelers' lives. For example, older travelers appreciate a slower pace than young travelers, and retired people typically have more time to spend on a trip than working people do; these understandings really focused our early product changes. In later years, we found that older Americans had become more sophisticated and adventurous travelers, and we changed our product line to keep up with them. Our strategies change, our tactics change, and our trips change, but our vision remains steady.

Grand Circle's Vision Today

We will strive to be the world leader in international travel, adventure, and discovery for American travelers over 50—providing impactful intercultural experiences that help change our travelers' lives.

We will establish this leadership position in the travel industry through application of our direct marketing expertise and the synergies gained from the acquisition of key nature and adventure travel companies.

We will generate significant annual growth for Grand Circle Travel, Overseas Adventure Travel, Grand Circle Small Ship Cruises, and future acquisitions. Each year, up to 5 percent of our after-tax profits shall be given to fund the Grand Circle Foundation in support of the people and environment our travelers visit.

We will strive to be a great company—providing a workplace that is stimulating, fulfilling, and meaningful to our associates; an environment where associates connect to their passions and to each other as we achieve professional and personal goals.

We know that our vision is bigger than most. We have never hedged our dreams. In fact, part of the Grand Circle culture is daring to undertake seemingly impossible things, confident that the encounter will be exciting. It is a true traveler mentality: There are no boundaries, only new frontiers.

Our Mission

While the vision says what we hope to become, our mission explains how we do business. The mission came a little later than the vision, in the early 1990s, and it was the result of some very deliberate work with our longtime friend and consultant Bob Weiler. Bob had been executive vice president of the Hurricane Island Outward Bound School, and he later founded Pinnacle, our leadership company. Like Alan, he was an early believer in the power of mission statements to direct corporate action in meaningful ways. Compared to other corporate missions, ours is a little unusual. It doesn't define a goal. Rather, it outlines our responsibilities— four responsibilities, in fact: (1) our responsibility to our associates; (2) our responsibility to our customers; (3) our responsibility to our financial well-being; and (4) our responsibility to society at large.

Grand Circle's Mission Today

Grand Circle Corporation is committed to a mission that creates a balance between our responsibilities to our customers, our associates, our shareholders, and our world.

ASSOCIATE RESPONSIBILITY
We will provide an environment that fosters professional development and encourages personal growth for our associates. We will maintain competitive compensation and benefits packages relative to the industry and community. We will conduct business with respect for each individual and his or her role within the organization.

CUSTOMER RESPONSIBILITY
Grand Circle Corporation, through direct marketing, is committed to providing active, mature Americans over 50 with the most exciting travel, adventure, and discovery programs in the world at unequaled value. We strive for 100% customer satisfaction.

FINANCIAL RESPONSIBILITY
We will operate Grand Circle Corporation in a sound financial manner, to create growth, and increase its value.

SOCIAL RESPONSIBILITY
Global citizenship is central to the success of Grand Circle Corporation. We will commit time, people, and funding through Grand Circle Foundation to local, national, and global communities in which we live and explore, thus creating a better world for our travelers to discover.

It wasn't easy getting the mission down to 179 words, but we accomplished it with a lot of work and arguing. The biggest argument was whether our customers or our associates come first. Most companies say their customers come first, but at Grand Circle we have always said, "Associates are Number 1." In the late 1980s, this position was almost completely unheard of, and many companies resist it even today. But we believe that if a company makes its associates its top priority, then its associates will do everything they can for its customers.

The proof is in the bottom line: The better we do by our associates, the better our financial results. We believe so firmly in the power of focusing on our people that we put "Associates are Number 1" at the top of the list of the Extreme Competitive Advantages that give us a three-to-five-year advantage over our competition.

We value our hard-working and challenging group of associates, and we want to channel their creativity toward common goals—goals that we have collectively agreed upon. Keeping our vision and mission in front of us keeps everyone pulling together in the same direction.

Our Values

The final component of our culture is our values. Like the vision and mission, the values are explicitly stated. They shape our day-to-day business decisions, give direction to our growth, and allow us to measure our progress.

There are six Grand Circle values, and they don't much resemble the ones most of us knew at our previous jobs. Executive Vice President Mark Frevert, for example, came to us from a Fortune 500 company, where the chief values were accuracy and fiscal conservatism. At TNT, where Alan was a co-owner for many years, the top three values were profit, profit, and profit. In that context, Grand Circle's values seemed revolutionary. Here they are:

Grand Circle Values

Open & Courageous Communication . . . Risk-Taking . . . Thriving in Change . . . Quality . . . Speed . . . Teamwork

The company values have affected my personal life in two important ways. First, I've gained the ability to speak up, even when saying unpopular things, and second, I remain calm and flexible even in uncertain—or scary—times.

—Kim McLaughlin
15-year as
Business F

Open & Courageous Communication. This is probably our signature value, the one outsiders most often remark on. We know that the combined intelligence of our organization is astounding, but it is valuable only if it is allowed to express itself openly. Honest feedback improves our products, discussion breaks down barriers, and challenges to leadership keep us all on our toes. When senior leadership listens to line associates, the *real* issues of the organization come to the surface. We want our truth unvarnished, warts and all.

What it looks like: Speaking up in meetings, asking tough questions, admitting ignorance, swallowing defensiveness, listening carefully, not whining, saying "thank you," offering suggestions, stifling gossip, confronting conflict, questioning political correctness, rewarding courage, respecting others' points of view.

Risk-Taking. Risk-taking comes directly from Alan, who enjoys it, but it is expected of every associate. We want everyone who works at Grand Circle to be able to lead at a moment's notice, and from anywhere in the organization, but that's only possible if everyone has daily practice taking risks. We encourage that by providing an environment where it is safe to make mistakes, and where important risks are rewarded whether they succeed or not.

What it looks like: Trying new things, expecting mistakes, stepping outside your comfort zone, moving forward without knowing the outcome, eschewing popularity, accepting new assignments gladly, embracing challenges, catching others when they fall.

Thriving in Change. This is the value that leaves many observers scratching their heads (more so, perhaps, in the early days, when we called it "Thriving in Chaos"). Change is a way of life at Grand Circle. We change everything—all the time. We change products, business practices, organizations, priorities, and work assignments. Every change has its reason, but most are course corrections dictated by world events, global competition, and the high volatility of the travel industry. Other changes are issued as deliberate challenges to our associates, to help them grow into stronger leaders. In all cases the goal is to maximize our effectiveness and success in an unpredictable and ever-changing environment.

What it looks like: Moving forward, turning on a dime, seeking opportunities, embracing chaos, lifting us up—not dragging us down, staying positive, remaining calm, stepping up to help, being part of the solution; no second-guessing, no regrets.

Thriving in Change Has Its Privileges

At 3 p.m. on April 17, 1986, Alan and I were at the Hotel National in Red Square, waiting to have lunch with the Russian Minister of Tourism. Lunch in Russia always began at 3 p.m. because on-duty officials could not drink alcohol before then.

The purpose of the meeting was to convince the minister to issue us tour operator credentials. Four gentlemen appeared and led us into a room with a long table covered with platters of cold cuts, salads, wine, and vodka chilling in ice buckets.

After formal introductions, the minister gave us some bad news. "Gentlemen," he said, "we regret that we are unable to discuss your request, as yesterday your government bombed Libya, the homeland of our comrade Colonel Moammar Gadhafi. This is most unfortunate."

There was a pause before the minister continued. "Instead, we will eat and drink well."

And that's what we did.

—Michael Shaw
Vice President, Product Planning

Quality. This value comes directly from the argument on the Salmon River. We needed to make it plain: No more "cheap and nasty" vacations. Most businesses believe cost and quality are constant tradeoffs. We believe it's possible to drive improvement in both simultaneously, but if an irresolvable conflict arises, then quality always gets the nod. It's not just that we have high standards. Quality also drives our repeat business, which is critical to our financial performance.

Once a group of outside investors described Grand Circle associates as being "Maniacs on excellence." They said it with misgiving, but we wore it as a badge of honor. Soon thereafter, Alan turned down their offer to buy the company.

—Denise Sablone,
17-year associate
Executive Vice President,
Worldwide Business
Operations

I've always prided myself on being a great team player. A short while after I started at Grand Circle, Alan commented that he thought I was a poor team player. I was shocked! When I asked him why, he said, "Because you would rather do it yourself than teach someone else or have them do it differently than you." It was a tough discussion, and I hated to admit it, but he was right. Over the years, I have learned that Grand Circle's idea of teamwork is both about supporting your team, which comes naturally to many of us, and about challenging your team to be better, which is harder.

—Martha Prybylo,
  17-year associate
  Grand Circle's first
  Vice President for
  Corporate Culture

What it looks like: Reading every traveler survey, considering every suggested improvement, not settling, celebrating progress, knowing the competition, exceeding expectations, holding our own work to high standards, aiming for 100%.

Speed. You need to move fast in the travel industry, but not everyone is comfortable with speed. We help by creating a safety net, quickly changing direction if a decision proves wrong and ensuring that mistakes are reversed without penalty. Open and courageous communication also puts the brakes on speed. A wrong decision can be costly, but if everyone speaks up when they see something amiss, it takes much of the risk out of speed.

What it looks like: Feeling urgency, setting deadlines, beating deadlines, wearing a watch, answering e-mails immediately, seeking clarity instead of certainty, not lingering over drafts; fast meetings, full date books, the thrill of the chase.

Teamwork. Our values define our behavior only if they are shared by all of us and we work as a team to benefit both the traveler and the company. At Grand Circle, "Teamwork" isn't a cheerleading slogan; it's the way we work on a daily basis.

What it looks like: Sharing knowledge and expertise, stepping in to help, committing to a common goal, accepting responsibility, deferring to greater skill, providing honest feedback, challenging the team, pushing for better results, showing compassion, supporting other people personally and professionally, celebrating success.

Putting the Values to Work

Our values are not idle words on a page; in fact, they get quite a workout. They are literally part of every business day because they govern how we behave. We use them to size up job candidates, plan strategy, evaluate performance, direct our growth, measure our progress, and decide awards and recognition.

We also insist that our leaders exhibit the values constantly—beginning with us, Alan and Harriet. We falter occasionally, but our associates and advisors always bring us back in line. That is what open and courageous communication does for us personally. It's invaluable. Our associates believe in our vision, mission, and values, and trust us to keep them whole. They are disappointed when they see us act differently, and they remind us to remain true to our principles.

Our associates also exhibit the values, and their actions can have far-reaching consequences. For example, late one Friday afternoon in 1994, after all the executives had left for the weekend, we sent out a company memo announcing an unanticipated shortfall that seriously cut into our associates' bonuses. Our timing was terrible, and our delivery was callous. At the corporate meeting the following week, Anne Marie Davis, one of our account managers, let us have it. "You can't just dump and run," Anne Marie said. "If you've got bad news, you've got to stick around for the fallout. That's what 'Responsibility to Associates' means."

Anne Marie was right. Since that day 16 years ago, we've made sure to deliver bad news honestly and face to face, in small group meetings. We don't sugarcoat it, but we relate the news personally and explain exactly what we are going to do about it. Anne Marie's feedback also resulted in another change that has become a signature piece of Grand Circle culture: our company Report Cards. Twice a year, each associate is asked to grade the company's performance on each of the Four Responsibilities—Associate Responsibility, Customer Responsibility, Financial Responsibility, and Social Responsibility—using letter grades, A to F. One the first report card, our grade for Financial Responsibility was a D-. Anne Marie reminded us that leadership requires accountability, and now our Report Cards keep us honest.

Learning Never Stops

As you can see from our early beginnings, we didn't do everything right. We still don't. Harriet, who trained as a teacher, never ceases to remind us that learning never stops. That's part of our culture, too, and we have found several different ways to integrate some powerful learning experiences into our business practice.

First, of course, are leadership offsites. Alan had long believed that taking people away from their usual place of business can help resolve tough issues; the change of scenery opens up thinking and generates ideas. Every traveler knows this, of course; new sights, new understandings, and new ideas are what make travel such a powerful learning experience.

Alan didn't go to business school. He succeeded through perseverance and a preoccupation with learning—especially from his mistakes. He reads endlessly, and when he runs into someone smart, he'll ask question after question. For someone who was impatient with formal education, Alan has been a lifelong pupil.

—Harriet Lewis

I knew it wasn't an ordinary company when . . .

It was the first loading dock party I was organizing, and I wanted it to be special. Could we AstroTurf the entire parking lot? Why not? How about a reggae band? OK. Cookout? Sure. Senior Team flipping burgers? Done. The steel drums called folks down, and most were wowed—it was a real party. Harriet came in a Carmen Miranda costume, and the dancing started!

—Priscilla O'Reilly,
17-year associate
Director, Public Relations

The Salmon River offsite taught us something different: Those ideas can sometimes be explosive, particularly when they arise in a challenging physical environment.

We learned to tackle the toughest issues first, and to be prepared to control the emotions around them. For years now, we've had rules of conduct for our offsites that keep the discussions on a direct but respectful footing. We make sure the team *owns* the issues and results—they're not handed down from the top. The focus is on learning, open communication, teamwork, and advancing the company—not conflict—so our offsites have become tamer and more productive. No one has brandished a burning log in years.

In the early 1990s, we began taking the entire Boston office on an annual offsite to Pinnacle, our leadership development center in New Hampshire. The program, called BusinessWorks®, involves leadership training, a deliberate effort to raise hot issues, and a requirement to bring actionable decisions back to the office to be put into play the next day. In addition to the hard business work, there are ropes courses, raft-building challenges, rustic cabins, and some pretty uproarious skits. Participants experience our company culture in new ways and come to see themselves in new ways, too. Today associates come to Business-Works from all over the world, in a cross-cultural exchange that takes learning to a whole new level.

The Freedom to Be Great

Our corporate culture has three formal components. Our vision is what we aspire to, our mission is what we'll do, and our values are the rules we play by. We believe that by making our corporate culture explicit, we have given our strong, independent-minded company of leaders the framework—and the freedom—to do their best work. The company has been very successful through some harrowing times, and we believe the culture is what has seen us through.

To a great extent, we've succeeded in maintaining the maverick style of our early days. Certainly no one walking through the door on Congress Street would mistake us for an ordinary company. There is a life-sized carved elephant in the lobby and a totem pole. On the garden level is the Grand Circle Gallery, which displays our personal collection of early 20th-century travel posters, along with some stunning black-and-white aerial photos taken by our dear friend Bradford Washburn, a renowned explorer, mountaineer, and great risk-taker. Upstairs, everyone is in motion. There is an air of expectancy and surprise, as if somebody, somewhere, might be up to something. As if someone might burst into song, or turn up in a hoop skirt, or throw a party on the loading dock because—oh, yeah!—that's happened before.

In the beginning we scrambled—first to survive, then to succeed. By the time the Berlin Wall came down, in the fall of 1989, we were positioned to do something great. In fact, in 1992, after offsites in the cloud forest of Costa Rica and in Cascais, Portugal, we dedicated ourselves to becoming not just a different company, but "The Great Company," a company capable of extraordinary things. Our culture, and our amazing associates, would take us there.

Harriet meets with children in Ahodwo, Ghana, where she was presented with the Tanzanian Humanitarian Award, May 2006.

CHAPTER 3

Vision Quest

In February of 1992, Alan and I went to northern Arizona for an unusual adventure. We were going to take part in an 11-day vision quest. We had studied Native American rituals, but were not sure what to expect. We weren't doing this for a lark; we wanted to discover more about ourselves, work on our personal relationships, and recommit to helping people. We had high hopes, but we never guessed that this would be the most powerful experience of our lives, or that a vision quest could wonderfully alter the way Grand Circle helps change people's lives.

We were all a little nervous as we settled in at the Wildflower Lodge, north of Prescott. We spent several days learning about vision quests and other aspects of Native American culture. Our instructor explained that our group of 28 participants would be split up into individuals or couples. Alan and I would be allowed to stay together, but we'd be completely isolated from the others for four days and three nights and we would have no food, no tent, no radio, and no phone. We would have sleeping bags and water. In fact, we had two sleeping bags, but we were so cold we zipped them together. The last rule would be the hardest for us: We were not allowed to talk at all those four days.

It was February and we were encamped at 5,000 feet, overlooking a craggy, high desert valley. It was bitterly cold. There were no people or facilities in any direction, so we started gathering odd pieces of wood for a fire. The sparse gambel oaks and scrawny junipers didn't offer easy pickings, and it took most of the day to build up a stack of firewood big enough for a bonfire.

The first morning we woke up to find two inches of snow on the ground and three dogs on top of us. The dogs, all different breeds, had just appeared in the night and had helped keep us warm. They stayed with us for the day, and then disappeared. We missed them when they left, but we think they knew we were supposed to be alone with our thoughts and feelings. The next couple of days, we listened to the wind, watched daylight play against the desert landscape, and wrote in our journals.

When we weren't huddled by our fire, we walked. Sometimes we walked together and sometimes we followed our own trails. We thought about each other, our family, Grand Circle, and ourselves. Although it isn't beyond either of us to break rules now and then, we never spoke the whole time we were away. At night, we lay on our backs for hours atop the high desert plateau. Above us, the unbelievably starry sky inspired wonder and introspection. Without speaking, we knew each of us was feeling something highly spiritual, a connection with the world and beyond.

On the third night, Alan woke up at three in the morning with a revelation: To really help change people's lives, we needed to make a stronger commitment. We had to use the entire company to make a real difference to our travelers and the places we visit. He shared his journal notes with me and I nodded agreement. His idea—a Grand Circle charitable foundation— would grow through the years to help countless people, but it was born in the still of the night without another soul around for miles.

For us, the vision quest was exceptionally powerful. Neither of us has felt anything like it before or since. It was life-changing. It didn't alter our path, but it showed us how to accelerate our pace toward the goal of helping to change people's lives.

—Harriet Lewis

Before 1992, we hadn't given much thought to corporate philanthropy. Instead, we donated our own time and money to various charities and community service projects. We were grateful for the opportunities we'd had in life and felt a responsibility to help others. Long before we bought Grand Circle, we gave money to charities like the Shriners, to help crippled children; to Neurofibromatosis, Inc., for research to cure this devastating neurological disease; and to Thompson Island Outward Bound, to help provide outdoor leadership training for inner-city youth in Boston. We supported many local causes and organizations, including our neighborhood YMCA and a holiday tree-lighting project on the Commonwealth Avenue mall, a block from our home. We also thought it was important for us to show up in person, to give our own time to local causes. We believed our personal involvement meant the money we donated would be used more effectively.

We wanted to share our ideas about personal giving with our children, so every year we would take Edward and Charlotte to help out at the Boston Family Shelter around the holidays. They were young then, barely in school, and they loved all the fuss and the Christmas tree. Perhaps they didn't quite grasp the problem of homelessness, but it was a good start. We also promoted the idea of "giving back" to our fledgling company,

encouraging associates to donate their time to community initiatives
in Boston and their hometowns. But until we launched Grand Circle
Foundation in 1992, our efforts at philanthropy were scattered. Although
we included the goal to help change people's lives in the Grand Circle vision
statement, we didn't have a formal structure in place to make it happen.

This was soon to change. On the way home from our vision quest
in Arizona, we made a list of people we admired who promoted peace,
education, and environmental stewardship all around the world. Today
we would call them "social entrepreneurs"—people who have vision
and courage, take risks, and adopt innovative approaches to creating
social change. We wanted people like that to serve on our Board of
Advisors. We aimed high; at the top of the list was Sir Edmund Hillary.

Then, almost as soon as we unpacked in Boston, we initiated the legal
steps to create a charitable foundation tied to Grand Circle Travel. We
committed to contributing at least $10 per traveler, per trip, toward the
various projects the foundation would support. Finally, we hired Martha
Prybylo to lead the foundation. Seventeen years later she serves as our
Executive Vice President for Worldwide People and Culture. We wager
there isn't another person in the world with that title; it is a testament to
how thoroughly all our efforts are grounded in our Grand Circle culture.

Founding Principals

We were thrilled when Sir Edmund Hillary agreed to join our board
of honorary advisors. We had long admired the spirit of adventure that
took him to the top of Mount Everest, and we shared his love of the
Himalayas and the Sherpa people. In fact, three years earlier we had
gone on a life-changing trip to Nepal, in honor of Alan's 40th birthday.
Later, we became friends with Sir Edmund and his wife, Lady June
Hillary, a relationship that developed over the years; it was an emotional
blow when Sir Edmund passed away in 2008.

Other prominent people from all over the world agreed to join us, too.
The original advisors included Dr. Rodrigo Carazo, former president of Costa
Rica; Ree Sheck, also from Costa Rica, from the Monteverde Conservation
League; Lars-Eric Lindblad from Sweden, one of the founders of adventure
travel; Dr. Robert Muller, from France, former Assistant Secretary-General of

*We make a living from what we
get. We make a life from what
we give.*

—Winston Churchill

the United Nations; Dr. Pedro Tavares, of SOS Children's Village in Portugal; Nancy Anderson, Director of the New England Environmental Network; Susan Ruddy, Vice President of the Nature Conservancy in Alaska; and Selahattin Erdemgil, Director of the Ephesus Museum in Turkey. Rounding out the original board were two friends from the Boston area, Bradford Washburn, a world explorer, photographer, cartographer, and mountaineer, and his wife, Barbara, the first woman to climb Mount McKinley. Together Bradford and Barbara founded Boston's Museum of Science.

We had a vision, a mission, and a great group of advisors. It was time to get to work.

In our eyes, Sir Edmund Hillary is a powerful role model for leadership and philanthropy. Over the years, hundreds of people have climbed Everest, and many succeeded in reaching the top, but only Hillary made it part of his life's work to help the local Sherpa people overcome their own challenges. His relentless fundraising and keen oversight of the Himalayan Trust, which he founded, have been an inspiration to us all at Grand Circle Foundation.

—Harriet Lewis

Original Honorary Directors of Grand Circle Foundation

Sir Edmund Hillary
International explorer; with Tenzing Norgay, first to scale Mount Everest; Founder, The Himalayan Trust

Bradford Washburn
Mountaineer, explorer, and cartographer; Founder, Boston Museum of Science

Barbara Washburn
Mountaineer and explorer; first woman to summit Mount McKinley

Susan Ruddy
Vice President, Nature Conservancy, Alaska

Ree Sheck
Writer and Conservationist Information Director, Monteverde Conservation League, Costa Rica

Lars-Eric Lindblad
Pioneer of adventure travel; President, Lindblad Travel

Dr. Rodrigo Carazo
President of Costa Rica, 1978–1982; Founder, University for Peace, Costa Rica

Dr. Robert Muller
Former Assistant Secretary-General, United Nations; Recipient, International Albert Schweitzer Prize for the Humanities, 1993

Nancy Anderson
Director, New England Environmental Network

Dr. Pedro Tavares
Vice President, Board of Directors, Associacao das Aldeias de Criancas SOS de Portugal

Selahattin Erdemgil
Leader of archaeological expeditions; Director, Ephesus Museum, Turkey

A list of our current Honorary Directors appears in the Appendix.

A World of Giving, Mistakes Aplenty

We began slowly, giving small amounts to organizations around the world as a way to say thank you to the countries that had so warmly welcomed Grand Circle travelers. In the first year we gave only $16,500, but we soon picked up the pace, and after we acquired Overseas Adventure Travel in 1993, we extended our reach. We set up a teacher training program in Nepal, raised a totem pole in Alaska, saved rhinos in Zimbabwe, and funded a clinic in the rain forest of Peru. We helped rebuild war-torn Dubrovnik, the beautiful city on the Adriatic that so many of our travelers had discovered on our Extended Vacations in Yugoslavia. We sent medicine to Rwanda and provided earthquake relief to Turkey. We supported a cancer hospice in Spain, bought ceiling fans for a school in Fiji, and gave computers to Buddhist monks in Thailand. Pretty soon, we were overseeing dozens of projects all over the world.

We found that giving money away wasn't as easy as we had imagined. We had big hearts, and were giving money to everyone, but in the early years we lacked clarity around how the money was to be used, and we had no measurements to ensure we were making a difference. We got robbed more than a few times. At least once, one of our own regional offices skimmed funds from the Foundation. Everything was piecemeal at the beginning. We were just happy to help, and everything felt good.

Willy Chambulo opened our eyes to the problem with one of his typically casual but profound remarks. Willy is the entrepreneur owner of Kibo Guides in Tanzania; he is our friend and business partner, and he now serves as an Honorary Director of the Foundation. When we were considering funding a science lab at a school in his country, he warned us, "This is Africa, people are hungry." We knew instantly what he meant. If you throw money around where people are hungry, much of it will be peeled off as it passes through different hands—unfortunately, not by the people who are *literally* hungry. In desperately poor countries, some well-fed folks often feel they are entitled to a piece of every economic activity.

Willy taught us another valuable lesson: Understand how far your American dollars will go abroad. In many developing countries, a dollar has colossal purchasing power, which means that more can be done with less money than you might think. It also means that unscrupulous

Grand Circle Foundation is a worldwide philanthropic organization, and worldwide philanthropy has special issues. Every country is different, and cookie-cutter solutions don't work. We learned this lesson the hard way.

—Martha Prybylo,
  17-year associate
  Executive Vice President,
  Worldwide People and Culture

people can pad estimates and fiddle the books so they can embezzle from naive Americans—and they seldom get caught.

Becoming Strategic

Over time, our efforts became more concerted. We saw the value in working with established charities and nonprofit organizations that had knowledge of local problems and could offer proven solutions. From this insight came our early partnerships with such organizations as the World Monuments Fund, AmeriCares, Sir Edmund Hillary's Himalayan Trust, and the Monteverde Conservation League—organizations that taught us a great deal.

Another big change was to involve our travelers directly in our philanthropy. We winnowed our list of projects to those that fell within range of our trip itineraries. Then we designed our trips so the travelers could visit our projects and see the Foundation's work in action. Soon our travelers were visiting the tombs we helped restore in Egypt's Valley of the Kings and discussing the Holocaust with the director of the State Museum of Auschwitz-Birkenau, to which we have given $400,000 over the years. By 1995, the same model was playing out in schoolrooms, craft workshops, historic churches, childcare centers, and game reserves all over the world. Our philanthropy was no longer conducted on the sidelines; it was now directly in the path of our travelers. It had become a strategic part of the business.

We knew that our philanthropy would benefit local people and interest our travelers, but we didn't anticipate how often the work of Grand Circle Foundation would actually change our travelers' lives. One of our travelers, Susan Rickert, of San Francisco, was so moved by the appalling condition of a school she visited in Tanzania that she spent the next several years raising $100,000 for five schools and finding sponsors for 17 student scholarships. Two more travelers, Mark and Naomi Hughes, of Hamilton, Virginia, raised enough money through their dog-grooming business to donate 40 bicycles to schoolchildren in the Tanzanian village of Karatu. The bicycles get the children to school and help their families transport such necessities as water and groceries. This kind of deep involvement with people who were once strangers happens to our travelers all the time.

Philanthropy has become part of our corporate culture and an integral part of our trips—not an isolated act of long-distance charity, but a vibrant part of our day-to-day business and a grateful expression of our global citizenship.

—Harriet Lewis

A Big Mistake

Our honorary advisors were totally committed to helping people, but they also saw themselves as advocates for their own corners of the world. In the early years of the Foundation, this kind of local interest posed no problem because our resources were limited and their enthusiasm made our efforts so much more effective. But as the Foundation grew, we wanted to branch out to places that our advisors did not represent, for example, Thailand, East Africa, China, Mexico, and Peru. As our advisors continued to lobby for their own interests, we had more and more trouble getting new projects off the ground. At the same time, we stopped seeking their counsel and didn't listen to them at a high level, where we really needed the benefit of their experience. What we learned is that leadership is much more important to philanthropy than mere advocacy. When you get a strong leader and passionate advocate in the same person—that's when philanthropy really catches fire.

—Harriet Lewis

Harriet Takes Charge

We had plenty of problems in those early days. The turning point came when Harriet got personally involved in a schools project in Costa Rica, in 2005. Harriet had served as the chairman of Grand Circle Foundation from the beginning and had often gone into the field to evaluate projects and approve donations. But this new project, which involved six schools, held special interest for her. Harriet trained as a special education teacher at Kent State University and had worked with special-needs children for many years in inner-city schools. Here was an opportunity for her to provide direct leadership in an ambitious new partnership.

Harriet had the support of Dr. Carazo, the former president of Costa Rica, as well as logistical help from local Grand Circle staff. Their contributions to the project were important, but Harriet soon saw the need for something else—local community involvement. For example,

When I think of global citizenship, I think of a tapestry. We're here in this world by ourselves, individually, but thread us all together and we're really something spectacular.

—Harriet Lewis

parents of children at the San Francisco School, outside San Jose, asked the Foundation to donate computers for the school, but there was a problem: Their classroom was open to the elements, and it had neither electricity nor air-conditioning—a huge obstacle at a time when computers overheated easily.

Harriet has a heart of gold, but she's also a realist; she knows wishful thinking can get you only so far. So she sat down with the parents and teachers and asked that they commit their own talents and energy to building a reasonable computer lab. And they did. One father offered to pay for the electricity. He had been driving his daughter from the village into San Jose to learn about computers—three hours for the drive and lesson each time. Some of the parents built the walls, others ran the electrical wiring. Then they put on a series of fundraisers to pay for air-conditioning. By the time the computers arrived, the community had already invested a lot of its own time and money. They had ownership of the project, and every parent made sure their children treated the equipment with respect.

Harriet had pioneered a new model of reciprocal responsibility, one that allowed our partners the freedom and independence to meet their own goals, and we had found a formula for global philanthropy that worked. Strong local leadership and a partnership based on shared responsibility made all the difference. Harriet's work in Costa Rica laid the groundwork for our *World Classroom* initiative, which launched in 2005 with the goal of fostering children's education and engaging the communities in which they live. Today the *World Classroom* initiative supports nearly 100 schools in 60 villages around the world. It is a program that resonates particularly strongly with our travelers, who visit these schools, for they care deeply about education and giving children opportunities for advancement in the global village.

Harriet's Rules of Philanthropy

Many lessons came out of the Costa Rican school project, and as we took the *World Classroom* initiative worldwide, we found we could apply them almost everywhere we went. Now we call them Harriet's Rules of Philanthropy, five guidelines for global giving that reflect our experience with many projects that worked—and some that didn't.

> **Harriet's Rules of Philanthropy**
>
> 1. Get personally involved
> 2. Work with strong local leaders on common goals
> 3. Foster respect, reciprocity, participation, and independence
> 4. Know the value of a dollar
> 5. Engage social entrepreneurs to magnify giving

Personal involvement. Global philanthropy is more than long-distance charity. Money is important, but close involvement with our overseas projects stretches our dollars further and lets the local people know there will be oversight. It also ensures that our donations are really meeting local needs, and that the recipients know their project is truly important to us. We can't personally supervise every project, of course, so we get commitment from our regional associates before we recommend any new endeavor in their areas; then they become our eyes and ears on the ground.

Strong local leadership on common goals. Strong local leaders are excellent community organizers, and we always try to get them on board at the very start of a project. That way, the excitement that outside support creates in a community can be given focus and direction. In many of our village projects those leaders are school principals, small business owners, or elected officials—people who know the local political landscape and can build community participation, which is essential to the long-term success of our projects. But local leaders cannot work effectively in isolation, so it's important to work as closely with them as they do with the community.

Respect, reciprocity, participation, and independence. Early on, we discovered many Third World communities are so poor they will take any kind of donation, disregarding their true needs to get it. If a charity is offering computers, for example, people will take them, though what they really need is clean drinking water. Sir Edmund Hillary reinforced this lesson, advising us that it is always best to begin a philanthropic enterprise with a face-to-face discussion. "Ask local people what they need," he said. "Don't tell them what *you* think they need." This is not only more respectful of local communities, it is also a better use of our money.

Travel is fatal to prejudice, bigotry, and narrow-mindedness and many of our people need it sorely on these accounts. Broad, wholesome, charitable views of men and things cannot be acquired by vegetating in one little corner of the Earth all one's lifetime.

—Mark Twain

Early on, I realized we had an important opportunity to change people's lives through travel—just as my own travels have changed my life and my outlook. I truly believe that if we all had more interactions with other cultures, we'd recognize more commonalities, we'd be more open-minded—and ultimately, we could change the world.

—Harriet Lewis

Once a project is decided on, we work hard to develop the kind of reciprocal responsibility that Harriet pioneered in Costa Rica. This means asking for community participation—helping plan the project, volunteering tools or labor, or raising additional funds. This kind of community participation mirrors our own personal involvement and creates ownership in the project from both sides. In this way, our projects become partnerships between equals and have a better chance at long-term sustainability.

The value of a dollar. Knowing the value of the U.S. dollar means understanding its purchasing power in every region we give to. It also means not over-committing funds, keeping tight budgets, demanding accountability, and safeguarding the money channel. By this we mean getting money into our recipients' hands as directly as possible, eliminating middlemen and even, in many parts of the world, official government agencies. Lax financial practices just invite graft; by keeping a tight fist and watchful eye we can give more money to more people who need it.

Social entrepreneurs. Whenever possible, we partner with social entrepreneurs who understand local issues and have experience delivering money and services in the regions where we give money. Besides being principled people and gutsy leaders, these entrepreneurs can give us some hands-on professional help—supervising distributions, meeting schedules, and auditing finances. Some of our partners are businessmen, like Willy Chambulo, the owner of Kibo Guides and our partner in Tanzania, who warned us that hunger would divert our investment in Africa if we were not vigilant. Others are village elders, local community workers, and even our own travelers and trip leaders. We believe that entrepreneurial leadership can come from anywhere, and we are constantly on the lookout for it.

All of these rules were learned in the school of hard knocks, and we made plenty of mistakes along the way. We still make mistakes, but there are fewer of them and we catch them earlier now that we know what they look like.

Our *Invest in a Village* Initiative

Sir Edmund Hillary had a common goal for every project he undertook for the Sherpa people in Nepal: sustainability. He felt strongly that once a project is complete, it should really belong to the community. That is only possible if the project is designed in such a way that the community can sustain it without ongoing financial support. It's like the old Chinese proverb, "Give a man a fish and you feed him for a day. Teach a man to fish and you feed him for a lifetime."

We have always taken Sir Edmund's philosophy to heart in the villages that we support through Grand Circle Foundation, and we formalized this commitment in 2009, when we launched our *Invest in a Village* initiative. Of course, we have always been deeply involved in villages around the world. Our *Day in the Life* program, which takes our travelers into homes, markets, fields, and craft workshops around the world, dates back to the earliest years of the company, before the establishment of Grand Circle Foundation, in 1992. The *World Classroom* initiative extended our local reach to village schools. The new *Invest in a Village* initiative goes yet another step, partnering with leaders in villages where we have already developed strong relationships to support the growth of entrepreneurial opportunities based on local community needs.

The model for this program is our micro-farm at the San Francisco School in northern Costa Rica, a three-phase project we began funding from the very first seed in 2006. In addition to providing hands-on learning opportunities for students, the farm supports the entire local community with high-quality nutrition and revenue from the sale of surplus produce, which goes to support the school. It also gives children from agricultural families a reason to stay in the village after graduation from school, rather than leaving to find work in San Jose, a pattern that has greatly concerned their mothers, who would like them to stay.

In another *Invest in a Village* project, established in 2010, the Foundation set up a women's sewing workshop in Bearat, Egypt, raising money to buy 37 sewing and embroidery machines so that village women can create traditional Egyptian *galabeya* dresses, school uniforms, and table linens for sale. Building on a tradition of hand-sewing in the area, the project increases both output and revenues, and creates jobs for at least 35 women who were previously unemployed. In these ways we hope to create sustainable change through local entrepreneurship.

It's a grand thing that Grand Circle Foundation is helping so many children. I find the visits very enlightening. I have an emotional connection with them because I grew up in an orphanage. It takes me back. These kids are in unfortunate circumstances, and the Foundation is helping them. A little bit goes so far in a poor country. These kids are so sweet and their expressions are so clear, it doesn't matter that we don't share a language. No matter where you go, there is some way to connect—and it's always these connections that we make for the rest of our lives.

—Mary Ann Trumko,
31-time traveler
Cudahy, Wisconsin

Grand Circle lit the fire of community service in me. I came here thinking that I was already giving back, but soon realized that I mostly just talked about the community service things I wanted to do! Grand Circle's community service events made it easy for me to get involved. I realized that if you make it easy for people to give back, they will. My husband and I founded a grassroots charity based on this same premise. We organize events that make it easy for families in our community to help local children in need. They keep coming back event after event—changing the lives of the people we help—and their own lives, too. I am so thankful to Grand Circle, Alan, and Harriet for teaching me this lesson.

—Kathy Wilder,
11-year associate
Vice President,
Data Warehouse

Philanthropy in Our Own Backyard

Grand Circle Foundation has a single mission—to help change people's lives—but it plays out in two spheres: "in the world we travel" and "where we live and work." The first sphere is global—and so is the second, for we are an international company with 38 offices worldwide. But the philanthropy we engage in at home is often different from the work we do abroad, because it happens in our own backyard, among people and in places we might see every day. It is the realm of community service.

In Boston, the tradition of community service actually predates the start of Grand Circle Foundation. It goes back to 1985, the year we bought the company. From the very beginning, we encouraged our associates to "give back" by putting their time, money, talents, and energy into local causes they believed in. We wanted them to experience the pride and connection that community service work brings, and we wanted to afford them leadership opportunities, too, as team captains, fundraisers, translators, and project organizers.

Since giving back is part of our business strategy, we make it easy for associates to serve. We develop a yearlong calendar of events from which they can pick and choose, and we help set up the events. We also publicly recognize our associates' efforts in our newsletters, at company meetings, and at annual awards ceremonies. In the late 1980s, we enshrined community service in our mission, as part of our commitment to social responsibility. In 1993 we created a Community Service Team to help organize associates' service work, and in 1994 we gave $25,000 in seed money for the Associates' Fund, which makes its own grants to Boston-area nonprofit organizations; in some years we have given as much as $100,000 to support extraordinary efforts. It is part of being The Great Company.

We are amazed by how enthusiastically our Boston associates have taken up the challenge. Over the years, we have joined them as they have walked for AIDS, biked for cancer, swum for clean harbors, and run marathons for more causes than we can count. We've given blood, sold pies, cooked meals, collected toys, painted houses, planted flowers, read to toddlers, sat with elders, and helped teenagers with their homework.

In 2006, one of our associates, Chris Penn, started a new program called Up & Out. Building on our longtime support of the Boston Family Shelter, Up & Out helps homeless families move into apartments by helping them acquire furniture, bedding, kitchen appliances, and even cleaning products. In 2010, the program relocated its 25th family. The previous year, our daughter Charlotte—who as a little girl loved handing out presents at the Boston Family Shelter with her brother Edward— bicycled 170 miles for the Dana-Farber Cancer Institute. Charlotte is an adult now, and works with us as Grand Circle's Marketing Director. Edward, who works for our commercial real estate company, Kensington Investments, has coached baseball for many years at the West End House Boys & Girls Club in neighboring Allston. For our family, community service has come full circle.

For the company, community service has spread all over the world, for as Grand Circle grew, so did our "backyard." We opened our first regional office in Germany in 1997, and today we have 38 regional offices from Cairo to Killarney. Community service looks different in each region, as our associates respond to different local needs. In Thailand, for example, associates once built a chicken coop, while in Mexico, a group of associates drove a mule team into the Copper Canyon to bring clothing to a remote Tarahumara village. Associates have baked mooncakes for elders in Hong Kong, renovated a classroom in Vietnam, and purchased musical instruments for children in Italy. It seems each office is developing its own tradition of giving. That's what we want them to do; it is the best way to ensure that the service is both heartfelt and helpful.

Over the years, Grand Circle associates have volunteered more than 25,000 hours to community service projects worldwide and donated more than $1 million of their own money to local causes. Participation is voluntary but enthusiasm is contagious, and today more than 90 percent of our Boston and overseas associates do some community service work every year.

Philanthropy Is Good Business

Philanthropy is not a cultural impulse everywhere, especially not in the corporate boardroom. In fact, we've found that the idea of giving back is given only cursory attention by most American CEOs; their charitable efforts are mostly window dressing. Part of the reason we wrote this book is to show that business success isn't hampered by philanthropy— in fact, it's enhanced. We believe philanthropy is part and parcel to building a great company and should be a key business strategy.

Community service brings our philanthropy mission back home, reminding us that our world community begins not in faraway places but in our personal connection with the people we meet every day.

—Maury Peterson,
10-year associate
Vice President,
Grand Circle Foundation

Alan and Harriet's personal and corporate generosity to Boston nonprofits is legendary. Altogether they have made donations and pledges totaling close to $15 million in the last 25 years to such organizations as the West End House Boys & Girls Club, Artists for Humanity, Boston Children's Museum, City on a Hill Charter School, Summer Search, Big Sister, Thompson Island Outward Bound Education Center, AIDS Action Committee, and the Greater Boston Food Bank.

In 1999, Alan gathered many of these long-term community partners to form the Foundation's Community Advisory Group (CAG). At first, the group met to advise Grand Circle Foundation staff on their Boston grants, but in recent years it has become a kind of incubator for social entrepreneurship, a place where nonprofit leaders can meet informally to share war stories and best practices. Alan and Harriet also attend the meetings, challenging the nonprofit leaders to get clear on their vision and mission and to become more focused on their leadership development. It is an innovative and collaborative model for philanthropy, one that seeks to pool experience to raise individual and collective performance.

Philanthropy is good for business because it attracts good people to the company, improves the motivation and retention of associates, creates a personal connection with customers, and builds trust in the organization. Associates and customers feel emotionally attached to an organization they believe is doing good as well as making money, and trust benefits the company in many ways, especially when it faces challenges.

Everyone wants to be part of something bigger than themselves. It's human nature. That's why professional sports teams draw ardent fans and why designer clothes are so popular. Companies that can turn their customers into fans do extraordinarily well—just look at Apple computers, BMW, Ben & Jerry's, Google—and Grand Circle. Because we have integrated philanthropy into our business model, taking travelers to visit our projects around the world, we have made strong emotional connections with our travelers; we know it is one of the reasons they travel with us again and again. We know because they tell us so in their trip evaluations. Our travelers also support our philanthropy through unsolicited donations to Grand Circle Foundation—more than $1 million to date.

A similar emotional connection propels our associates' performance into overdrive. Our associates voted Grand Circle one of the Top 25 Best Companies to Work for in America, an award sponsored by the Great Places to Work Institute and the Society for Human Resource Management. They also voted us one of the Best Places to Work in Boston through an award sponsored by the *Boston Business Journal.*

Another benefit of our philanthropy is that it brings responsive assistance from local people when problems arise in faraway places. We're considered gracious visitors all over the world because we give back to the world we travel. Our regional associates appreciate the recognition they receive in their countries for directing our donations, and they are proud to work for an American company that encourages them to become involved in local philanthropy. All of this pays dividends when we need effort or support above and beyond the norm.

We don't engage in philanthropy to elicit favors or build morale or even to attract travelers, but we've seen the results. Here's our advice: If you want to build a great company, make philanthropy as important to your business as marketing and finance. If you don't feel the impulse for philanthropy in your own heart, give the responsibility to someone in your organization who does have the passion for it. You'll find you'll do very well by doing good.

Since 1992, Grand Circle Foundation has donated or pledged more than $50 million to 163 projects worldwide. Today we support projects in more than 40 countries, including more than 100 schools in 60 villages, and the company has won many industry awards for social responsibility (see Appendix). We feel really good about it.

"I Can't Believe You're Still Alive."

It was at the dedication of a new math and science building at the Rivers School in Weston, Massachusetts, in the spring of 1998 that I became reacquainted with Alan Lewis. He and his family were being honored as the benefactors of the project. Though I'd seen his name in the program, I had no expectation this was the Alan Lewis I had known as a teenager. More than 30 years had passed since I last saw Alan, when he was a camper at the West End House Boys Camp in East Parsonsfield, Maine, where I served as a counselor.

When the master of ceremonies called Alan and his family to the podium to accept the honors, I recognized him from our camp days. As a youngster Alan always stood out for his size and physical strength. My most vivid memory, however, was his intense, competitive nature. To say the least, he was a handful.

After the ceremony, I approached Alan to introduce myself, and we began to reminisce about those summer days. At one point I blurted out, "I can't believe you're still alive." Luckily, we both laughed at my discourteous comment.

When I told Alan I was now serving as the president of the West End House Boys & Girls Club, he immediately asked how he could help the organization. We met later to discuss replacing the aging facilities in Allston, Massachusetts, where we serve approximately 1,200 children from the most diverse neighborhood in Boston.

What we have done for ourselves alone dies with us. What we have done for others and the world remains and is immortal.

—Albert Pike, 19th-century American explorer and philosopher

When a devastating earthquake hit Haiti in January 2010, we sent an e-mail appeal to our associates and travelers asking for help raising money fast. Grand Circle Foundation offered to match any donations received within two days—up to $150,000. Within 48 hours, 2,500 travelers and many associates had responded with contributions that totaled nearly $400,000 with the Foundation's matching funds. Follow-on donations exceeded $100,000 from an additional 1,500 travelers. That's 4,000 travelers who responded to our appeal right away, helping us to raise $541,000. What a great bunch of travelers to partner with us so enthusiastically.

—Alan Lewis

Alan and Harriet were the major catalysts for bringing together the resources needed to raise $8 million. Today we have a renovated 40,000-square-foot facility, the Lewis & Gordon Center, with a Kids' Café that serves 65,000 meals a year—all because of the generous spirit of this man who did not forget his roots.

—Henry L. Barr, former President
  West End House Boys & Girls Club, Allston, Massachusetts

A Final Lesson

There is something about our vision quest in Arizona that we didn't tell you. After the third night, as we were climbing down from the plateau, eager to get back to Boston to start work on the new Grand Circle Foundation, Harriet suddenly slipped and fell. She landed hard, spread-eagled across a prickly pear cactus. It hurt—*really* hurt. That night we had to pull each needle from her body one at a time. Harriet asked herself why this had happened after such an inspirational journey. She decided it was a message—a message to prepare herself to return to reality. Like our vision quest, changing people's lives would be hard, but it would be an experience that would change our lives, too.

Sawyer Park and the Global Village

Harriet and I have a home away from home called Beaver Dam, in Kensington, New Hampshire. Beaver Dam has been in my family for four generations and I've been going there since I was a kid, so we have deep roots in the community. It is a small township, really, just 1,800 people scattered around a 12-square-mile area.

We love Kensington, and we wanted to do something for the township, so in 2004 we began discussions with the town to build a nice park on some land we owned there. With all our experience with Grand Circle Foundation, you would think this little philanthropic project would go smoothly, but it didn't. I broke a few of Harriet's Rules, and they came back to bite me.

For one thing, I didn't really want to get personally involved, so I appointed a liaison, a guy I knew, to work with the town, and he managed to piss everyone off. Also, we threw around a lot of ideas for the park without really listening to town officials or asking what the townspeople themselves wanted or needed. There were too many chiefs, not enough trust, and no shared vision for the project. At that point I just walked away.

A couple of years later, one of the early project supporters, Michael Del Sesto, approached me hoping to get the park back off the ground. This time things were different. The selectmen formed a committee of town officers, youth and recreation staff, and representatives from our Pinnacle Leadership Center, which is also located in Kensington. We listened harder, and I got a new point man, Kensington resident Bruce Cilley, who not only was a strong project leader but also got along very well with the townspeople. Everyone involved was a townie, and before long the project got neighbors out of their homes, united in the excitement of getting the job done.

One day, Harriet remarked, "This is just like Costa Rica. The project didn't really get started until you started listening, found a good leader, and made sure everyone in town got involved. Really, Alan, good philanthropy *does* take a village."

Sawyer Park opened in 2008. It is a grander place than we had first imagined, with three lighted baseball diamonds, an all-purpose field, a basketball court that converts to an ice-skating rink in winter, a playground, a skateboard park, bathrooms, a full-kitchen concession stand, and walking paths that connect with the town trail system. The entire park is organic—no pesticides or herbicides allowed. Four fertilizer companies each adopted a field, and residents help with turf care.

We donated the land and the funds to build Sawyer Park, and we will make annual contributions toward its maintenance. It's been worth all the early trouble to watch the community come together under the lights for hot dogs and a Little League game. I learned a lot, too. You need to listen before you can work together, and you need a strong leader to keep projects moving along. This is one of the most meaningful philanthropic donations I've ever made, and I've made a lot. Who knew it would take a world of giving to know how to bring charity back home?

—Alan Lewis

One generation plants the trees, another gets the shade.

—*Chinese proverb*

Two chairmen meet in Sinya, Tanzania: Maasai Tribal Chairman Kipuloli Napiteeng and Alan Lewis, 2001.

CHAPTER 4

Unforgettable Experiences

In January of 2001, Harriet and I set out to climb Mount Kilimanjaro. It was Harriet's idea, really. She had been feeling kind of stuck that year, in need of an adventure. Ever since we went to Nepal together in 1988, Harriet has said that fresh air, hard exercise, and open spaces are good for her. Something about the difficulty breathing actually opens up her mind and body. She gets a powerful clarity. So she started training like a maniac, and off we went.

At the last minute, Harriet got sick and we had to change our plans. After Harriet felt better, we picked up our old friend and partner Willy Chambulo, owner of Kibo Guides, who arranged for us to camp at a Maasai village called Sinya. It was market day, and people were converging on the village from all directions—just streams of people dressed in the traditional red cloth of the Maasai, coming to market with sugar and trinkets, their spears rattling and their jewelry tinkling.

Somehow we found ourselves in a grassy area under a grove of trees where the villagers were slaughtering a goat. We later learned that this grassy spot was Sinya's only restaurant. Pretty soon we were attracting a crowd. At one point Harriet was surrounded by throngs of chattering women dressed in boldly printed fabrics, all eager to see and touch this white-skinned, red-headed visitor. They were smiling, and singing in a high-pitched way, and ducking their heads towards her and away from her. It was like being caught up in a raucous celebration of some unexpected victory.

The warmth of the people and their eagerness to share their culture made this one of Harriet's strongest memories. It was truly an unforgettable experience. But it was also a little scary. The crowd was too close; Harriet couldn't get any air. Suddenly a man appeared, carrying a spear, and the crowd dispersed. It was Kipuloli Napiteeng, the chairman of the village. Something in Harriet's expression had persuaded him to intervene, and for the rest of our stay, we were Kipuloli's honored guests.

That evening, Kipuloli, Harriet, and I shared a meal around a campfire. Kipuloli brought a goat. We had a long and fascinating conversation about our respective lives. In our discussion, we learned that Kipuloli was elected chairman by the male elders of the village, and that he shared our passion for education. He understood that education would irrevocably change his village and its culture, but he wanted the children to make their way and prosper in a modern world. We saw that Kipuloli was a compassionate and visionary leader and liked him immediately. We didn't want this unusual cultural exchange to end, so we made an impromptu decision: We invited the chairman to come to Boston.

That's when we found out that Kipuloli possessed another leadership skill: He knew how to bargain. He would come to Boston if we could meet three conditions; we agreed to them all, and even imposed one of our own. Around that campfire, with the surrounding villagers looking more and more confused, we settled the terms of Kipuloli's visit to the United States: The chairman could bring along his chief warrior; they could both wear their traditional dress; and they could carry their spears—except on the airplane, of course. Kipuloli agreed to our sole condition—that he keep an open mind. The deal was made. He would come in June.

What were we thinking? Kipuloli had never been on an airplane, and had seldom been more than a few dozen kilometers from his village. He spoke no English, and we spoke no Maasai. The chairman had never seen a building taller than a few stories, and he had only a rudimentary understanding of money. How would we even feed him and his warrior? Although we have plenty of trees, there are no Maasai restaurants in Boston.

As we walked away, Willy shook his head and started laughing.

"What's so funny?" I asked.

"Mr. Napiteeng thinks you're the chairman of a faraway village called Boston."

—Alan Lewis

We love to travel and interact with other cultures, and when we talk to our travelers, we find they feel the same as we do. Travel is fun, enlightening, and it keeps us young. We always return from a trip feeling fresh and rejuvenated. Some might say we're lucky to be in the travel business, but luck had nothing to do with it. We picked travel because of our keen enthusiasm to experience the world. We wouldn't be as happy in any other business.

We like going to unusual places and doing something out of the ordinary. Over the years, we've visited more than 100 countries, seen six continents, and traveled more than a million miles. We've trekked in Nepal and camped in the Serengeti. We've traveled together, we've traveled separately, we've traveled with our children and friends, and we've gone on countless trips with the company.

What we've learned in our travels is that it's not possible to fully understand another culture and people in a short trip, but if the experience is genuine and, as they say, *up-close and personal,* we can get a better appreciation for other lifestyles and points of view and learn something about ourselves in the process. Our hosts may learn something more personal about Americans, too. This is our travel philosophy, and this is what we strive for in all of the trips we offer with all of our travel companies —Grand Circle Travel, Overseas Adventure Travel (OAT), and Grand Circle Small Ship Cruises. We want every trip to offer unforgettable experiences that can help change people's lives.

Honey Has an Idea

The idea of offering "Unforgettable Experiences" goes way back at Grand Circle. Honey Streit-Reyes coined the phrase in 1989. We have known Honey for more than 40 years. She grew up in East Prussia, then came to the United States and worked for a while as a housekeeper and car dealer on Long Island. Later she ran trips to Mexico with her husband, Rodolfo. Rodolfo was another character. He knew all the shady tricks of the trade and he could smell trouble a long way off. In later years, Rodolfo was a great ally to us, our special agent on the ground, letting us know who was taking advantage of us as our business expanded around the world.

Honey was one of our early hires after we bought Grand Circle in 1985; she was our European buyer, and she designed many of our early trips in Germany, Austria, and Switzerland. She was an expert on ground delivery, fashioning hour-by-hour itineraries that were carefully designed for appreciation and discovery. Honey and Rodolfo wanted our travelers to have adventures that would last a lifetime—experiences that were unavailable with any other travel company.

Honey designed our very first *The Best of Eastern Europe* trip in 1991. It was an exciting time to visit Eastern Europe. The Berlin Wall had come down just 18 months earlier; there were celebrations in the street and electricity in the air. It was new territory for American travel companies, and Honey made the most of her eyes and ears on the ground. Because she had grown up in Germany, she knew firsthand how to make the trip unforgettable—by staying in family-owned hotels close to city centers, arranging home-hosted meals, eating in local *schnitzel* and *goulash* restaurants, visiting places where Americans didn't usually

When the music and images of a trip remain in your head on a daily basis, when you smile without realizing it's because you remembered something from the trip, you know you have had the best experience of your life.

—Michelle Sewing-Sohn,
First-time traveler
Lake Worth, Florida

go, and pacing the 18-day trip so there was enough time to really engage with the culture. While other companies were herding their travelers through empty cathedrals and tourist-trap *biergartens*, our travelers were having conversations with lifelong Communists. Now, almost two decades later, *The Best of Eastern Europe* continues to be a popular trip.

Getting to Unforgettable

Our travelers tell us we have excellent trips. In fact, 81 percent of our travelers rated their trip as "Excellent" in 2009. We use three tools to achieve excellence: We design all our trips around four Product Pillars; we evaluate our trips using the best quality-assurance system in the industry; and we hire and train the greatest Program Directors and trip leaders in the world. It is a three-pronged approach, and each component supports the others. The Product Pillars discipline trip design and delivery. Our quality surveys give us feedback so we can improve the products. And our Program Directors and Trip Leaders work every day to keep the unforgettable experiences coming.

Our Trips Rest on Four Mighty Pillars

We established our four Product Pillars over the course of several years. The first pillar—Value—came in 1988, shortly after we returned from our difficult offsite on the Salmon River. Our president and vice president for product development had both left the company, unwilling to let go of the cheap, mass-market tours they were used to. The other three pillars emerged from the offsite to the Costa Rican cloud forest in 1991 and the offsite to Portugal in 1992, the one that also produced the commitment to becoming The Great Company. Alan himself announced the new vision to the associates. Grand Circle would offer meaningful cultural encounters at unsurpassed value that could actually change people's lives, and we would do this by building all our trips on four pillars: Value, Pacing, Choice, and Discovery.

Value. Not just good value, but *unsurpassed* value. We're not talking about price alone. We look at value as the combination of price and the experience you get for that price. The easiest thing in the world is to cut back on trip features until you have the rock-bottom price. But what's the point of traveling at the bottom? You'd get a better experience watching a travel special on TV. Instead, we strive to keep our price as low as possible, while maintaining excellence and offering high-quality included features. For example, a home-hosted meal with a local family costs less than a

I met a family in Costa Rica that had been offering home-hosted dinners to our travelers for years. I wondered if they ever got tired of the cooking and polite conversation, so I asked the father why he kept doing them. He was surprised by the question, and then said, "I've had doctors, lawyers, authors, and even an astronaut at my table. Do you know how much my son has learned?"

—Maggie Nevins,
6-year associate
Renewal Traveler Counselor

restaurant meal for the group, but it gives our travelers a much more authentic cultural experience. On a per diem basis, we offer the best value in the industry, without exception. For example, on our best-selling River Cruise from Amsterdam to Vienna, our travelers pay at least $100 less per day than they would with our strongest competitor, saving between $1,000 and $2,000 per trip.

Pacing. Good pacing makes for an enjoyable trip, and that goes double for older travelers. We pay special attention to the first 48 hours, when travelers are tired from their overseas flight. We limit early wakeup calls whenever we can. We train our Program Directors and Trip Leaders to walk at a leisurely pace. When we travel by road to a featured site, we try to find a route and time that avoids the worst traffic. We don't jam everything possible into an itinerary, because memorable trips allow travelers time to savor small events like having a cup of coffee at a sidewalk café. As a rule, we spend at least two or three days in each location on land trips—on some GCT trips, six to eight—enough time to settle in and feel comfortable.

Choice. We know Americans prize their freedom and independence, so we build a lot of choice into every trip. We offer land trips, River Cruises, small ship coastal cruises, Extended Vacations, and adventure trips in 100 countries around the world. Each trip can be customized with a choice of optional excursions, as well as the opportunity to add days at the beginning or end of the trip so travelers can do as they like on their own. We build in plenty of free time for travelers to follow their Program Director or trip leader's advice on good restaurants and sights to see, and open seating on our River Cruises lets travelers explore different vantage points on the ship and sit with whomever they please. We also encourage our Program Directors and Trip Leaders to offer choices to travelers on the fly, so if unexpected opportunities arise, they can decide whether to follow them. We have always found the most successful kind of leadership empowers others to make their own decisions.

National Week in China

National Week in China is like our Fourth of July spread over an entire week. The Chinese people flock to Beijing for the festivities. Our first day was very crowded. In the evening, the Trip Leader explained the next day's itinerary and said that the planned sites would be mobbed and traffic horrendous. She also described an alternative itinerary that would avoid the worst of

Alan and I have always believed in having sharp contrasts when we travel. One day we might ride camels across the Sahara and spend the night in a tent or a tree house lodging. The next day we might take an easy stroll through a market and stay in small, warm, inviting lodgings where we can relax, reflect, and renew our energy for another day of discovery. We like to mix things up. That's what good pacing is all about.

—Harriet Lewis

Bilbo used to say: "It's a dangerous business, Frodo, going out your door. You step onto the road, and if you don't keep your feet, there's no knowing where you might be swept off to."

—J. R. R. Tolkien, *The Hobbit*

the crowds. Then she asked what we wanted to do. We all chose to stick with the original itinerary. The crowds were as promised and we got jostled a bit, but we didn't mind because it was our choice. Besides, we literally rubbed elbows with the locals!

I've been on trips with other travel companies where we were overprotected the whole time and were constantly told what to do. Grand Circle treats its travelers like adults. They respect us and let us make decisions. I appreciate that.

—Diane Best, *5-time traveler*
Paradise Valley, Arizona

Discovery. Discovery is the most important pillar, the one that helps us create unforgettable experiences. When we travel together, we like to interact with the locals and discover the local culture firsthand. Harriet likes to poke around markets and talk with teachers; Alan likes to take long walks to find places tourists don't usually see. We assume our travelers want to do these things, too.

So over the years we've created a series of signature discovery events for our travelers, including school visits, home-hosted meals, excursions to native markets and bazaars, exclusive tours of some of our Grand Circle Foundation projects, cooking, crafts, and discussions with experts on "hot-button" local political and economic issues. These kinds of programs can be difficult to set up, but they pay off in customer satisfaction. When discovery is high on a trip, we get high scores on our post-trip evaluations. When we fail, we see low scores.

Go Where Americans Don't Go

We have a saying at Grand Circle: *Go where Americans don't go.* It's part of our discovery formula, to visit places that other American companies don't usually take their travelers. For example, we visit the City of the Dead in Cairo, tour native townships in South Africa, and take our travelers to Palestine and Albania. In China, we visit an undeveloped section of the Great Wall where no other tourists are present—a section of the Wall that Grand Circle Foundation helps maintain. We include unusual modes of travel on our trips, too, like camel rides, river rafting, sailing on *sampans* and *feluccas*, and an overnight train ride in China. We go off the beaten path whenever we can.

We also push the boundaries of conventional tourist conversation. In fact, we train our trip leaders to raise sensitive issues that other travel companies consider "non-discussible"—and get our travelers talking about them. In Vietnam and Croatia, for example, they discuss wars involving American and U.N. troops. In India, they talk about the caste system. In China, they talk about Tibet and censorship, and in Egypt they discuss the role of women in a Muslim society.

We also train our trip leaders to *Stop the bus.* If a trip leader sees something interesting happening on a walking tour or bus excursion, they will ask travelers if they would like to stop to watch or participate. Trip leaders have stopped the bus for parades, political demonstrations, roadside craft sellers, cattle auctions, wedding processions, and street performers; they have even stopped the bus to help out with a rice harvest. This kind of ad hoc discovery event has the double benefit of showing our travelers something unexpected and completely unscripted, and giving the trip leader something new to talk about, too.

A Day in the Life of a Village

Our four Product Pillars come together especially well in a program that we call *A Day in the Life,* which has been a popular feature of many of our trips since 1989. The program is different each time, but usually involves spending a full day or half day in a small, out-of-the-way village experiencing local life firsthand. In Thailand, for example, travelers take a walking tour of a village, meet the principal of an elementary school supported by Grand Circle Foundation, learn a simple dance from the children, tour the village's new agricultural cooperative (another Grand Circle Foundation partnership), and try their hands at making traditional bamboo baskets and grass brooms. In Mexico, travelers visit a Mayo home and learn how to make tortillas. In each case, the *Day in the Life* program engages our travelers in relaxed, hands-on cultural exchanges with the community at large.

These village programs are difficult to design and deliver, and we have spent a lot of time on them. Making them an included feature imparts value to the trip and helps vary its pacing. Although structured, the program leaves plenty of opportunities for travelers to choose whom they will talk to and what they will do. Most important, these village-based discovery programs are enthusiastically received by our travelers, who invariably rate them very high on their post-trip evaluations.

Once, on a family trip to Zimbabwe, we had just finished dinner and were walking to our tents at the lodge when I suddenly froze. I said to Alan, "What's that noise? I think it's an elephant."

"No," he said. "It is not an elephant."

I could still hear it, though—and it sounded heavy. Then I looked around and I said, "Oh, really?"

The elephant was just a stone's throw away. He was walking along, just pulling up trees like they were nothing. We were right by the kids' tent and we went up on the porch to watch him. Suddenly, this huge trunk came toward us, like a big serpent. It got so close ... so we decided it was time to go inside. He lost interest then, and continued on his way, walking through the campsite and pulling up trees.

Things like that happen in Africa all the time.

—Harriet Lewis

A Big Mistake

When the dollar weakened dramatically around 2005, we took some included features out of our trips and made them optional excursions instead. This strategy allowed us to keep our base prices low, because optional excursions are priced separately, but it hurt our quality scores by undermining two of our Product Pillars: both value and discovery. When we saw the results, we put these excursions back into the base trips. Like magic, the scores went back up.

This was a very big mistake because it tampered with our second Extreme Competitive Advantage—Unsurpassed Value and Excellence, which is the foundation of our product strategy and the key to our dominance in the industry. Lesson learned: Stay with our Extreme Competitive Advantages. They are what made us successful and set us up for future success.

How Our Trips Became More Adventurous

If all this emphasis on discovery and unplanned detours sounds familiar, there's a reason. As a family, we Lewises have always been adventuresome travelers. Small group, wilderness-based adventures thrill us, and our travel journals are full of adventure travel stories. We went trekking together in Nepal for Alan's 40th birthday. We took the kids hiking in the Costa Rican rain forest and took them rafting on the Zambezi River from the base of Victoria Falls—a very adventurous trip that involved whirlpools, an overturned raft, and alligators on the shore. Chasing adventure is how we ended up in Sinya, off the beaten path in the shadow of Kilimanjaro, swapping stories with Kipuloli Napiteeng.

So it is perhaps not surprising that we bought Overseas Adventure Travel (OAT) in 1993. There were strategic reasons for the acquisition, of course: We wanted to broaden our traveler base; Baby Boomers were coming into retirement with big adventures on their minds; and we needed to build a roster of trips outside of Europe and the Middle East, where American travel had been devastated by the first Gulf War. But the reasons were equally personal; for us, "adventure travel" is pretty much synonymous with "unforgettable experience."

There were difficulties. The small, Cambridge, Massachusetts-based company was losing money, and its trips were too fast-paced and expensive for our market. Our strategy was to apply Grand Circle's four Product Pillars to the design and delivery of the OAT trips, then watch the quality reports like a hawk until we were sure the trips suited our travelers' wishes and met our high goals.

The biggest challenge—and greatest opportunity—arose from OAT's signature feature: small group travel. Our traditional Grand Circle land trips have an average group size of 38 travelers, a number that fits comfortably into a standard-size bus, but OAT land trips take no more than 16 travelers per trip. Small groups offer a more intimate travel experience, and make it easier to get to out-of-the-way places, but it's hard to make money on them because their high costs have to be spread over few travelers. It was a challenge to make our value proposition work for small groups, but we did it by making the trips longer (to bring down the per diem cost); dealing directly with local vendors in the destination countries; including airfare in the package price; and focusing our marketing on the unique and unforgettable experiences.

Two Brands, One Vision

We believe that a great company does a few things well, so when we make a new acquisition or start a really big initiative, we take care not to reinvent ourselves. We look to our leaders to keep us focused and disciplined, remembering our mission, vision, and values, and applying our proven strategies to the new opportunity. So when we acquired Overseas Adventure Travel, we stayed true to our winning formula, rigorously applying Grand Circle's four Product Pillars to the OAT trips. Within two years, we had turned the company around, turning a half-million dollar annual loss into a $3 million profit. In 2010, more than 50,000 people traveled with OAT, and the brand brought in $269 million in sales.

If I hadn't had so many travel experiences when I was growing up, I would not be the person I am today. Traveling has genuinely made me more open-minded and more open to risk. Mom and Dad made me do things I would never have imagined doing. Sometimes I didn't want to do their adventures, but nine times out of ten, I enjoyed the experience and 100 percent of the time I tried something new.

I am very grateful for the challenges and risks that I've come across while traveling. I learn something new about myself every time. The adventures experienced with my family became infectious. I travel so much now that I think Mom and Dad wish I'd just park my butt at home for once! We miss each other when we don't travel together.

—Edward Lewis

Our Amazon trip was spectacular. Our guide brought some villagers on the boat for a visit—three families, with their children. They were curious about us. They wondered if we were too cold in our air-conditioned cabins and thought it strange that we slept in beds. We showed them the dining room and kitchen and they were amazed with the stove and refrigerator. They had no electricity, so they fished every day and salted some for later. It's good to be home, but we will never forget the lovely, generous people of the Amazon.

—Margaret and Richard Southwick,
6-time travelers
Bakersfield, California

The last part was easy. Small group travel really *does* change the travel experience. Small groups can get access to restricted sites like antiquities that have been jeopardized by too many people trampling through them over the years. Small groups can stay in family-run inns and eat in cozy restaurants that can't accommodate bigger groups. Small groups create a special camaraderie among travelers, who often make friends with whom they travel together again later. They connect more easily with children during school visits, engage in deeper conversations at our Grand Circle Foundation sites, and get more individual attention from trip leaders.

But as every adventure traveler knows, the "unforgettable" part of adventure travel is the adventure. Once you've slept under a starry Botswana sky, or eaten rice cakes with villagers in Thailand, or pulled a new friend under a towering waterfall in Peru, you'll never be the same again.

How Our Trips Got All Wet

Grand Circle had been chartering small ships for excursions on the Nile and Yangtze rivers for years, but in 1996 we decided it was time to get into a new category of travel: river cruises and coastal cruises. We jumped into the European river cruise business headfirst: first chartering some ships, then buying a cruise line. The first was an impulse buy, the second a misunderstanding (we'll talk about that later), but the reasoning was sound: River cruises offered a different kind of unforgettable experience that would appeal to older Americans.

Most civilizations grew up first next to water, so the oldest and most picturesque towns are frequently found along rivers and coastal waterways, making sightseeing easy. Small river boats and coastal cruisers can dock in shallow-water ports and at islands that can't accommodate large ships, getting travelers off the beaten path. Plus the ships serve as floating hotels, so travelers can unpack (just once!), settle in, and move effortlessly between ports that promise new adventures every day.

We didn't know much about ships at the time, but we knew how to deliver unforgettable experiences. We leveraged our company strong points—value and discovery—and used our land expertise to design unique onshore excursions, then presented the trips to our travelers, who were clamoring for River Cruises. In time we were able to price our cruises on the assumption of 96 percent shipboard occupancy— far above the industry norm. This tipped the scales for us. Because most ship profit comes from selling the last cabins, we could offer our river cruises at prices far below those advertised by our competitors.

Today, Grand Circle is the world leader in small ship cruises, operating more than 60 owned or chartered ships all around the world. Our ships cruise the rivers of Europe, South America, Asia, and Africa, and our small ocean ships cruise the coastlines of Scandinavia, the Mediterranean, and South America. We also have deep-water cruises to Antarctica and the Galápagos. That's pretty unforgettable right there.

Quality Begins at Home

How do we know so much about what our travelers think about our trips? We send them an especially elaborate post-trip questionnaire. Travelers find it in their mailbox when they arrive home, and we get an astonishing response rate of more than 70 percent. Some travel companies are pleased to get a 3 to 20 percent return, but we find that travelers arriving home after an unforgettable experience are eager to tell us about their trip—the good, the bad, and the ugly. They not only answer the check-the-box questions, they also write copious longhand comments.

Our questionnaires are long—typically five to seven pages—and they cover everything from the traveler's first phone call to the company to their arrival home. The questionnaires are customized for each trip and coded by departure date so we can track the quality of the trip in different seasons and under different trip leaders and drivers. The questions probably look excessive to people accustomed to customer-response postcards, but this information is our lifeblood; it literally determines how we manage future departures. Leadership in the travel business requires a vision, but it also requires *information*.

On an OAT trip to Egypt, I heard music coming from a restaurant. As a retired music teacher, I simply had to stop and listen. I even asked to join the musicians on stage to play the drums. As I jived along with the band, dressed in a *galabeya* and headdress, I was one of them. It made me aware of the global society we share, even in our own country.

Returning home, I saw this firsthand at my church, where we normally have two services: one for our elderly church members and another for our Hispanic congregants, spoken entirely in Spanish. Recently, we had a combined service, and I was the organist. Again it was the music that provided the shared experience, overcoming the language and cultural barriers. My trip taught me we can all create bridges of connection.

—Billie Blakeney,
3-time traveler
Augusta, New Jersey

We talk a lot in this book about changing people's lives, and I wonder sometimes if people know what we mean. Well, we get letters all the time about life-changing trips big and small. It can be something simple, like returning home from a trip and finding you're reading the international report in your newspaper—for the first time. Or suddenly seeing all the curry restaurants in your neighborhood; they were there before, you just didn't see them. One woman recently told us about her trip to Slovakia, where she saw a picture of her grandfather for the first time. Another wrote of celebrating Shabbat with relatives in Israel, and hearing their personal accounts of the Holocaust. Several travelers have even taken up second careers after going on our trips—as authors! You never know what will come of traveling. That's the fun of it.

—Harriet Lewis

Another Big Mistake

We believe in cutting products that don't meet our standards. Years ago, our Russia trip came up short on quality scores. A big problem was the food. The travelers said it was awful—boring and repetitive—with way too many potatoes. Another problem was that two of our senior leaders didn't really believe in the trip; they were concerned about the quality of the ship. Though our associates in Moscow and St. Petersburg said they were making progress, we cancelled the product. Our big concern was that if the trip didn't meet expectations, we would lose loyal travelers. We couldn't risk it.

It turned out to be a mistake. The quality scores for the final trip departures actually *exceeded* our goals, but it was too late, because we had already released our inventory. Our travelers were right all along—the food was boring and then it got better —we had just acted too fast. But we had also made another mistake—we failed to listen to our associates in Russia, the ones who had the most current information and who really had their eyes and ears on the ground. We lived to regret it, because it took us five years to get back into Russia. All that time we kept kicking ourselves, saying: *Listen to the travelers and the folks on the ground.*

Most companies ask for feedback from their customers, but few of them act on it as obsessively as we do. We scan every questionnaire electronically, tabulate all the quantifiable data, create a database that is accessible to our associates all around the world, read all the handwritten comments, and send the results both to the regional office to which the trip is assigned and to the appropriate departments here in Boston. When a consistent problem arises, our regional offices immediately work to develop an action plan to address it.

A team of outside observers once famously characterized us as being "Maniacs on excellence," and they are right. We believe if you want to build a great company, you have to ask your customers how they feel about your products, listen to what they have to say, and then *act* on what they say. We believe all our trips are excellent, but our travelers have proven us wrong again and again. Fortunately, they also teach us how to improve. We change trips all the time in response to what travelers have told us. For example, we recently added an additional night in Jerusalem to our Israel trip, along with a new *Day in the Life* of a Bedouin community; on our Panama trip, we took our travelers' advice to move the transit of the Panama Canal to the end of the trip, to serve as the climax of the adventure.

Over the last five years, we have raised our overall excellence rating five points, to 81 percent, and we've done it by listening to our travelers. Good leaders listen. Our experience is that travelers know what they want, and when we deliver, they become unassailably loyal to the company, traveling with us again and again.

A Traumatic Decision

Most American travel companies use American tour guides on their overseas trips. We did, too, for the most part, until 1996, when we began thinking about hiring more local guides. We wanted our travelers to have authentic cultural encounters abroad, experiences that other travel companies couldn't easily replicate. Could we deliver more unforgettable experiences if our trip leaders were born and raised in the destination country? Would their cultural knowledge, national pride, and local connections make enough of a difference to make up for the difficulty and cost of completely changing our system?

As it turns out, we had our answer in our travelers' post-trip evaluations. At the time we were using both American and local trip leaders in some of our more far-flung destinations. When we compared their quality scores, we found that our travelers preferred the local trip leaders. It made a certain amount of sense. Even the most experienced American guide would have trouble delivering the kind of insider view and behind-the-scenes information that a local guide can. But that sample was small. Would the conclusion apply across all our trips?

It may seem odd, but our quality scores for the *air portion* of our trips supported the case for using local guides. Our air scores were never very good in those days, but they were better when we used a foreign airline. The seats and service weren't very different, but the excitement of

I have been interested in yoga and Indian philosophy for more than 20 years, first as a yoga practitioner and later as a teacher. Part of my training included studying the origins and philosophy of yoga in India—but all of these lessons came from books and teachers—until I went to India on an OAT trip.

I was grateful that our Trip Leader, Sujay Lall, was so knowledgeable and willing to discuss spiritual philosophy with me. He shared readings about different religious beliefs, gave me a Sanskrit lesson, and went out of his way to give me as many opportunities as possible to experience the spiritual side of India. We visited many temples, were introduced to a "holy man," and met with a guru in Varanasi, where we received astrological and spiritual advice. It was a special experience for me.

—Cynthia Moltenfort,
 4-time traveler
 Burke, Virginia

going to a faraway place started as soon as the traveler boarded the plane and was greeted by a foreign accent. Travelers liked that immediate connection with a different culture, and they liked the personal touch.

To be honest, we were a little surprised. The image of the Ugly American dominated American tourism in the 1990s, and many travel companies operated on the assumption that American tourists didn't really want to rub elbows with foreigners, that they preferred their cultural encounters filtered through an American guide who could lead them safely through dirty streets and get them back to the hotel in time for cocktails. Most companies cocooned their travelers, keeping them away from trouble spots and out of uncomfortable conversations because they thought that's what American travelers wanted. We thought our travelers were different—more educated, more curious, and more open-minded—and were delighted to learn that was true.

Still, switching to all-local guides would be painful. We had close to 300 American trip leaders working for us, and many of them had been with Grand Circle from the beginning. Some were friends. How could we cut them loose? We considered phasing them out, but that could take years, and while we were transitioning, we wouldn't be able to guarantee our travelers a local guide.

After weeks of mulling the issue over, we made one of the most difficult decisions of our business lives: We let all our American guides go and replaced them with trip leaders native to our destination. A suit from a group of California guides wasn't resolved for five years, and the settlement was costly. It may have been a difficult decision, but the data from our traveler questionnaires after the change showed that it was unquestionably the *right* decision. As we expected, our quality scores soared.

Getting the Best

We didn't just want local guides; we wanted the *best* local guides the country had to offer. We had learned a lot about trip leaders over the years. Alan, in fact, had served as a trip leader early in his career with United Travel, taking travelers to Switzerland and the Caribbean. It was maybe not his finest hour in the travel business—he was young, restless, and perhaps not as patient as he might have been—but he

> When an organization thinks big, leadership matters a lot. At Grand Circle, we believe that true leadership is grounded in courage and conviction. Courage allows us to think big and take risks; conviction charts our course.
>
> —Alan Lewis

learned a few things. He learned that leading trips is hard work, that a great trip leader can make all the difference in a trip and in a company's reputation, and that a fair number of them are pretty aggressive entrepreneurs in their own right.

Getting the best native guides would be challenging, so we reviewed compensation in every country and made sure we offered the best total package, including year-round work and high per diem rates. In return, we set challenging goals and rigorously measured our trip leaders' performance.

By hiring native guides, we broke the tourism model wide open. Our competitors thought we were crazy. Most of them still do; in fact, 95 percent of travel providers worldwide continue to use guides from the home country. Certainly, using American guides would be cheaper and easier. But the benefits of having local guides are tremendous. They know the language, they understand cultural cues, they have friends and family in the country, and they have personal stories to tell. They know where the bad guys and the bargains are. Local guides deliver unforgettable experiences. We might be crazy, but we made the right decision and we have never looked back.

Bending the Rules

We make one exception to our local trip leader guideline. When a trip visits several different countries, the trip leader will be from the first country on the itinerary. We call this *continuous leadership*, and we implemented it after reading our post-trip questionnaires. Travelers grow attached to their trip leader and don't like to see a change just because they have crossed a border. We believe paying attention to what travelers tell us is crucial to creating excellent trips.

When the SARS epidemic hit China, I was reminded that our trip leaders do more than handle minor problems. They are responsible for the safety of our travelers. Unfortunate incidents can happen anyplace. It makes me feel good that our trip leaders are more than educators with engaging personalities, they are highly capable leaders.

—Jim O'Brien,
   15-year associate
   Chairman, Kensington
   Investment Company

Transformational Encounters

Travel can change people's lives, and sometimes travel can transform a company. When we look back on our accidental trip to the village of

Sinya, we're startled by its many ramifications. After our encounter with Kipuloli Napiteeng, we expanded our presence in Tanzania; today we have two safari trips to Tanzania with OAT, and another trip that combines the two. Though Sinya is not on any direct travel route, we have included it in our Tanzania itineraries, and travelers rate it a memorable experience. We knew they would. It was certainly a memorable experience for us.

Our visit also affected our Foundation work in the region. On our visit there in 2001, we stopped by the local school, as we usually do. Harriet was dismayed. The schoolroom was tiny, filled with hornets, and students shared space with stored food and other provisions. The books were literally moldy. After observing class for a few hours, she asked herself, "What chance do these kids have?"

We knew we had to do something, but how much difference could we make alone? Luckily, we knew a social entrepreneur in Tanzania, the same individual who took us to Sinya in the first place: Willy Chambulo. Willy had built Kibo Guides from scratch. He also loved to build physical things. We had been partnering with him for years as a ground operator; now we decided to take our relationship to a new level. We made Willy a proposition. We would help capitalize him so he could build wilderness camps and help us fix up the school in Sinya. He would pay us back with reduced rates when our travelers stayed at his camps.

We saw this as a way to buy direct in Tanzania and simultaneously help the children of Sinya. We would work the business side through Overseas Adventure Travel and Grand Circle Travel, and the social side through Grand Circle Foundation. Little did we know we were breaking social norms in Tanzania. Willy was the first native Tanzanian to own lodges and permanent tented sites in the country. Other lodge owners were not happy that we were bypassing them and financing a competitor, but it all worked out in the end. Willy did a magnificent job building the lodges and school, and we've had a loyal partner ever since, one that we view as a true friend.

Great Travel Experiences

When we design and improve our trips, our goal is to give travelers experiences they will remember for a lifetime. Unforgettable experiences come in many packages. Sometimes they involve the kinds of cultural encounters or awe-inspiring sights that we deliberately build into our trips. But our travelers mention little, unexpected things, too, like having breakfast at dawn on a dune in Morocco. Our travelers' unforgettable experiences often seem to involve food, like grabbing falafel on the streets of Luxor, trying chicken feet for breakfast in China, or drinking snake wine in Vietnam.

Unforgettable experiences can also be simple human connections, like buying fruit in an open market, singing along with a bunch of Hungarians to American rock-and-roll, trading sign language with Tibetan monks in another bus while caught in traffic, or just making friends with fellow travelers. Our travelers tell us about these kinds of experiences all the time.

The great thing about travel is that you don't need to plan every aspect of a trip to make it memorable. The world is a fascinating place. If you do the pacing right and give trip leaders permission to stop the bus to pursue unscripted experiences, then serendipity will immeasurably add to the trip, and pretty soon you will have an unforgettable experience. We are happy to sit back and let it happen.

The real voyage of discovery consists not in seeking new landscapes, but in having new eyes.

—Marcel Proust

CEO Nick Lento and Vince Cook clown around while exemplifying leadership at a recent BusinessWorks®.

CHAPTER 5

You Can Lead from Anywhere

We stood in a serene meadow that had been mowed so recently that we could still smell the freshly cut grass. There were about two dozen of us waiting patiently with a tall African man dressed in a red robe and carrying a spear. Except for a gently flapping American flag, the New Hampshire morning was exceptionally still. People casually milled about, some in muted conversation, while others wandered over to long tables covered with coffee urns, juice pitchers, fruit, and pastries. A few kept expectant eyes on the forest trail that led from a distant dirt parking area.

Then we heard them, far off at first, but gradually drawing closer. They were coming. When the boisterous chattering became louder, we knew they were about to break clear of the woods and into the meadow.

Pretty soon, a long line of people emerged from the woods, laughing and cheering. The buses had delivered all the Boston associates to BusinessWorks, our once-a-year company event that brings together associates from all over the world. We had been meeting for two weeks with our Boston and overseas leaders to resolve business issues at Pinnacle, our leadership development center; this was the final day of the offsite, when the entire company came together for a day of learning, challenge, and some irreverent fun.

In years past, we had shaken hands, slapped backs, and even hugged as everyone joyfully filed through our welcome line. This year would be different.

Kipuloli Napiteeng, the chairman of the Tanzanian village of Sinya, had joined us at BusinessWorks as part of his American visit. The chairman didn't speak English, but he didn't need to be told that this was a tribal gathering. He is a great leader, and he knew just what to do. Pretty soon a chant went up from Kipuloli and his warrior, and the two men started leaping into the air in time with the rhythm of their chant. Within seconds, hundreds of people, including Alan, were leaping into the air. A few even tried to join in the chant.

Something was happening—something spontaneous, foreign, and yet completely in keeping with the Grand Circle culture. For 15 minutes, pandemonium consumed the previously quiet meadow. The Maasai chairman and his warrior had never been out of Africa and had never flown in an airplane. But they sure knew how to jumpstart a gathering of the clan.

It was impulsive. It was raucous. It was an unforgettable experience.

—Harriet Lewis

ood leadership is the force that holds a company together and simultaneously moves it forward. Good leaders meet new situations head-on. They inspire others to action. They jumpstart new initiatives and find opportunities wherever they go. Good leaders move the world. Kipuloli Napiteeng is that kind of leader. Standing in a meadow in New Hampshire, 7,000 miles from home, he sized up the advancing crowd and turned what could have been a ho-hum reception for a visiting dignitary into a crazy, cross-cultural celebration. He saw the opportunity, raised his spear, and got jumping.

We love that kind of leadership, that willingness to engage right then in the moment, to create something from nothing, to keep the engine running. Over the years, we have seen just how powerful that kind of leadership can be. We see it in our trip leaders, whose leadership skills make our trips so memorable. We see it in our leadership team in Boston, who have courageously navigated us through crisis after crisis. We see it in our best overseas leaders, who get the best quality scores from travelers on the trips in their regions. We see it in our Grand Circle Foundation projects, which flounder without strong local leadership. We believe to the depth of our being that we need good leaders to help change people's lives. Leadership is important at every level of our enterprise.

Leadership from Anywhere

Some businesses may be best served by a top-down, rule-based leadership model, but international travel isn't one of them. International travel is a volatile business. Disruptions and calamities occur with surprising regularity in one part of the world or another. When a volcano erupts in Iceland, when an airliner falls into the sea, when a group of travelers gets stranded at the Pyramids, we need action fast and locally. The company can't wait for someone from Boston to turn up and decide what to do. The comfort and safety of our travelers and the success of our business depend on responsive action by those closest to any emergent problem.

The volatility and global nature of our business require that everyone in the company be willing and able to make decisions at any time, in any place, and at every level of the organization. This is asking a lot, because it is not only asking for action and direction, but for speed. People unaccustomed to leadership roles are especially speed-averse, but we cannot afford hesitation or second-guessing. That means we must develop leadership at all levels of the company—that *everyone* be given opportunities to lead from wherever they are. That expectation is inherent in the values we talked about earlier; it is why we put such stress on open and courageous communication, risk-taking, speed, teamwork, and the ability to thrive in change. These are values that build leadership skills, and they are values we expect all our associates to embrace.

That means the moment you sign on to work at Grand Circle, no matter what your title or area of responsibility, you are required to think and act and speak up like the company depends on you. Like leadership could fall in your lap tomorrow—because it can and it will. You are a leader-in-waiting.

This isn't just talk. It happens all the time. In fact, we *make* it happen. Our associates may be called upon anywhere and any time—in a training session, at the lunch table, on a site visit to a Grand Circle Foundation project—to tell us what they see as the company's hot issues and how they would help us improve our performance. It makes some people nervous, at least in the beginning, but like public speaking, leadership gets easier with practice—and we practice all the time. We are fixated on empowerment and readiness. We call it our "Culture of Leaders" and we say, "You can lead from anywhere."

We would like every person in the company to be a leader. That may be impractical, but nevertheless we've made a commitment to help people all over the world become better leaders. We do this through attention to the Grand Circle culture, through coaching and mentoring, through leadership development programs, through company practices like open corporate meetings and BusinessWorks, and through the work of our subsidiary, the Pinnacle Leadership Center.

Come to the edge
We can't, we are afraid
Come to the edge
We can't, we will fall
Come to the edge
They came
And he pushed them
And they flew!

—Guillaume Apollinaire

Failure is the opportunity to begin again, more intelligently.

—Henry Ford

A Big Mistake

Modern corporations run on computer systems. The one Charlie Ritter built for us back in the late 1980s was called GERT, which stood for Grand Circle Enters Revolutionary Technology—the winning entry in a company naming contest. GERT had gotten old and cranky, so in 1999 we launched a company-wide initiative to build a new system we called BRAVO. As we always do when making a big business change, we created a transformation team to lead the transition.

The project had plenty of leadership and expertise, including our new President, who brought in people from his old company to lead the technology team. Among them was our new CIO. Our first mistake was allowing this "elite" team to design the system without full input from our associates. It soon became clear that the big-shot technology team needed to understand *our* business, not somebody else's.

Momentum carried the project forward even as a few associates began raising red flags. The technology team dismissed them saying the naysayers were just resistant to change. Soon the company split into warring camps: for and against BRAVO. The tech team kept saying they could get it to work, but they couldn't. It finally became obvious that we had made a bad decision. After spending $11 million over two years on the project, we killed it.

Afterward, we gave BRAVO a huge Irish wake. We laid out a mock coffin below the loading dock, then formed a procession so all the associates could throw their BRAVO manuals into the coffin. Then we had a feast and made toasts with Irish whiskey to send off the dearly departed. Then we hired Charlie Ritter back from another company to re-engineer GERT, the system he had designed many years before.

This was a case of over-reliance on formal leadership and expertise. Had we listened to our associates who raised the alarm— courageously leading from right where they were—we would have saved a lot of time and money.

—Alan Lewis

Three Essential Qualities of Leadership

First and foremost, a leader must have a vision and be able to communicate it effectively. As Alan says, if a leader doesn't know where he is going, who's going to follow him? The leader must also see the world realistically and approach problems pragmatically, so he will know what it takes to actually achieve the vision. This means the leader must look and listen objectively, to gain information and new perspectives from others who have them.

Second, leaders must be gutsy. "Gutsy" is Harriet's word, and by it she means that in any given situation, leaders must be willing to tackle the toughest issues first and make decisions about them; only then can they move the world toward their vision. Tough issues remain unresolved because they frighten people, so gutsy leadership requires courage. It also requires humility. Good leaders must recognize and acknowledge mistakes; in fact, the best leaders revel in mistakes because mistakes mean they're learning and growing.

It is often said that the best leaders are fearless. This is a misconception. In fact, people who have no fear make poor leaders. While they may take a company into new territory, even to new heights, they cannot be depended on because they do not see the world clearly; if they did, they would have some healthy concerns. Sooner or later, a fearless leader will do something reckless and irresponsible—and he will take the company down with him.

Third, good leaders empower others. They develop other leaders because they know they cannot achieve their vision all by themselves. They recognize and celebrate other people's successes, and they give back to the people and places that support them in ways that help them grow into their own potential.

Harriet's sister, Nancy Lyon, is a great example of an empowering leader. Nancy was a famous negotiator, one of the very best, and she was fiercely dedicated to developing other women leaders. One year she took Sue Harvey with her on a do-or-die buying trip to South America. She trained Sue nonstop for two weeks— what to wear, how to sit, who to flatter, when to stonewall—and then, on the last day of the negotiation, handed Sue the remaining contract and insisted she close the deal herself. "You can do it," Nancy said, and sure enough, Sue did.

Standing in front of 20,000 people during a timeout and you're designated to take the last shot to win the game. Why?

Well, if it's not you, it's somebody else. Who is going to do it better? What's the problem? You're either going to be the hero or the goat. What's the problem with being a hero? It's a great experience! What's the problem with being a goat? People are going to think ill of you?

If your major concern is people thinking ill of you, you'll never be able to make a decision to do the right thing. Why worry about what people think—you are not in control of what anyone thinks anyway.

—Tommy Heinsohn, 6-time All Star player, Hall of Fame honoree, and 2-time championship coach for the Boston Celtics, in remarks to GCC leadership at the Basketball Hall of Fame

Chairman Kipuloli Napiteeng Answers Some Questions

- What does it take to be a leader in your village?

  A leader has to listen to all the people, challenge them, until you get through to the decision. You don't tell them what to do, you all decide. A leader helps you get there.

- When you go home, what might you do differently?

  I would like my children to come and learn in the U.S. And I would like to sell my cattle here.

- What is the future of the Maasai?

  Education, land, water. We need education to compete with the life that is coming.

The World Needs More Leaders

Leaders like this are in short supply. We know this because we're always searching for leaders all over the world, both for our companies and for Grand Circle Foundation, and we've found they are few in number. This is not a small issue. Many parts of the world and many aspects of the human condition need to improve, and that is going to require good leadership.

The good news is that leadership can be taught. Or at least good leaders can learn to become better leaders, and some, with proper encouragement, will step forward to become first-time leaders. People all over the world have been conditioned by schools and bosses in the workplace to suppress their opinions, to show deference to their elders or to those higher in the chain of command, and to conform to the supposed needs of the larger organization. We've learned that when people are encouraged to act as leaders, more than a few jump at the chance. They respond like it's some repressed need they can suddenly fill.

Age doesn't seem to matter; a person can rise to leadership at a young age, or in old age, or at any time in between. Titles and fancy offices don't matter, either; in fact, they can sometimes hamper leadership by putting up barriers between the officeholder and the things they need to know. After all, a title only bestows the *opportunity* to lead. What counts is decision-making and action—resolute action that is guided by vision, undertaken courageously, and directed toward the greater good of the company and the world at large. Understood this way, leadership can truly come from anywhere. This means that wherever you are in the organization, you can provide leadership for others, including the chair and vice-chair on occasion.

Our Leadership Model in Action

One way to understand our leadership model is to sit in on one of our monthly corporate meetings, which are held in Boston during the last week of every month. These are all-hands meetings; everyone from the mailroom to the boardroom attends—about 480 Boston associates— along with any overseas associates who are in town on business. Cheerful rock music welcomes the crowds as they gather in a big open space on the fourth floor of our building on Congress Street. It's a high-energy event, full of anticipation, excitement, and sometimes dread.

Martha Prybylo, our Executive Vice President of Worldwide People and Culture and Corporate Responsibility, opens the meeting by welcoming new associates and honoring those who have reached milestone years with the company. Ten-year associates are expected to say a few words, and though most are scared to death to speak in front of such a large gathering, their stories of roads traveled and risks taken with the company are always inspiring. They often tell us that their work with us has changed their lives. One associate said the company has taught her to be fearless; another told how a trip to Egypt helped her overcome a lifelong fear and suspicion of Muslims, a cultural barrier she had grown up with in her native Philippines. We hear such stories all the time, and they are gratifying.

Next come awards for outstanding performance during the past month. We believe that recognition not only honors the recipients, but also lets all associates know we are constantly looking for success stories in the company. Leadership expects excellence and rewards it.

After Nick Lento, our Chief Executive Officer, gives a business update and reports on ongoing initiatives, another member of the Executive Team presents the month's financial results and quality scores.

Grand Circle has taught me to face challenges directly and quickly. I have come to realize that you gain nothing by waiting to be certain— because you can *never* be certain. If you take action right away based on what you see in the moment, and if you are willing to correct your course along the way, you will almost always end up with a better result. Over the years I have applied this philosophy professionally, with other organizations, and personally, when faced with difficult medical, financial, or other decisions. It is a lesson that I have repeated over and over to my children as well. It has made me a better leader— and a better person.

—Joe Cali,
12-year associate
Executive Vice President,
Analysis

Maybe the most important change in my life came from our culture. I speak up now and give feedback to my family and friends. Grand Circle gave me a voice. I never really did this before—especially with my husband—but I do now! I am a stronger woman for working here and I thank Alan and Harriet every day for providing this to me.

—Esther Canter,
17-year associate
Call Center Help Group

We don't fudge them or wrap them in public relations-speak, either. We produce the profit and loss statement, a summary sales report, and the quality scores from travelers' evaluations. Everything is disclosed, especially our mistakes. This is seldom done in public companies, even those that pride themselves in their "corporate transparency," and it is practically unheard of in privately held companies like ours.

But we believe in full disclosure, not only because we are honest and candid people by nature, but because we think full disclosure is the only way to ensure that everyone is aligned on the same issues and goals. Besides, how can we expect leadership from all levels if we withhold vital information? Open and courageous communication is our first value. Leadership means walking the talk.

The corporate meeting goes for an hour. The second half is the tough part. That's when the Executive Team "sits on the hot seat" while associates ask them tough questions. It's all about direct accountability, and there are rules. We have to answer every question; we can't pass the mike back to the audience. If we've made a mistake, we must say so; if we don't have an answer, we must commit to getting it. It can get intense. You can feel 480-people's-worth of apprehension when a tough question is lobbed to the front of the room, but you can also feel the empowerment that swells up when other associates rise to their feet to applaud the question that has been on everyone's mind.

We have trained our associates well: They don't hesitate to challenge equivocation. In fact, we think they look forward to it. That's just as we want it. We're looking for honesty, not blind loyalty. The proverbial "yes man" is not a leader. In our opinion, he's not even a good follower. He's just taking up space.

Our corporate meetings serve many purposes. They keep associates well informed about past performance and future plans; they facilitate conversation among all levels and departments of the company; they remind the senior leadership to exhibit our values in public and productive ways; and they allow associates to take the lead on issues of importance to them by questioning decisions and proposing changes. At Grand Circle, open and courageous communication is a two-way street, and leadership demands participation from every level.

Learning by Doing

We strongly believe in experiential learning; in fact, we think the best way to learn is by doing. This is Alan's personal legacy. Never a devoted classroom student, Alan got his early leadership education on the streets; later he learned from his travels and from some unusual teachers like Kipuloli. He sees leadership learning as a lifelong project, and we take the same approach with our associates. At Grand Circle, we foster leadership on a daily basis by periodically giving associates new job assignments that change their work group and stretch their skills.

Group Hug

During a corporate meeting, an associate asked a question about a temporary spike in workload. A member of the senior leadership gave a long, convoluted answer. Instead of sitting back down, the associate said, "We had the same problem last year. Management should have foreseen it. What are you going to do about it and how are you going to avoid the same problem next year?"

Alan leaped off the stage and ran down the aisle to give the associate a hug. He had always said we should embrace tough questions. Until that moment, I didn't know he meant literally.

—Jim Best

At Grand Circle, everybody moves among departments—and frequently. A transfer does not always mean a promotion, or a demotion, for that matter; more often a lateral move is made to give an associate experience in a new area of the company's operations. In more hierarchical companies, such a move might be resented. In such companies, corporate advancement—at least in the middle ranks of the organization—depends on increasing competence in a narrow field of expertise. But the price of this kind of advancement is high, both for the associate and for the company. Because the worker's contribution to the company demands specialized knowledge within a small segment of the company's operations, he or she can never become a true leader of the enterprise.

A few years ago, Sir Edmund Hillary was in Boston visiting Grand Circle. He was asked what he was thinking when he finally reached the summit of Mount Everest. His response: "I was looking over to Makalu across the way and mapping my route up." Makalu is another peak in the Himalayas and the fifth-highest mountain in the world. That's what great leaders do. They always have their eyes on the next prize.

—Harriet Lewis

We believe associates can lead from anywhere, but it takes knowledge to offer opinions about areas outside a person's immediate responsibility. By shifting assignments, associates gain broad experience in different operational areas and come to feel comfortable offering up solutions and expressing their opinions openly. Lateral movement also prepares associates to work as a team when they are promoted to higher leadership positions.

Cross-Training in Morocco

We were planning an offsite in Morocco, with the goal of improving learning and discovery on our top 20 products all over the world. Associates from every region and key departments would be there, and a disagreement arose over how to organize the associates into teams. Most people wanted to distribute the finance people amongst the teams because the finance people didn't know much about the trips. This is our usual approach, but this time Alan disagreed. Instead, he put all the finance people from all over the world onto one team. We could tell that the associates thought this was a crazy idea. They had low expectations for the team of number-crunchers.

The offsite included visits to small coastal towns, a Jeep trek through the desert, tent camping, a home-hosted meal with a Moroccan family, a visit to a hammam, and a sunrise breakfast at the top of a dune. During each activity, the teams would brainstorm ideas for creating unforgettable experiences. On the final night of presentations, the finance team astounded everyone by making the best recommendations. Emboldened by the challenge, and finding freedom in their outsider position, they had imagined activities no one else had even considered. Alan just smiled, because he knew you always get great ideas when people are given an opportunity to get away from their daily routine and work outside their chosen field of expertise.

—Mark Frevert
Executive Vice President/Chief Architect

Cross-Training and Transformation

Another way we promote company integration is by forming cross-functional teams whenever we need to resolve big issues or change the way we do business. Assignment to one of these transformation teams is an honor, and it means a lot of work; team members must quickly learn the needs of all departments and come together, through a group leadership plan, to move the company forward. Cross-departmental training is of great help to us during crises because we can count on many associates bringing firsthand experience to the crisis room.

For example, in October 1999, we experienced a terrible tragedy when EgyptAir Flight 990 crashed off Nantucket, killing 54 of our travelers. Family members called us for days, first for information, later to arrange transportation to Boston, and finally for help with memorial plans. All our associates wanted to help. In fact, we had more volunteers for the Call Center than we had phones available. Because of our policy of making lateral assignments, every one of those volunteers had Call Center experience and could step right into to the job. Similarly, two years later, after 9/11 disrupted air travel all over the world, we were able to call on many associates with air-routing experience to help us get travelers home.

Good Programs and Best Practices

Over the years, Grand Circle has developed many leadership programs for associates. A typical program might take a group of 10 or 12 established leaders on a two-day offsite to focus on a couple of really hot issues—for example, how to increase sales after a terrorist attack in Europe, or how to build stronger relationships with our solo travelers—with the intention of developing the values of open and courageous communication and risk-taking. During feedback sessions, the participants come up with their own professional development plans which they execute when they get back to the office.

These leadership groups also meet monthly with Alan and other executives to help each other make tough decisions—like firing a high-performing associate who does not fully support the culture, or making an unpopular recommendation to the Executive Team. The group helps the individual develop an action plan and timetable to make the

I was a leader of a LEAD trip to Italy back in 1998. It was a strong trip with many unforgettable experiences, including a walking tour in Pompeii and an amazing drive along the Amalfi Coast. But the most memorable part was the leadership learning. One night, each of us received feedback from the entire group. It was a very powerful night, a difficult night, and a real turning point. I saw how open and courageous feedback should be given— consistently, directly, and in a timely way.

Personally, I learned that I don't always stay open to tough feedback. Realizing this has helped me recognize situations where I begin to close down. Now I see feedback as a gift. It's not to tear someone down, but to help build them up.

—Kurt Therrien,
22-year associate
Executive Vice President,
Kensington Investment
Company

necessary action happen; the group literally chants, *"When? When? When?"* to force the commitment.

One of the great things about owning a travel company is that we can offer leadership training in really exotic locations; we can literally use the world as our classroom. For example, travel figures prominently in our signature Leadership, Exploration, Adventure, and Discovery (LEAD) program, which takes 10 to 12 high-performing associates from all levels of the company on a 10-day version of one of our Grand Circle or Overseas Adventure Travel trips. The second day of the trip usually includes a challenging team-building activity. In the past, LEAD groups have slept in caves, hiked through mountains, camped in the Arctic Circle, taken part in a road rally in Egypt, and gone bungee-jumping in New Zealand. As always, there is a business component, for while the focus of LEAD trips is leadership development, all participants are expected to return to the office with recommendations for improving the quality and profitability of the trip.

Not everyone gets to go on a LEAD trip, but all associates get support for their personal growth and development. The company is generous in its reimbursements for such things as language courses, experiential learning programs, and college courses and graduate school, and we offer many opportunities for travel and community service. We also have a strong record of promoting from within.

Grand Circle also supports the leadership development of its community partners in Boston through the Foundation's Community Advisory Group (CAG), which we organized in 1999. This group, which includes the directors of Artists for Humanity, the West End House Boys & Girls Club, the Greater Boston Food Bank, Big Sister Association, Summer Search, City on a Hill Charter School, StreetSafe, SquashBusters, and several other important inner-city nonprofit organizations, meets quarterly to brainstorm and share best practices. Sometimes they will share solutions to common problems, like homelessness; other times they will offer help with one member's new initiative, as when four CAG members offered community service opportunities for a fifth member's teenaged clients. The Foundation helps by providing professional business advice, training resources, and free use of the Pinnacle Leadership Center in Kensington, New Hampshire; in return, the

TOP: Grand Circle Chairman Alan Lewis, Sir Edmund Hillary, and Executive Vice President/Chief Architect Mark Frevert in Antarctica aboard Grand Circle's 35th Anniversary President's Cruise, December, 1993.

BOTTOM: Members of Grand Circle's Executive Team, senior managers, and regional worldwide leaders bond onboard the M/S *River Anuket* during an offsite in Egypt, April, 2002. Charlie Ritter is on the right in the back row, in blue.

TOP: Honey Streit-Reyes (upper left) presides over one of her famous strategy sessions with Program Directors and regional staff aboard one of Grand Circle's river ships, 2003.

BOTTOM LEFT: Alan Lewis with Nobel Peace Prize recipient, former President of Poland, and Honorary Director of Grand Circle Foundation Lech Walesa during his visit to Grand Circle's headquarters in Boston, May, 2006.

BOTTOM RIGHT: Jim O'Brien emcees a loading dock party.

TOP: Skit competition winners perform on stage at BusinessWorks, Kensington, NH, 2000.

BOTTOM: Harriet and Alan Lewis enjoy the ride in Madeira, Portugal, 1994.

TOP: Vice Chairman Harriet Lewis leads an associate group on a Recognition Journey to China, 1996.

BOTTOM LEFT: Alan Lewis in Moscow, Russia, April, 1987.

BOTTOM RIGHT: Director of Product Marketing Vinette DiGregorio and Executive Vice President Lisa Norton don traditional garb in the Sahara, Morocco, 1995.

TOP: Jim Best and his wife, Diane, prepare to enjoy a "sundowner" in Namibia, 2009.

BOTTOM: Willy Chambulo (second from left), owner of Kibo Guides, and Maasai Chief Kipuloli Napiteeng (center) get BusinessWorks jumping, 2001.

LEFT: Grand Circle associates take one more step than they thought they could during a BusinessWorks "high" initiative, Kensington, NH, 2000.

ABOVE RIGHT: Grand Circle associates compete in a race across Reflection Pond aboard rafts they built from barrels, PVC pipe, and rope, BusinessWorks, Kensington, NH, 2000.

BOTTOM RIGHT: Alan Lewis rallies the crowd at BusinessWorks, Kensington, NH, 2000.

TOP: Alan Lewis with one of his best friends, Sophie, at BusinessWorks, Kensington, NH, 2000.

BOTTOM LEFT: Edward Lewis in Antarctica, 35th Anniversary President's Cruise, 1993.

BOTTOM RIGHT: Edward, Harriet, and Charlotte Lewis on a family vacation in Barcelona, Spain, 1992.

TOP: Alan Lewis and the Grand Circle Advisory Board, Boston, MA, 1986.

BOTTOM: Harriet Lewis receives the City on a Hill award, Boston, MA, 2006.

partners give us invaluable advice on how to improve the Foundation's community giving in Boston.

BusinessWorks

One of our most powerful leadership development programs is Business-Works, our annual summer offsite held an hour north of Boston, near our second home in Kensington. Each June, hundreds of associates from as many as 60 different countries come together at our conference site in the woods to solve business issues, reinforce our company values, participate in hands-on experiential learning, and practice leadership skills. It was at BusinessWorks that Kipuloli Napiteeng raised his spear and got the place jumping.

Providing Leadership to Social Entrepreneurs

Greg Zaff had an ambitious dream: He wanted to use his love of the game of squash to help young people from the inner city become better students and responsible citizens. So he founded SquashBusters, a nonprofit group that would do just that. The squash was the easy part (Greg is a pro), but the schoolwork and citizenship proved harder. As a member of Grand Circle's Community Advisory Group (CAG), SquashBusters received help with this from fellow CAG members. One organization in the group set up the SquashBusters teaching program; four others offered community service projects for the kids. Greg also brainstormed with fellow group members to improve SquashBusters' grant writing and fundraising efforts.

"No other funder in the city does this kind of collaborative work," Greg says. "There is real power in the informal learning, encouragement, and inspiration we get working with other CAG members. It has been so energizing; it has given us so much perspective, and we've met really tremendous people. This is a new kind of philanthropy—open, visionary, and empowering—and it has really made our work better."

I attended the first BusinessWorks in 1995. We slept in tents pitched on a slope. And it rained! And Alan seemed to love that.

— Dave Lubchansky,
20-year associate
Director, Community Relations

Charlie Ritter had a fear of heights. When we do high-ropes exercises at BusinessWorks, it doesn't matter how far you step out onto the wire, only that you try. But Charlie's fear was palpable. He would hug the tree until he willed himself to step out. Once started, he refused to give up. He never made it even halfway across the wire, but he showed more courage than those that made it all the way across. He was an inspiration to everyone at BusinessWorks and at Grand Circle.

—Alan Lewis

Many of the participants at BusinessWorks are already company leaders; the senior leadership team comes from Boston, for example, as do the leaders of many of our overseas offices. High-performing associates, including trip leaders and Program Directors, also receive invitations. In the past, principals from schools supported by Grand Circle Foundation have come to BusinessWorks, and so have some of our travelers.

Each year, the participants come to the woods—a setting deliberately chosen to be outside most people's comfort zone—to tackle a set of what seem to be outrageous business goals. One year we challenged participants to find ways to save $52 million in the cost of goods. This emphasis on setting big business challenges—as well as our relentless focus on our top people, top products, and top vendors—is part of our ongoing commitment to "The Great Company." In fact, the precursors of BusinessWorks, three companywide offsites held in the early 1990s, were called "Great Company Outings."

The business portion of the offsite can last as long as two weeks. During that time, regional and departmental teams meet in rustic cabins, under tents, in the fields, and in barns to brainstorm ideas around the tough issues that we have brought to the offsite. The goal is to make significant, actionable decisions about such things as company performance, organization, associate assignments, product design, quality scores, and vendor delivery. All meetings end with measurable commitments for each participant. On the final Thursday, Boston leadership joins the regional leadership for a leadership summit.

On Friday, the final day of BusinessWorks, participants are joined by most of the Boston staff for a final day of learning, challenge, and fun. In some years, we've even shut down the Call Center. This Friday of BusinessWorks is widely known around Congress Street as "The Day We Love to Hate." First there's the insanely early wakeup call. By 7 a.m., associates are already worrying about missing the bus and being embarrassed in the "icebreakers" session, knowing someone might be called on to moo like a cow.

Next thing you know, we're flying through the trees on the high ropes course and building rafts from loose barrels and lengths of rope. The challenge is to construct a raft that can support six people and paddle it across a pond. We work as departmental teams, and by midday we are beginning to appreciate unsuspected qualities in people we've worked with for years. We call it "action learning," and we learn a lot from it about the way we set goals, handle conflicts, reign in the bossy members, buck up the scared ones, and persevere together until we get the job done. The same behaviors we exhibit on the ropes course are the ones we will see in the office. The point, of course, is to bring our new understandings back to the office, where we can use them to improve our teamwork.

In the afternoon, everyone gathers under a giant, white-peaked circus tent to watch uproarious skits. There is rollicking laughter and spirited balloting for the most irreverent, particularly toward senior leadership. Bad singing and cross-dressing are often involved.

All these experiences—the intense business work, the physical challenges, and the unbridled fun—push our associates outside their comfort zones, underscoring our values of risk-taking, teamwork, and open and courageous communication. They consolidate our corporate culture and contribute to leadership development by affirming the principle that leadership comes from every level of the company. Associates find out what they are capable of at BusinessWorks, and the experience can change their lives.

Alan Hands Out Some Free Passes

At a recent BusinessWorks, one of the tough issues on our agenda was to find ways to improve our discovery scores by ten percentage points across the board. When Alan put the challenge out there, he was met by silence. Trip leaders were hesitant to try anything new if there was a risk that it wouldn't work. They were afraid an innovation would backfire, lowering their own performance scores—scores that determined their incentive pay and the number of trips they could lead.

So Alan gave them all *free passes*. If the trip leaders wanted to try something new and unusual on a trip, we wouldn't count that departure in their performance scores. The results were amazing. In total, the free pass departures outscored the regular departures by more than ten points. Not only did we provide more discoveries for our travelers, but the whole exercise was a great lesson on leadership and risk taking.

A Free Pass to Jump into the Main River

I had promised Alan to use my free pass for a jump off one of our river ships into the Main River—all the willing travelers and me. When I described the idea to the captain of the M/S *River Concerto*, he gave me a critical look, but he eventually agreed.

We were just outside the quaint village of Wertheim, at the confluence of the Main and Tauber rivers in Germany. The water at this juncture was 69 degrees Fahrenheit. The Wertheim fire brigade positioned a rescue boat with three volunteers in case of emergency, and the captain provided towels and onboard safety personnel. We were all set to go, but I was worried that no one would want to jump.

I announced the voluntary jump at dinner and offered a sign-up sheet for those interested in joining me the next day. Within minutes, 60 people had signed the sheet. Oh, boy.

Just before lunch the next day, all 60 showed up. They were dressed for fun. Some wore bathing suits, but most just wore shorts, knickers, knee socks, T-shirts, and even sneakers. A few wore their life vests, but others had somehow found funny-looking air wings. To my surprise, the captain said he would jump first to prove it was safe. He jumped to great applause, and then everyone else leaped into the water to the sound of clicking cameras. Soon the crew started jumping from the plank, some even in their duty uniforms. It was a huge success; the town newspaper wrote a great story about the "Big Jump," and it became an unforgettable experience for all the travelers.

—Jan Bryde, Program Director

Among the free pass excursions were a visit to a women's jail in Quito, Ecuador; a short ride on Tito's private Blue Train in Serbia; a visit to the Kings Cross red-light district in Sydney; and a visit with a caravan of Tinkers (Gypsies) in Ireland. Some of the excursions, like a visit to the City of the Dead in Cairo, were so popular that they became standard offerings on our trips.

Did all of these experiments work? No, not all of them. We measured their success from traveler feedback and retained the ones travelers liked, made changes to others, and discontinued the excursions that were rated poorly. The whole process exemplifies our approach to business: tackling tough issues, listening to our associates, empowering them to make decisions, reversing mistakes with impunity, and celebrating success. In this kind of business climate, associates really can lead from anywhere.

Pinnacle Leadership Center

BusinessWorks is held at the Pinnacle Leadership Center, a 500-acre site in Kensington, New Hampshire, that we own and operate. The Center is staffed by professional organizational advisors and offers a comprehensive business and leadership curriculum. The facility has cabins and studios for indoor meetings, several different venues for outdoor meetings, a network of trails, several fields for orienteering and team problem-solving exercises, a huge pond, and an eight-station ropes course in the treetops.

Over the years, Pinnacle and Grand Circle have contributed significantly to each other's success. Pinnacle staff have developed many business and leadership training modules for us, including single- and multi-day sessions on such topics as "Building a Common Worldwide Organizational Culture" and "How to Turn Trouble to Opportunity"—all using leadership principles and business models that have made Grand Circle such a great company. Pinnacle has trained scores of leaders for Grand Circle from countries all over the world, including all of our overseas offices. We also make the center available free to our Community Advisory Group, social entrepreneurs, and not-for-profit organizations.

WHAT GOOD LEADERS DO

- Hold a vision
- Communicate effectively
- See the world realistically
- Listen
- Deal with the tough issue first
- Make courageous decisions
- Recognize mistakes and reverse bad decisions
- Develop other leaders
- Recognize and celebrate success
- Give back

Leadership for Entrepreneurship

These days we are devoting more of our time to developing leaders outside the company. I am particularly interested in helping business entrepreneurs and social entrepreneurs who share our desire to help change people's lives.

We believe that business and philanthropy go hand in hand. Good companies do both, and *great* companies make philanthropy a part of their business strategy. In the same way, nonprofit organizations of all kinds can benefit from more entrepreneurial approaches to their work. We know this from the success of Grand Circle Foundation.

We founded the Pinnacle Leadership Center in 1992 to help nonprofits and social entrepreneurs develop better leadership skills. In 2009 we launched the Lewis Initiative at Babson College, in Wellesley, Massachusetts, which supports leaders who embrace social missions. We are heartened by the commitment to philanthropy we see in the rising generation of young entrepreneurs. In 2010, we launched Grand Circle Leadership to teach our leadership model.

—Alan Lewis

Nominal Group Process

At our Pinnacle Leadership Center, we use a methodology called "Nominal Group Process" to help us examine and resolve tough issues. The methodology is simple. Breakout teams or buddy pairs write their top concerns and ideas on flip-chart paper. When the team regroups, all the lists are compared. After redundancies are eliminated, everyone votes to prioritize the issues. The top vote-getters are put in rank order, and these become the issues and concerns that will be resolved. The same nominal process is then used to come up with the solutions and action sets.

We also use this process every day in our offices and on all our company offsites, wherever they are held. In all cases, an associate acts as facilitator, insuring that everyone has a chance to speak, that the other participants listen and ask only clarifying questions, and that there is consensus on the rank order of issues. This is a very different approach to problem-solving than coming in with an agenda and predetermined talking points. It raises everyone's concerns and ideas, allowing a consensual leadership to emerge from all levels of the organization, whose members then own the issues and actions.

Leadership Is Not for Spectators

More than anything else, leadership means engagement in the here and now. This was the brilliance of Kipuloli performance at BusinessWorks; he saw people on the move—and immediately joined them.

We love the fact that Grand Circle associates are engaged with travelers, their workmates, and the community. What makes our travel business fun is watching people stepping forward with great ideas, ignoring organization charts to challenge authority, demanding to have ever greater challenges, and jumping into the middle of a crisis to help. We are rarely disappointed and often astounded by our associates. "People are Number 1"—that is our first Extreme Competitive Advantage. It has been first since the beginning of the company, and we continue to nurture our associates as our most important resource.

We work with them to cultivate a corporate culture that propels performance and gives everyone opportunities for growth and leadership experience. Our associates want career growth, personal growth, income and security, and the sense of belonging to a fun-loving and winning team. Our travelers want quality, value, a long-term relationship, and unforgettable experiences. If our culture delivers what our associates need, then we feel confident that our associates will deliver what our travelers want. By empowering our associates to lead from everywhere, we guarantee the success of the business.

In today's cost-cutting corporate climate, employees are too often regarded as liabilities—resources to shed if there is a way to get the work done more cheaply in China or India. This kind of thinking emerges when companies are run by managers instead of by leaders. Managers herd people, while leaders chart a course and inspire others to follow. We see our employees very differently; to us, today's associates are tomorrow's leaders. And we don't mean some tomorrow in the distant future. We mean literally *tomorrow*. We know that our associates will step into any leadership vacuum whenever they are needed and that they will help lead the company to ever greater achievements.

Alan and Harriet explore Egypt with fifth-generation tour guide, Farid el Fayed.

CHAPTER 6

Locals Know Best

The senior leadership team was on an offsite at the Algonquin Hotel in New Brunswick, Canada. I woke up on a brisk morning convinced that Grand Circle had to open offices overseas. It was 1996, and up until that time we had run the company pretty much from Boston. I knew we had to change or we'd never achieve our vision to be the world leader in quality and value. Harriet wasn't with me on that offsite, but I could hear her voice inside my head. Wherever we traveled, she loved meeting and talking with the local people. She always said, "Locals know best."

When I wandered outside, I found my team happily sipping their morning coffee in cozy rocking chairs positioned around the hotel's big old porch. I was about to disrupt their peaceful morning.

"We're going over the water," I announced.

Heads whipped around. "What?"

The startled response didn't surprise me. We had been arguing about this for days.

"That'll drive up costs," said Joe Kurosz, our Vice President for Operations.

"Not if we handle it right," I countered. "We can do it with only nine or ten people."

Joe looked unconvinced. "Where?"

"Munich."

"No! Munich's way too expensive."

"That's where Honey is. She knows the town and she'll get us a reasonable lease. It'll be easy."

Kate Cooney also objected. "We'll lose control of quality," she said. Kate was president of Overseas Adventure Travel (OAT), and she was worried because OAT had just launched its first trips in Europe; she didn't want some relative stranger making decisions about her trips.

"How would we monitor what they are doing?"

"We'll coordinate by using videoconferencing every day," I said.

We went around and around on it, but I was sure I was right. We needed to cut out the middleman, be our own local knowledge. I had an answer for everything.

"It'll work," I insisted.

So we did it.

And it didn't work, not at first.

—*Alan Lewis*

We always do things different. It must be in our blood. Even today, most travel companies manage their worldwide operations from their home offices, but we began building a network of overseas offices back in 1996. It wasn't a smooth build-out by any means. The launch of the first office, in Munich in 1997, proved to be expensive, contentious, and hard on morale in Boston. But we survived and pressed on. Within two years, we were in Cape Town, Hong Kong, and Bangkok. Then came Rome, Sydney, Paris, and Warsaw. Today we have 38 offices and do business in 100 countries. We have 220 associates working for us in the regional offices, and more than 1,600 trip leaders and crew members on our ships. We are the most international company in the travel industry, a truly global enterprise.

Business and philanthropy leaders often ask us how we run this worldwide organization. They're puzzled by our success because they've stubbed their toes many times managing people from different cultures, even in such sophisticated business centers as London, Paris, Rome, Hong Kong, Singapore, and Buenos Aires. Our success in more exotic and far-flung places like Egypt, Vietnam, China, and Croatia leaves these executives scratching their heads, and they're less than thrilled when we tell them our secret: Just get out there and make mistakes.

They really don't have much choice. Today's organizations must look beyond their own borders. The world is becoming smaller, and both businesses and philanthropic organizations must learn to raise their sights to the people who populate the entire globe. Grand Circle may have had more confidence going global—we are, after all, a *travel* company, and we don't mind taking risks—but there is no magic recipe for dealing with other cultures. The encounter will be different for different industries and different corporate cultures, and the logistics are always difficult. It just takes experience, and experience comes from making mistakes.

Here's how we've done it. It's not the only way, but it has worked for us.

Locals Know Best

It may sound strange, but we went global so we could become more local. This isn't true for every company. Other companies go global to expand their markets, or to outsource their manufacturing, or to increase their visibility to foreign governments. We weren't looking for any of those things. We began opening offices overseas so we could get in-depth, in-country knowledge to make our trips truly unforgettable, and to get direct purchasing power to improve our pricing. One of our Extreme Competitive Advantages is "Unsurpassed Value and Excellence." Going global would improve both sides of that advantage.

It might help if we explained how we operated before 1996, and how most travel companies operate to this day. In those days, Grand Circle booked hotel rooms, rented motor-coaches, and arranged meals through independent ground operators in the host region. The ground operator also coordinated with unions to get us tour guides. In other words, the ground operators acted as a middlemen to arrange all the elements of a trip, and they took a healthy cut for their services—up to 50 percent. In many parts of the world, there were layers of kickbacks and favoritism built into the system that increased our costs. Replacing underperforming vendors was slow and difficult; it was always excuses, excuses, excuses. In our view, the ground operators had too much control over the trips. We needed to manage them ourselves.

A Big Mistake

Opening the Munich office turned out to be a mistake. I had underestimated the difficulty of running an overseas operation. The lease turned out to be expensive, we needed far more than ten associates, and Munich resisted everything that came from Boston. We even lost money from embezzlement. We moved too fast, and without good controls. But without taking this first step, Grand Circle would never have built the best worldwide organization in the travel industry. We knew that locals know best, but it took us awhile—and a few big-ticket mistakes—to learn how to direct a worldwide organization to take advantage of local knowledge and expertise.

—Alan Lewis

I bond with my fellow travelers, and my experience reflects the ancient Sanskrit verse, "Vasudhaiva Kuttumbakam," which means, "The whole world is my family."

—Padmaja Bharti,
  Trip Leader since 1997

We knew there was another way because we had already tried it. Soon after we acquired Grand Circle, we hired Honey Streit-Reyes to organize many of our European trips from her native country, Germany. Honey was our first direct buyer in Europe, which at the time was our primary sphere of operation, accounting for 75 percent of our travelers volume. Honey bypassed the ground operators in Germany, Austria, and Switzerland, which saved us a lot of money. She also improved our trips —significantly by arranging for home-hosted meals, surprise excursions to out-of-the-way places, and unscripted encounters with local people. Honey's trips always scored high on our travelers' quality surveys.

In time, we came to understand that it wasn't just Honey. Local people *always* know their country best and *always* deliver the best trips. Today it is obvious to us. Our local buyers negotiate face to face with our vendors, and they get better prices because middlemen aren't taking a cut. Our local finance people resolve vendors' problems on the spot and in the native language; they also deal easily with local currencies. Local managers select and train trip leaders better than we can from Boston; they also understand local laws and deal effectively with their governments. Local people make our operations run smoothly, and they help overcome inertia when problems arise. They are that important personal presence when a phone, fax, or e-mail from Boston can be easily ignored.

Similar benefits appear on the product side. Local people make our trips less "touristy." They find family-owned hotels and restaurants that reflect their own culture; they know places where Americans don't ordinarily go; they find locations for our discovery programs, like our *Day in the Life* program; and they design our travelers' visits to our Foundation projects. Because they are on site, they are the first to know when local conditions change, like when train workers go on strike or the quality of a hotel suffers under new management. And our local trip leaders do a much better job explaining their culture and history to our travelers than even the most experienced American guides. In 1996, the advantage of local control wasn't quite as clear to us as it is now, but as we looked harder at our quality survey data, we found that the more local people controlled the design and delivery of our trips, the higher the quality scores from every region.

Here is another way to look at it. Suppose a Russian travel company wanted to offer Russians a trip to the United States. Russian trip designers would research travel guides and visit America to choose some destinations. Russian buyers would negotiate a deal with an American ground operator who would supply hotel rooms, transportation, and meals. During the trip, a Russian guide would explain the significance of the Statue of Liberty, the Empire State Building, and Wall Street. This same guide would answer questions about 9/11, the Vietnam War, baseball, hush puppies, *Saturday Night Live*, and the U.S. government. We don't believe this approach would give Russian travelers a genuine and culturally enlightening experience in our country. Surely an American guide would have better information and a truer perspective on all these matters. And the same is true abroad—locals know best.

Going Global

By 1996, we understood that we would never gain control over the quality of our trips until we broke free of the self-serving ground operator system. We also understood that we would never break free of this system from Boston. We didn't have the knowledge, the networks, or even the languages to do it.

Bucking the system would be difficult—even risky in some countries. In many developing nations, the travel industry is tightly controlled and protected by the national government, and most countries require that foreign companies create a legally incorporated subsidiary before dealing directly with vendors; that's a lot of bureaucracy and paperwork. In many areas, deep-seated guilds control the assignment of tour guides to trips; we knew they would fight to distribute plum jobs to our big-tipping American tour groups. Ground operators have power, too; they can threaten to take business away from vendors who deal directly with us. In fact, this has happened to us many times.

With governments, guilds, and ground operators lined up against us all over the world, our office in Boston was overmatched. We were clear on our strategy: We needed to establish a local presence to increase value and excellence. But to do that, we needed to make an organizational change. We needed to open overseas offices and staff them with local

Travel is an unusual business. Nowhere else is a company representative with customers for 14 to 21 days, in a strange locale, for almost every waking moment. This is why local trip leaders are a crucial element of our worldwide strategy—they can make or break the trip.

—Alan Lewis

When the Munich office opened, we wanted them to feel like they were part of the Grand Circle team. So we set up a video-conference link for our monthly corporate meeting. The Munich associates would huddle together in a tiny conference room, and in Boston, we would all yell, "Hello, Munich!"

Due to the lousy technology at the time, we would all sit around with slowly fading smiles until about a minute later, when we heard back, "Hello, Boston!"

This only lasted a few meetings before we dropped it.

—Harriet Lewis

people who knew the ropes. We opened the doors to our Munich office in May of 1997—and a high-tech place it was too, with five desktop computers, four laptops, Internet access, and videoconferencing. The idea was to have Munich manage all our European products—at that time numbering 35 trips with 1,000 departures a year—while Boston retained sales, marketing, finance, and customer service functions. Later we brought accounting over to Munich, too … and then everything else. We had high hopes.

There were glitches. The rent was high, the associates were sometimes *too* independent, and one absconded with some money. But the Munich office showed us that local control of our program services, e.g. hiring and training our trip leaders, could greatly improve our quality scores. It also helped us expand the practice of buying direct in Western Europe, securing our hold on our most important market. We had our sights on new markets, too, especially with our fast-growing OAT trips. Unfortunately, we soon discovered that the Germans were just as hesitant as the Americans to tackle the more remote parts of the world.

Munich taught us that if we were going to buy direct all over the world, we needed offices all over the world. In 1996, we already had about 30 people working for us in several countries overseas, but they worked on their own, mostly out of their homes, and their responsibilities were limited. Now we were thinking about an entirely different kind of overseas presence. By 1999, with footholds in Europe, Africa, and Asia, we were committed to building a geographically dispersed, multinational, and multicultural workforce of several hundred people.

Boston Revolts

People resist change, and our Boston office resisted the move to a worldwide organization pretty much from the beginning. There were logistical difficulties for one thing, like dealing with different languages and different time zones, but the discontent ran deeper than that. It was hard for the Boston associates to let go of the trips and responsibilities they had nurtured for so long, and even more difficult to put trust in strangers who were thousands of miles away. Some associates who were terrific trip developers in their own right didn't have the interpersonal skills to support others in that job. Others didn't have the temperament; they were too competitive.

Boston associates dragged their feet, second-guessed, and withheld important information from the regional offices. They resisted trip design changes from overseas associates, were slow to train them in our computer systems, and put up barriers to transferring financial control. The Boston associates truly believed they knew best how to provide trips for American travelers. They didn't believe as firmly as we did that locals know best, and they didn't see that they were running the risk of cocooning our travelers in an American envelope as they passed through every foreign country.

People especially resist change if they think it threatens their livelihood. In fact, the build-out of our overseas offices put few Boston jobs at risk, but there was a certain amount of paranoia on Congress Street all the same. After all, we had already fired all of our American tour guides and replaced them with local trip leaders. How far could we be trusted with the jobs in Boston? Would all the work be transferred overseas? This was a very difficult period for us personally, not only because we were at odds with longtime employees, but also because we were not getting the cooperation we needed to transform the organization.

The only thing to do was press ahead. We got people out into the field to train overseas associates, brought regional people to Boston, hired capable people in the regions to handle new tasks, held offsites on how to get the job done, and communicated our goal and our reasoning over and over again. Grand Circle has a goal-oriented culture, so setting hard deadlines for the roll out and holding individuals specifically accountable for making it happen probably had the most impact in turning the tide.

Eventually, people saw that we were growing so fast that saving jobs really wasn't the issue—getting help for the snowballing workload was the issue. In 1998 alone, our associate ranks grew by 30 percent to more than 600 people worldwide; by 2000 we had 16 offices and 2,500 employees. Boston and overseas associates started to get to know and trust each other better, and that also helped. It took longer than

Not everyone thought Munich was a good idea. It was emotional because we had the full support of Alan and Harriet, but lots of push-back from many others. There were moments when I wondered if the office would ever open. It was a lot more work than anyone ever anticipated. The ironic thing is that the constant back-and-forth travel I did between Boston and Munich made me understand firsthand how inefficient and time-consuming it can be to work with an ocean separating you from your business.

—Charlie Ritter

expected—several years in fact—but momentum kept building until we were really moving at Grand Circle speed.

Building the Worldwide Operation

In 2004 alone, we opened offices in Quito, Tokyo, Istanbul, the Galápagos, Phnom Penh, Buenos Aires, Copenhagen, Dijon, Budapest, Lima, and Letchworth, England. We also transferred responsibilities formerly assigned to Boston to all of our worldwide offices. Besides buying trips and managing vendors, the regional offices were now responsible for training and managing trip leaders, performing accounting functions, maintaining the computer records for their products, designing trip itineraries, preparing pre-trip information for travelers, handling any problems or dislocations that might occur on our trips, and managing every aspect of our ship operations in their regions.

At the same time, we were building new Grand Circle Foundation partnerships around the world. In 1996, we began working with the Auschwitz-Birkenau Museum and the World Monuments Fund to support some of the world's great cultural and historic sites. As we rolled out our new overseas offices, we realized we could use the new organization to support more local projects, too, like village schools and orphanages, and even to help develop projects directly with local communities, like the organic micro farm we support at the San Francisco School in northern Costa Rica. Our regional managers found new partnership opportunities for us; our overseas associates helped us oversee the projects; and our local trip leaders gave compelling tours of the sites when our travelers stopped by to visit.

We felt this kind of radical decentralization was necessary. Keeping a tight rein from Boston might have been easier—certainly less nerve-racking—but it would have been counter to our vision, values, and corporate culture. Unless we devolved critical operations and responsibility on the overseas offices, we would never get leadership from everywhere. We would lose the sense of associate ownership for the success of the company, lose our nimbleness in seizing business and philanthropic opportunities, and lose our responsiveness in crisis.

In typical Grand Circle fashion, we went a little *too* far, and we have since pulled some operations back to Boston. We have also changed some reporting lines. For example, certain overseas financial operations—

When we decided to go worldwide, Charlie Ritter, our technology guru, emerged as the unlikely champion of the overseas offices. His official role was to put in the technology that would allow us to communicate with the offices in real time, but he did much more than that. Charlie was a great listener. He had enormous empathy for people and enjoyed working in foreign cultures. The overseas associates really trusted him, and he became an aggressive advocate for them. Charlie had some rough moments, but to this day, he is remembered as the grandfather of Grand Circle worldwide.

Charlie passed away a few years back. I miss him and his wisdom. In his honor we created the Charlie Ritter Award, which is given annually to a Boston-based associate who supports our regional colleagues at the highest level.

—Alan Lewis

finance, accounting, and payables, for example—now report directly to Boston rather than through their regional managers. But we're still far more reliant on our worldwide associates than are other travel companies.

Most importantly, the regional offices are responsible for delivering the best possible travel experience in their region, and our quality ratings have gone up dramatically since we decided to "go over the water." In 1995, our "Excellent" rating was 60 percent; in 2005, eight years into our worldwide rollout, our "Excellent" rating was 73 percent. In 2009, we hit 81 percent. Not all of that gain can be attributed to the regional offices, of course, but we know they are the prime mover. This result has changed how we think about our business. At Grand Circle, we periodically evaluate and realign our business initiatives against what we call our Extreme Competitive Advantages, the handful of advantages that will take our competitors three to five years to overcome. We began building our overseas offices in 1996 to support one of our most important Extreme Competitive Advantage: the Unsurpassed Value and Excellence of our trips. The leverage that local control has had on both value and excellence has been so powerful that we added our Worldwide Organization to the list.

Running a Worldwide Organization

Over the years, we have come up with a set of simple rules for running our worldwide organization. The logistics are more complicated, of course, and are somewhat particular to our company, but the seven rules give us guidance for many different situations. Here they are:

7 Rules for Running a Worldwide Organization

1. Speak the same language
2. Build on company values
3. Communicate, communicate, communicate
4. Set clear goals
5. Impose financial controls
6. Give back everywhere you go
7. Respect people and cultures by treating everyone the same

OUR WORLDWIDE OFFICES

In 2010, we had 38 offices in 31 countries on six continents.

Here they are:

Amman, Jordan
Arusha, Tanzania
Bangkok, Thailand
Basel, Switzerland
Beijing, China
Boston, USA
Bratislava, Slovakia
Buenos Aires, Argentina
Cairo, Egypt
Cape Town, South Africa
Chiang Mai, Thailand
Cusco, Peru
Delhi, India
Dubrovnik, Croatia
Guatemala City, Guatemala
Hanoi, Vietnam
Ho Chi Minh City, Vietnam
Hong Kong, China
Istanbul, Turkey
Killarney, Ireland
London, England
Luxor, Egypt
Lyon, France
Marrakesh, Morocco'
Moscow, Russia
Panama City, Panama
Phnom Penh, Cambodia
Quito, Ecuador
Rome, Italy
San Jose, Costa Rica
Santiago, Chile
Siem Reap, Cambodia
St. Petersburg, Russia
Sydney, Australia
Tel Aviv, Israel
Tokyo, Japan
Tunis, Tunisia
Warsaw, Poland

Many people warned us not to try to impose Grand Circle values in some regions of the world. They particularly warned us that Asians couldn't engage in open and courageous communication because they worried about "face." We learned the opposite lesson at an offsite in Morocco, where some of our women associates from Thailand and China rated their male leader, who was also Asian, as a poor communicator. It was a stressful afternoon, as the leader shut down in anger. After some additional feedback and coaching from a group facilitator, the man reluctantly accepted that he needed to improve his communication skills. By the end of the day, he was genuinely grateful for the women's honesty. The women later told me it was insulting to put limits on our expectations for people because of cultural stereotypes.

—Alan Lewis

English Required

All our overseas associates must speak English. This applies to everyone from the regional manager to the accountants in the back room. We can have lots of differences, but language cannot be one of them; a common language is a prerequisite for effective global communication. Even though everyone speaks English, we constantly remind ourselves that English is often not the first language of our associates. For this reason, we always ask for feedback on important communications to insure that the message has been correctly understood.

Values First

As in Boston, values count far more than work experience when we hire for an overseas position. We believe that if an associate shares our values, then we can teach the job skills. If the values are missing, even in an otherwise great resume, we can never get that associate to become a full member of the Grand Circle family. We're not talking about cultural values; we want our associates to hold on to the values of their national heritage and family upbringing. We're talking about the six company values we mentioned in Chapter 2: open and courageous communication, risk-taking, thriving in change, speed, quality, and teamwork. Adherence to a common corporate culture allows us to operate as a single, cohesive team, even though we come from very different national cultures.

Values assessment begins even before the job interview. For key hires, we use a Leadership Effectiveness Assessment tool designed to reveal the candidate's priorities, attitudes, values, and leadership style; it is the same assessment we use for key hires in Boston. We also interview for values. This may sound hard, but it's actually easy. There are no tricks involved. We are completely open and above-board; we just explain our corporate culture to the candidate. Whenever we can, we do two-on-one or three-on-one interviews; when candidates see several associates espousing the same values and reinforcing the importance of those values at Grand Circle, they begin to get the picture. Many don't believe us at first—some of them have gotten snow jobs about company values at other American job interviews—but if we stay consistently on values throughout the interview, most candidates see that we're serious.

One of the reasons we're so frank is that we don't want to hire someone destined to fail. We want prospective associates to walk away if they don't believe they can fit in with our culture. For a 90-day period after hiring, we reinforce our culture and assess the associate at every opportunity, to be sure that our goals and roles are clear. On occasion, we have to tell an individual that we've made a mutual mistake.

Is this hard? You bet. Many parts of the world value formal, highly structured relationships, especially in business. In these cultures, speaking up doesn't come naturally in the workplace, never mind risk-taking. But even in highly patriarchal societies, we've always found courageous people who don't hesitate to express their opinions, take risks, and work fast to get the job done, even in pretty chaotic circumstances. In fact, when they're given the freedom to do their best work, they often become some of our most valuable leaders.

Constant Communication

It is difficult to overestimate the importance of communication, especially face-to-face communication, in a global enterprise. At Grand Circle, we actually strive for over-communication. We say, "You can lead from anywhere," but we can't get leadership from our overseas offices unless our overseas associates are absolutely clear on their assignments. So we hold a weekly teleconference with every office, send Boston associates to help in the regional offices, and bring overseas associates to Boston whenever we can.

The big event, of course, is our annual BusinessWorks, when the entire overseas leadership team—all the regional managers, along with other associates who have distinguished themselves the previous year—comes to the Pinnacle Leadership Center in Kensington, New Hampshire, for two to three weeks of business meetings. We deal face-to-face on the hot issues of each region, starting with the performance of the top people, and then addressing the top issues with each of our top products.

Written communications are also important. E-mail messages are traded constantly. If an overseas associate needs an answer from Boston, his primary contact in Boston tracks the query until it is resolved. Regional associates read our weekly electronic update, *Bridges*, as well

At one BusinessWorks, an overseas associate remarked offhandedly that our Grand Circle values are easy for Boston associates because Boston associates are Americans. He didn't understand the laughter that met his comment. Since we were the only American company he had worked for, he assumed that our values were common in the United States. Little did he know! Grand Circle is a different kind of company—here *and* abroad—and we have as much difficulty living our values as people from Thailand or Argentina.

—Sue Harvey,
20-year associate
Executive Vice President,
Pacific Rim, Americas & Africa

as other associate publications; they also approve all our catalogs, brochures, and website content to make sure we represent our trips correctly and don't promise more than they can deliver. At Grand Circle, communication is a two-way street, and one that is very well traveled.

Goal Tending

We want consistent high-quality scores from our travelers, and that requires a high-performing global team. We achieve this by making sure every associate has specific goals attached to his or her name at all times. These may be product excellence goals, inventory goals, cost goals, discovery goals, trip leader goals—whatever pertains to the associate's position. For example, a region might have a goal to improve Excellence by two points, or to acquire hotels and meals to accommodate another 1,000 travelers on a particular trip, or to hold total costs flat over the prior year, or to institute additional training for trip leaders who score below 80 percent in Excellence. The goals will change from year to year, but the goals are always explicit and always tied to individual associates.

Our overseas associates live our values. They are dedicated and industrious workers, always on call to serve our travelers. Getting stuff done is not a concern. Getting the *right* stuff done is the hard part. Clear and measurable goals get associates in Phnom Penh working in unison with associates in Cairo and Boston, and tending to goals is every associate's full-time job.

Financial Controls

Early on, we made the mistake of throwing too much out to the regional offices without instituting adequate financial controls. Large contracts are always tempting, and in some parts of the world skimming a little off the top is considered standard business practice. Regional offices also handle a lot of cash for tips, entrance fees, and emergencies. They say a few bad apples can spoil a barrel, and it was certainly true in our case. After a few incidents of pilfering and outright embezzlement, we went against our natural aversion to paperwork and implemented strong financial controls in the overseas offices. Because a few unscrupulous people took advantage of our weak controls, every office now has to file monthly financial reports—and they had better balance!

Another Big Mistake

When we first began building our overseas offices, our financial accounting wasn't what anyone would call rigorous. When we visited overseas offices, we were chiefly concerned with the traveler experience, not possible financial shenanigans. We paid the price for this mistake. In Munich, a rogue associate faked a list of vendors and issued checks to an Italian shell company for fabricated goods and services. Once a month, he would fly to Italy and transfer the funds to his own account. Needless to say, we've now established strong financial controls around the world.

—Alan Lewis

Give Back to Get Ahead

Grand Circle Foundation's motto is "Giving Back to the World We Travel." Giving back is good for the people we help, of course, but it's also good for business. The village innkeeper remembers that we support the local school when we come by to negotiate our contract for the next few years. Historic towns help us deliver unforgettable experiences because they know the Foundation has made contributions to preserve local antiquities. When we search a country for people willing to provide home-hosted events, we get lots of applicants because people know we've helped their community through the Foundation. Travel is always a symbiotic relationship, and giving back to the world we travel returns more than feel-good rewards—it makes it easier to lead a global enterprise.

We reinforce this reciprocal relationship by encouraging regional offices not only to support the Foundation projects that our travelers visit in their countries, but also to engage in local community service. Community service is not always the local cultural norm. In India, for example, it is customary for philanthropically-minded people to donate money to a cause rather than do the work personally, so when Mohammed Iliayas, our general manager for India and Bhutan, organized a community service event in July 2009, the effort was all the more surprising for the recipients. In all, 44 volunteers, including

Recently I met with two of our vendors from Cusco, Peru, who are also the maternal heads of their households. They offer home-hosted meals to our travelers. These ladies had just lost their homes and all their belongings in the floods of 2010, and were living under tarps at a local soccer stadium. They both cried and hugged me in a powerful way—not because we were raising money to help them (though we did), but because we were happy to allow them to continue earning money as hosts while they temporarily used relatives' homes. Alan has always taught the importance of never leaving a place because of difficult circumstances. I will never forget those two ladies.

—Mark Shionis,
11-year associate
Senior Vice President,
Worldwide Contracting

OAT Trip Leaders, staff, and vendors spent a day renovating the Surdas School for the Blind in Agra, near the Taj Mahal. It was a nice example of putting corporate values to work to make a cultural difference.

Kindergartners on the Danube

Manolache Ambrose, captain of the M/S *River Aria*, one of Grand Circle's private river cruisers in Europe, is a man constantly on the lookout for new things. In November 2008, he got something totally unexpected: a passenger list that included 89 kindergartners from three schools and a local orphanage.

The children's cruise was a special community service event organized by the staff of Grand Circle's regional office in Bratislava, Slovakia. The idea was to "create a beautiful experience for all the children." The ship's captain and crew certainly succeeded. Happily blowing on the whistles attached to their life vests, the children played games, toured the ship, and enjoyed a special, nutritious feast as the M/S *River Aria* sailed along the Danube.

"The kids really enjoyed the day," Captain Ambrose says. "I like working for a company that cares about people."

Respect for Other Cultures

Finally, leading a worldwide organization requires a genuine respect for other cultures. We share our six Grand Circle values with our associates worldwide, but we don't try to impose American culture onto other societies or individuals. Overseas associates wear what they want, eat what they like, and decorate their offices as they please. They speak their native language among themselves and observe their national and religious holidays. They perform community service work that supports cultural traditions, and we never question their political convictions.

There is a business reason for this. Cultural disrespect makes people resentful, and a resentful associate is seldom productive. But there is a better reason to respect other cultures—because different cultures are interesting and, differences aside, we are all human beings. As Harriet says, "In every new place, no matter how different, I find people engaged in the same dance of life. In every person, regardless of language or dress, I see more commonality than difference. In travel, I discover true hope for global understanding."

This attitude comes easily to us at Grand Circle because all our associates—wherever they work—are travelers, and real travelers approach the world with an open and inquisitive mind.

Two Common Mistakes

Building and leading a worldwide organization is difficult. It can be impossible if you make one of two common errors. The first is to treat your overseas offices like vendors, i.e., not providing leadership and parity, just telling them what you want. This kind of relationship relegates overseas associates to second-place status and they notice fast. Our overseas associates have the same access to us as our Boston associates do, and we share with them all the information that we disclose at our monthly corporate meeting. There are no closed books and no arm's-length dealings. If you do not want to treat your overseas associates as co-workers, extending them the same opportunities and responsibilities as your home associates, you would probably be better off contracting with an independent ground operator.

The second error is to manage overseas associates as if they were all Americans. We believe this is a lazy way to run a global enterprise—lazy and arrogant. People who grew up in Tennessee are different from people who grew up in Southern California; Cambodians may have a hard time relating to either. We encourage all our associates to bring an open and fair mind to work. We also encourage them to do their homework, not just on the business operations in our overseas offices, but also on the business norms in our many far-flung regions. Misunderstandings are common in global enterprises; cultural sensitivity can head some of them off.

Locals Really Do Know Best

If you are going to lead a global enterprise, you must actually believe that locals know best. If you don't, you will be forever micro-managing your

It's easy for people in the field to blame headquarters, so we made a rule that the nebulous word "Boston" could never be used as a scapegoat. "Boston" can't make people do anything. If an overseas associate can't put a name to the complaint, then the issue is dismissed. This may sound harsh, but we can't resolve tough issues if we don't know who generated the demand or otherwise caused a problem. Regional associates are often reluctant to identify the person in Boston who is giving them difficulties. This is understandable but counterproductive. In a situation like this, we remind overseas associates that open and courageous communication is one of our values, and we encourage them to demonstrate that value by being as honest and forthcoming as they can be. We treat it as a leadership issue, and an opportunity for personal growth.

—Martha Prybylo,
17-year associate
Executive Vice President,
Worldwide People and Culture

overseas offices and sabotaging their work. Like company values and corporate culture, a commitment to overseas associates cannot be empty words.

Our advice to other companies is this: If you find yourself uncertain about whether locals know best, look to your company performance data. In our case it was obvious: whenever we let local guides lead, local buyers buy, local trip designers make the itineraries, our quality scores went up. The way our business works, the higher our quality scores, the better our customer retention, and the greater the profit for the company. Our worldwide organization not only delivers value and excellence, it *generates* value and excellence. For this reason it has become our Number 1 Extreme Competitive Advantage. Whatever metric you use in your company—sales figures, customer retention, or bottom line—measure it local vs. headquarters. That will get you past any unsuspected cultural stereotypes or prejudices. If you don't believe us, believe your numbers.

Once Alan was at a meeting in our office in Dubrovnik, and an associate raised a concern about the security of some of our company information. The associate felt we should protect our business models and strategies better. "They are very valuable," he said. "The competition would love to get their hands on them."

Alan just smiled and said, "I would willingly hand them over. Maybe the competition would learn something. But I'm not worried, because no other company will ever have the people and culture that we do. Our people are Number 1. *You are our Extreme Competitive Advantage.*"

—Harriet Lewis

On the Record

Our travelers depend on our trip leaders to provide truly authentic experiences in the places they visit. They are not interested in the government's official version of current events or the tourist board's prettified "spin." They are looking for the truth from people who know their country firsthand.

Sometimes they even use our trip leaders as sources for books they are writing. One traveler, Freddie Remza, a retired teacher from Apalachin, New York, spent many hours in conversation with her OAT Trip Leader, Helen, as she researched adoption practices in China for her book for middle schoolers called *The Journey to Mei*. Another traveler, Judith Hudson, a retired teacher from Decker, Michigan, published a book called *Bayo: A Good African Boy*, based on a story told by her Trip Leader, Modest Bayo, on an OAT safari in Tanzania. Travel is all about stories, and we are delighted that our travelers honor the powerful stories that local people have to tell.

—Harriet Lewis

Since that morning on the porch of the Algonquin Hotel in New Brunswick, we've stumbled many times—sometimes badly. But we have remained focused on the goal and have learned from our mistakes. We still don't do it perfectly, but each year we're getting better at leading a vastly diverse workforce that spans the globe. Our worldwide organization has been great for our business, and it has also been a lot of fun. Put dozens of nationalities together in a common enterprise and the results are as exuberant and surprising as life itself.

We are two very fortunate people and we owe it all to the nearly 50 different nationalities that work with Grand Circle around the world.

In 1991, an exhausted management team emerged after a 24-kilometer hike through Costa Rica's Monteverde Cloud Forest—the first American group to do so.

CHAPTER 7

Transformation and Turmoil

It was 1994, and Alan and I were amazed at the pace of change at the company. We had recently taken two major actions: launching Grand Circle Foundation, and acquiring Overseas Adventure Travel. We were very excited about these new ventures, but we weren't sure how to integrate the changes into the company. We needed advice and some time away to think, so we scheduled an offsite in Costa Rica.

We had taken the children to Costa Rica in 1991, when they were about seven and nine, and I had wonderful memories of hiking through the cloud forest, dodging sticks thrown by howler monkeys while the kids laughed and laughed. The offsite would be more serious, of course. We invited our senior leadership, our board of business advisors, their spouses, and members of the honorary board of Grand Circle Foundation. We had never gone together on an offsite, but with all that brainpower, we were sure to have a productive offsite, and have a little fun along the way.

When they asked what to expect, it's doubtful anyone said, "Intense heat. Torrential rains. Dysentery. Riding horseback through uncharted jungle in total darkness." Somehow we had misjudged the adventure quotient of the trip. But that was the least of our troubles. Four days into the eight-day trip, after our Foundation board had gone back home, it became clear that Alan and I had a mutiny on our hands.

Several of our business advisors saw the acquisition of Overseas Adventure Travel as an excellent opportunity to take Grand Circle public. They reasoned that the acquisition would result in a big jump in the valuation for the company. But Alan and I didn't want to take Grand Circle public. Adding to our consternation, several of our business advisors couldn't understand how our vision for worldwide philanthropy related to our business venture. To us, the connection was obvious, but they just couldn't see it. As we hiked through the jungle and wheeled around in Jeeps, the different factions kept pressing their case. The last straw came when a cadre of dissenters met secretly to strategize a public offering—without informing either Alan or me of their plans.

Of course, the dissenters could not force their way; we are a private company, and our board has purely advisory powers. But a breach in trust is difficult to repair, and soon after our return to Boston, we asked four of the board members to leave, including one of Alan's relatives. We were shocked and crestfallen at the fallout from the trip. This was not the change we were after.

—Harriet Lewis

Our travelers are Americans over 50, and they are well-acquainted with change. Most are old enough to have grown up with a single black-and-white television. The family station wagon was built in the USA and it didn't have seat belts or even air-conditioning. Travel was a retirement dream, but the Cold War was hot, and a good part of the world was off-limits for Americans. In fact, 50 years ago, most Americans had never flown in an airplane, except perhaps as soldiers, and only a tiny fraction of the citizenry had a passport. Today, those Americans travel the world with Grand Circle. They have seen the world change, and they have changed right along with it. They know that change is necessary, often thrilling, but not always easy. That is the lesson of this chapter, too.

Then and Now

When we acquired Grand Circle Travel, the business was pretty simple. Our traditional, coach-based tours were purchased from ground operators and managed from Boston. Our associates were primarily American, as were our trip leaders, and most of our trips went to Europe. We marketed directly to our customers through catalogs printed in huge press runs, and we made do with a workforce of about a dozen people.

Boy, have things changed. Today, our products include small group adventure travel, River Cruises, and small ship coastal cruises, as well as the traditional Grand Circle Travel products. Our trips are no longer traditional sightseeing tours, but rich, cross-cultural experiences that include home-hosted meals, school visits, and *Day in the Life* programs. We now offer trips to all seven continents, including destinations we never dreamed of 25 years ago, like Russia, Vietnam, Tibet, Albania, Jordan, Namibia, and Mongolia. In fact, in the not-too-distant future, we hope to offer trips to Cuba.

The company has changed, too. Today we have a worldwide organization with 38 offices in 31 countries and more than 2,300 associates. We buy our trips direct from vendors in the host country wherever we can, eliminating ground operators and their commissions. We've switched from mass mailings to targeted marketing and have, belatedly, embraced the Internet. In 25 years, we have transformed ourselves from a small, money-losing travel company into a global enterprise—leader in our industry.

Change—A Way of Life

These were not minor changes in the company. They were huge, and they came at a dizzying pace, sometimes with little warning. We don't mind that. We like change. In fact, people often remark that neither of us is very good at sitting still. And we know that change is a way of life in the travel business. That's why we made "Thriving in Change" one of our company values.

As chair and vice chair of the company, we feel it is our responsibility to look outward and ahead. Most companies forget to look outside. Then when a big change happens, they're blindsided and have to scramble to catch up. We strive to stay ahead of changes by spotting trends in their embryonic stage.

We do that by actively seeking information. We peruse dozens of competitor brochures every week. We both read books constantly, two or three at a time, and we keep up with the world political scene. We talk to our advisors all over the world and ask them what they see coming in the way of travel trends and business changes. We pay special attention to information from our own travelers, who tell us what they think of our trips and where they want to go next. We read business journals, and we stay close to forward-thinking business professors, especially at Babson College, in Wellesley, Massachusetts, which houses our own Lewis Initiative for Social Enterprise. Last, but certainly not least, we travel the world, and wherever we travel, we listen to the local people and keep our eyes open to new opportunities.

Do we have perfect 20/20 vision? No. We've made many mistakes, but most of our mistakes have been in execution, not vision. Usually, we have thought so hard about a change that we get the direction right, even if we're not sure how to get there.

Two Big Transformations

We have already talked about several major changes in the company, including the launch of Grand Circle Foundation, the termination of our American tour guides, and the opening of our offices worldwide. Two other big changes—the acquisition of Overseas Adventure Travel in 1993 and our investment in River Cruises in 1997—radically changed

Do not suffer life to stagnate. It will grow muddy for want of action.

—Samuel Johnson

the world of travel for us and our customers.

These two changes came at a time of turmoil in the industry. The first Gulf War, which began in 1991, had brought travel in Europe and the Middle East to a standstill. At Grand Circle, we had two rounds of very painful layoffs, and we experimented with a number of domestic trips, none of them very successful. In 1991, the United States declared war on Iraq, and 40 percent of American tour operators went bankrupt. We were determined not to be the next casualty. Clearly, we needed to find new destinations and new styles of travel that would appeal to our travelers.

A Company Blind Spot

In spite of all of our efforts to anticipate change, we sometimes get surprised, especially around technology. That's our company blind spot. Like most of the people at Grand Circle, Harriet and I gravitated to travel because we love people and places, not gadgets. We can turn on a dime in a world crisis, but technology can sneak up on us. For years, we insisted that our travelers didn't use the Internet. We were wrong, and we've been playing catch-up for the last couple of years. When introduced Harriet's Corner on website in 2009, we discovered how really wrong we had been. The response to Harriet's travel musings and tips has been overwhelming. Imagine how much closer we could have been to our travelers if we had been listening in all the right places!

—Alan Lewis

First Came OAT

We saw adventure travel coming from a long way off. We have always been attracted to adventurous trips ourselves. Harriet went to Africa with girlfriends after college; Alan did a fair amount of outdoor adventure activities in the 1980s; and together we trekked in Nepal with friends in 1988, to celebrate Alan's 40th birthday.

We were convinced that our travelers would like adventure travel, too. They were curious, educated people; some had been to Europe, Africa, and Asia in the service; many had already "done" all the traditional European sightseeing tours. And then there were the Baby Boomers, coming up hard and fast—and in big numbers. The first wave of that famously independent-minded generation would hit 50 in 1996, and there were 70 million more right behind them. Our plan was to meet them with a wide range of trips in Europe and beyond. Acquiring an adventure travel company would broaden our reach both demographically and geographically, ensuring our longevity as a company and protecting it against regional travel disruptions.

We started searching out adventure travel companies right after we returned from Nepal. Alan took a hard look at Mountain Travel, but ultimately walked away. Then, in 1991, on the heels of the Gulf War, we found our opportunity right across the river, in an old, three-story house in Cambridge, Massachusetts. The company was Overseas Adventure Travel (OAT), which offered custom treks and small group tours around the world, especially in East Africa, Nepal, Turkey, and Peru. OAT's associates were mostly in their 30s and 40s, and they were *passionate* about travel. They reminded us of ourselves. It seemed like a good match, and in 1993 we bought the company.

Paving the Way

It was a good match but not a perfect fit. We loved the exotic locales and the small group concept—a maximum of 16 travelers per trip—but some of the trips, like the Mount Everest and the High Alps trips, were too strenuous for our market. We were looking for something more like "soft adventure" than "high adventure." We were also alarmed by the balance sheet. The company was bringing in $4 million in annual sales, but was losing about $500,000 a year. The trips were expensive, and yet many were unprofitable; some had only one or two departures a year, and as few as 12 travelers.

We had seen this sort of thing before—in the trips we inherited from Colonial Penn—so we weren't worried. Our goal was to offer small group adventure travel to older Americans at a more affordable price; we wanted them to experience the amazing cultural interactions that come when groups are small enough to get off the beaten path and relate one-on-one with people very different from themselves. We knew we could get there by rigorously applying our Grand Circle business

The mutiny in Costa Rica was a shock and disappointment. We liked and respected our business advisors, but they didn't understand what we wanted from OAT. They thought we didn't see the money-making opportunity in the acquisition. In their view, OAT was a nice addition to our portfolio; we could use it to increase our stock valuation if we went public with Grand Circle. We got that, but we didn't care about a big short-term gain. We were looking for long-term gains in discovery and market share. It was a tough, agonizing decision, but we needed to force a big change in our board so we could continue to build our dream. We asked the four dissenting board members for their resignations, and we received them.

—Harriet Lewis

practices: weeding out the worst-performing trips, buying direct, lowering the per diem cost, building on our four Product Pillars, and including international airfare in the package price. Maybe we pushed too hard and too fast for these changes; the founder of the company, Judi Wineland, moved on after a year, saying our vision for the company no longer resonated with hers. We understood. We are vision-driven people, too, and we were sorry we couldn't see eye to eye.

Within two years we were offering adventures priced $2,000 to $3,000 less than our closest competitors, and our trips included international airfare (theirs didn't). More importantly, we had opened the world of small group adventure travel to folks who'd never known it was possible to travel like this, and we took them to places they'd never dreamed of going. That was our vision: to help change people's lives.

The Adventure Continues

In 1994, Overseas Adventure Travel officially joined the Grand Circle family. For a while, we ran it as a separate operation in Cambridge, but in 1999, we brought OAT's associates to Congress Street to work at Grand Circle headquarters. The move was unpopular with some of the OAT staff—OAT had always had its own, off-the-beaten-track kind of culture—and there was another round of resignations. From this we learned that managing an office across the river can be as hard as managing an office on the other side of the world. Culture is culture, and you have to be careful to respect it, not to step on people's toes.

We also learned we had to honor promises. OAT had long offered a "Small Group Guarantee"—not more than 16 travelers on any trip. It was a big part of OAT's value proposition. But after OAT moved to Congress Street, we started to make some exceptions; larger groups are, after all, more profitable. Passenger counts on some departures crept up to 17, even 18. Our OAT customers let us have it. They let us know in no uncertain terms that this trend was unacceptable; we needed to make our money some other way. In 2004, we created an internal team charged with safeguarding this guarantee and controlling costs, and we've been true to our word ever since.

Today, Overseas Adventure Travel is the fastest-growing tour company in the United States. In the past ten years, the passenger volume has more than doubled (to more than 50,000 travelers a year), and sales have more than tripled (to $269 million). In fact, most of our company's growth now comes from the OAT brand, and what was once a sideline business for us accounted for 43 percent of our travelers and 47 percent of our sales in 2009. Our OAT Small Ship Cruises have appeared on both the Gold List and Readers' Choice List in the annual *Condé Nast Traveler* awards ever since 2002, and we've been on the list for Best Tour Operator/Safari Outfitter for seven years running. When we returned from Nepal in 1988, we knew small group adventure travel would change our company, but OAT's progress has exceeded all expectations.

A Bicycle Detour

It was 1997, and we were very pleased with our success with OAT. We were starting another new venture, too, building our first custom-designed ship for our European River Cruises. We were on fire. So we decided to buy *another* company: Vermont Bicycle Tours, which we later renamed VBT. Now we really had the Old World covered—by plane, train, foot, ship, bus, and 10-speed, soft-saddled, specialized bike.

This was a whole new world of travel we had never experienced before. That was the problem, of course. Bicycle enthusiasts are their own breed. They are generally younger than our GCT and OAT travelers, for one thing, and more competitive. They wanted to cover a lot of ground every day, and they wanted to bring their own bikes.

Despite years of trying, we were never able to mesh VBT with our Boston-based travel companies. A big part of the problem was that we tried to force VBT into the OAT mold, when their travelers, products, and culture were too different. We eventually found a solution—we sold VBT in 2006. We broke even on the deal, but considering the loss of time and focus on our core business, it was a big mistake.

—Alan Lewis

In 1998, OAT was hit hard by troubles in East Africa, one of its principal spheres of operation. Bombings at the American embassies in Nairobi, Kenya, and Dar es Salaam, Tanzania, had hurt bookings on one of OAT's most popular programs: tented safaris in Tanzania. We hustled to offer new trips to China, Tibet, and Borneo, drawing on the expertise of our new office in Hong Kong. The trips were very successful. It was one of the first signs that our worldwide office strategy was on the right track.

—Alan Lewis

I don't like boats, it's true. I like having my feet on the ground when I travel. But even I could see the appeal of the *M/S River Symphony* and the rest of our *River*-class ships—sleek, bright, comfortable, and friendly. Ten years later, those ships are still winning awards from *Condé Nast Traveler* and *Travel + Leisure*, even against competition that includes brand-new, all-suite ships. We didn't know much about shipbuilding in those days, but we knew our travelers and what they would like.

—Harriet Lewis

Then Came River Cruises

We bought OAT because we understood adventure travel, and we molded it carefully to fit our vision for Grand Circle's future. The ships were different. We waded into River Cruises chasing an opportunity, and we soon found ourselves in over our heads.

We had run a very successful special event in October 1996, a Rhine River Valley cruise to celebrate the 38th anniversary of Grand Circle's founding. It sold out in a matter of days, and soon our travelers were clamoring for more. This was a demand we hadn't really foreseen, but there was a problem. The charter cruises available in Europe at that time were mostly downscale affairs; we had pulled off a winner for the anniversary cruise by chartering one of the better ships and customizing every detail of the trip. We couldn't replicate that success on a broad scale (though we tried, garnering at one point one of the worst "Excellent" scores in our history—17 percent on a Russian River Cruise in 1997).

The biggest problem was the ships. The European fleet was old; the ships were dark, cramped, eccentrically decorated, and in dire need of refurbishment. They really didn't meet American standards. Then, in 1997, a golden opportunity fell in our laps. The best of the charter companies, a Dutch firm, was about to build a new ship. The keel had not yet been laid. We bought in on very favorable terms, becoming full partners and having the ship built to our specifications. Honey Streit-Reyes secured the contract and oversaw the build-out from our new office in Munich. The new ship, the *M/S River Symphony* was a ship Americans would sail on, with all outside cabins, air-conditioning, floor-to-ceiling windows in the dining room, bathrooms outfitted to ocean cruise standards, and balconies.

We built two more ships with our Dutch partner, but it wasn't enough. Demand outpaced inventory; we couldn't keep up. And though the ships were terrific, the onboard experience still wasn't up to our standards. We had to contract with local providers for food, service, entertainment, and housekeeping, and the results were erratic; sometimes even the electricity didn't work. So we bought out our Dutch partner, built seven more ships, and got some outside help on the service side. We were in the ship business—big time.

A Big Ship Mistake

We made a lot of changes to the company in the 1990s. Every time we made a change, it seems we also made some humdinger mistake. In late 1999, we were thinking about buying European Cruise Lines (ECL), a small river cruise operation, to expand our ship operations. As was customary in American business, our CFO wrote up a letter of intent; he then flew to Holland to present the offer. In the United States, a letter of intent does not have the force of a contract, but in Holland, it turns out, it does. Who knew? Not us. Suddenly, Grand Circle owned a river cruise line.

There were four ships in ECL's fleet, and not one was up to our standards. We sold off two of them the first year, and sank a lot of money into refurbishing the others. But in the end the venture was a bust. After a couple of years, we had sold all the ships and dismissed or reassigned all the employees. We had wasted $14 million, but we had learned a valuable lesson: Never sign anything in a foreign country without knowing what you're getting into.

—Alan Lewis

How Did We Get Here?

It's hard to overstate how big a change the River Cruise business was for Grand Circle. Our expertise was land tours; we knew nothing about shipyards, or docking rights, or running a housekeeping operation. But all of a sudden we owned all these multimillion-dollar ships. For 20 years, Alan had been an outspoken "no assets" guy. When we travel, we travel light, and Alan applied the same principle to the business: *Assets just weigh you down*. But we know an opportunity when we see it, and we are not afraid to take risks if we think it will get us closer to our dream.

So there we were, at the start of a new millennium, trying to figure out how to guarantee our trademark "unforgettable experiences" and not take a bath. Early on, Alan, Mark Frevert, and a team of senior executives from Boston went to Spain for an offsite to brainstorm and set goals; the group then traveled to the new Munich office to get input from our buyers and

Getting into ships was a crazy thing to do, really, and a lot of our advisors said we would live to regret it. It was a time in business when there was a lot of focus on core competencies—and ships sure weren't ours. We had to bring in a lot of expertise, and for a couple of years it was a fiasco. But we had a tiger by the tail, and Alan wasn't about to let go.

—Mark Frevert,
25-year associate
Executive Vice President
and Chief Architect

program developers there. Among them was a Croatian associate who by sheer coincidence was a certified master mariner and experienced ship's captain. We thought that was a good omen.

Over time, a formula emerged. We knew our travelers liked the convenience of river cruising; it is an easy way to get from place to place, and they only had to unpack once. But that didn't mean they wanted to sit on the ship all day. We distinguished ourselves from our competitors by pairing the best ships in the business with the best onshore excursions. Other river cruise operators didn't have our expertise on land, so we were able to deliver much better experiences, such things as winery tours, home-hosted meals, school visits, walking tours, and visits to local markets. We also divided each ship's passengers into several smaller groups, each with its own program director, to keep the experience up-close and personal.

Smooth Sailing

Two initiatives finally nailed River Cruises for us. First, we set up a yield management team in Boston to really push our load factors, i.e., the percentage of berths filled on each sailing. Our competitors' ships were running at 70 to 80 percent occupancy, but because we had so many travelers on our mailing list and our marketing was so successful, we were able to fill 96 percent of our berths, which allowed us to lower our selling prices. Soon we were offering better cruises for far less money than the competition—often more than a $1,000 less per person. We still have that price advantage.

Second, we developed an action plan to get more direct control of the shipboard experience. After several bad experiences with outside vendors, we began hiring crew and training staff ourselves. We also established our own nautical and hospitality division, based in Dubrovnik, to deal with food, beverage, and housekeeping services. We now controlled the whole operation. Before long, we had complete vertical integration of the river cruise enterprise—something we never attempted in any other aspect of our business. We became the only river cruise company catering exclusively to American travelers.

As we expected, once we had control of the entire operation, our quality scores soared. By 2001, our River Cruises were off the charts, and by 2004, we had 43 ships of our own. The next year, we took a new step, building a line of small ships for OAT. We had been chartering small ships and large yachts for OAT trips in the Mediterranean and Galápagos for many years, but had encountered the same problems of quality control that had plagued us on European rivers. Same problem, same solution: build and outfit them ourselves. Today we own or charter 60 ships all around the world, and small ship travel is a growth market for us. Like our OAT small ships, our Grand Circle River Cruise ships regularly receive awards and recognition in industry publications. For example, ten of our ships made the list of Top 50 Small Ships in the 2010 *Condé Nast Traveler* Readers' Poll.

When we got started in ships, we were chasing an opportunity and running on instinct. We knew it was a big change for the company, and our execution wasn't perfect. But if we hadn't taken that risk, we would literally have missed the boat.

Big Changes, Extreme Advantages

The acquisition of OAT, in 1993, and the venture into shipbuilding and ship operation, in 1997, radically changed our company. Today we count Leadership in Small Group Travel and Leadership in Small Ship Cruises as two of the Extreme Competitive Advantages that put us years ahead of our competition.

Complacency Can Be Fatal

We believe when something quits changing, it's dead, and that includes business and philanthropic organizations. Grand Circle is always in flux. That's the way we want it, and that's the way it has to be, because travel is a volatile industry. Complacency can be fatal. We have seen many travel companies fail because they thought their business model was bullet-proof or because they just weren't paying attention.

In this business, you must be ready to change at a moment's notice. This means more than staying open to suggestions. It means having a corporate culture that values speed, encourages risk-taking, and thrives in change. It also means having a process ready to go.

How to Transform an Organization

There is no easy way to direct transformational change. It takes a clear understanding of what the change will mean at every level of the organization, a determination to make it happen, and some careful tracking. We've messed it up more than once. But we think it boils down to these seven simple steps:

---

7 Steps for Change

1. Set clear goals and focus change where it will make the most difference
2. Communicate the change at every opportunity
3. Use offsites to draw on the brainpower of the entire organization
4. Get everyone on board
5. Build transformation teams to direct the action
6. Make good use of action sets and deadlines
7. Measure results and change course if you have to

Stay Clear and Focused

Look around you. Lots of things need to change, but you can't do it all. We believe it's crucial to pick *the next most important change* and then see it through to completion. A lot of companies fail at making transformational change because as soon as they get started on one change, they run off to fix something else. This is a formula for failure. An organization needs sustained focus to transform its business.

Communicate the Change

Communication is key. Leaders must formulate a clear goal and explanation for the change, one that everyone in the organization can understand. This is a challenge at Grand Circle, because our associates speak dozens of different languages. We must craft our message in simple but powerful English and then repeat it over and over again—in company memoranda, in newsletters, in conversation, in our weekly teleconferences with overseas managers, and in our monthly corporate meeting. It may get repetitive, and associates will sometimes roll their eyes, but we have found that as soon as you quit talking about change, you lose momentum.

Use Your Collective Brainpower

The best brainpower seldom resides with senior management, and the best ideas don't always arise in the office. That's why we always start a major transformation with an offsite dedicated to visioning the change. Put a group of smart, experienced people together in a new environment, preferably outdoors, and their solutions will never disappoint you. We reach deep into the organization to include people who know the day-to-day workings of the company and can see the landmines we might step on if we were to run willy-nilly through the landscape. Our offsites don't always go as planned, but they always surface the hot issues.

Get Everyone on Track

Over the years, we have developed a very structured approach to brainstorming and consensus-building. We've had to do this because our company values encourage a kind of high-energy creativity that can sometimes go off in a thousand directions at once. The approach is based in Nominal Group Process, a decision-making practice that identifies key issues and considers all points of view, regardless of where they come from in the organization. We use techniques developed at the Pinnacle Leadership Center, which has been honing methodologies for this work for more than 20 years. Group facilitators keep the process moving forward in a speedy and predictable fashion. We have done this so many times, we know exactly what to do.

Build a Transformation Team

Transformation teams are charged with making the change happen. Whether it's a new computer system or a new way to train trip leaders, the process is the same. One member of the senior leadership team is identified as the sponsor and is held accountable for the initiative. Together the team identifies hot issues, determines necessary actions, sets deadlines, and reports progress to the Executive Team. Associates

The Worst Offsite Ever

When Alan asked me to facilitate the offsite in Costa Rica, I accepted with no sense of foreboding. It turned out to be the worst offsite ever. There was all the trouble with the board of directors, and there was that harrowing moment when Alan found himself literally driving down a hill with no brakes. On an excursion down into a valley, I got thrown off my horse, banged my head, and made the balance of the trip in a Jeep.

I was glad when we finally arrived at the San Jose airport for our flight home. Suddenly, Alan asked me if I had seen Mark Frevert. He had been out of sorts due to some parasitic disease. We searched high and low, and found him just before final boarding—asleep behind a potted palm. Everybody was thrilled when we got settled on the plane and finally heard the wheels go up.

—Jim O'Brien,
15-year associate
Chairman, Kensington
Investment Company

vie to get on these teams because we have a history of using them for testing and developing new leaders.

Hold the Presses

One of the biggest changes in our business has been in marketing. For more than 20 years, we operated as a direct-mail mass marketer, mailing truckloads of big catalogs out to customers many times a year. It was heavy work in every sense of the word—and costly—but it was effective. Today, we send highly targeted communications in many different formats, including letters, postcards, single-product brochures, Web discussions, and electronic news. We're able to target our communications because we know where our travelers have been and they tell us where they want to go next.

The changeover from mass marketing to targeted marking was a big undertaking that affected many departments. Instead of dictating the change, we formed transformation teams to tell us how to get it done. It more than a year, but it was accomplished with little disruption to the business because it was guided by the people who had the most knowledge of the work and had the most at stake.

—Lisa Norton,
  Executive Vice President, Marketing

Make Actions Happen

The action plans are the important thing. At Grand Circle, action plans are always very specific. Every issue around a change generates a set of specific actions; each action is assigned to a specific person, who is responsible for getting it done by a specific target completion date. Since the goal is clear and everybody has participated in the plan, the transformation gets broad support and every associate helps make it happen.

Measure and Reassess

Experience has taught us that when faced with a problem or a need for change, speed is more important than being exactly right. We can get away with fast action because we have an understanding with our associates that if an idea or action isn't working, we will quickly change our direction— *without penalty to the team.*

This practice has two prerequisites. First, our associates must feel free to say, "Hey, this isn't working," and second, we need to measure our actions to confirm progress. Measurement takes the emotion out of the assessment; it allows us to move forward in confidence and without blame. For this reason, all of the actions in our action sets are *measurable;* our metrics include such things as quality scores, sales figures, cost figures, and traveler volume. We constantly check the numbers to confirm that our change is on the right track. If we don't see what we expected, we reassess and make any necessary midcourse corrections.

Another Big Mistake

As we moved into the 21st century, we saw surprising growth for Overseas Adventure Travel. At the same time, sales on the Grand Circle Travel side remained relatively flat. The world seemed to be moving to small group adventure travel, so we initiated a big transformational change to phase out the older GCT land trips in favor of OAT trips.

Boy, did we get that wrong! Letters and phone calls came pouring in. Loyal travelers who had been with us almost from the beginning beseeched us not to drop the GCT brand. Luckily, we have no problem reversing direction when we see we are on the wrong path, so we held another Irish Wake to officially lay the mistake to rest. Then we reinstated our old GCT trips, and even added some new departures. Reinvigorated sales told us this was the right move. Lessons learned: Listen to your customers; admit mistakes.

—Alan Lewis

The biggest lesson I have learned over the years is how to deal with change. At Grand Circle you either go with the flow or you just can't work here! There have been many changes over the years, and some have not been easy. I don't really like change, but over the years I have learned to deal with it. I have become a much more flexible person in my personal life as well.

—Sally Hughes,
20-year associate
Traveler Support

It Helps to Be a Traveler

We didn't always follow these Seven Steps for Change. In fact, it took many years to come up with this list. We have learned a lot from the many transformations that we have chosen for the company. In the case of our River Cruises, we didn't really know what we were getting into; we just saw the opportunity, took the risk, and developed the transformation plan on the fly. That's the hard way to do transformation, but it's not impossible, and it can be very rewarding—and very profitable.

What we know for sure is that change happens fast in the world, and a change can devastate a travel company caught flatfooted. We always try to stay on our toes, but it isn't easy. These days, when we contemplate a major change, we focus hard on vision and planning. We know that if the goal is crystal clear, we will be alright. The path to get there may have a few unexpected detours, but that's OK with us. After all, we are travelers, and detours are sometimes the best part of the journey.

As the World Turns

There has been a lot of change in our lifetimes. Change will not only keep coming, it will continue to accelerate. It seems almost like a law. As developing countries adopt modern technologies and market-based economies, they go faster and push us to go even faster to keep from being run over. Change can be stressful. It can also be exhilarating. Individuals can make a choice about how much change they want in their personal lives, but organizations must thrive in change if they want to survive and prosper. We may wish it were different, but no one can change the dynamics of a worldwide economy that keeps getting compressed in time and distance.

All this emphasis on change probably has something to do with our own personalities. We like change and challenges, and we seek out the road less traveled. We surround ourselves with people who have a similar mindset, too. We think it's the right attitude for our business and a major reason for our success. We don't manufacture semiconductors or automobiles. We deliver unforgettable experiences in every part of the world. When that world changes, we have to change, too. Some say you have to be a "change junkie" to work at Grand Circle. There's truth in that statement, and we say it with pride, too. For us, change is a constant—and a constant source of pleasure. We love travel, we love our business, and we love our travelers. And we love watching Grand Circle constantly evolve into something new and unforgettable.

Harriet and Charlotte Lewis at the women's gathering, Kensington, New Hampshire, 2009.

CHAPTER 8

Loyalty Is a Relationship

Harriet had a grand idea. Women travelers have always been important to Grand Circle, but recent numbers showed them growing in strength. Harriet's Corner launched on our website in March 2009 and was already generating a huge volume of mail from women travelers. Harriet's idea was to meet with some of our longtime women travelers at the company's Pinnacle Leadership Center in Kensington, New Hampshire.

The goal was to get the travelers' feedback on how we could improve our trips to meet the needs of women. We didn't worry about the number of attendees because the training center was more than 500 acres and we would conduct the get-together under a massive tent. Plenty of room. So we decided to invite every woman within a hundred-mile radius who had traveled with us three times or more. We figured we'd get maybe a hundred.

On that fateful June morning, a seemingly endless line of animated women hiked up the dirt path from the parking lot. Soon, our site director grabbed me and took me aside, concerned.

"The parking lot's full," he said. "And the access road is clogged with cars parked on both sides. People can hardly get through."

"Direct them up the path and have them park in the field," I said.

We had planned entertainment, food, and discussions about travel. The event was literally standing room only with more than 250 attendees. The crowd was boisterous, engaged, and eager to talk about travel—with their friends, their seat-mates, and Harriet. As I worked the crowd with Harriet, it became obvious that these women were interested in talking to my wife, not me. I'm competitive, but not with Harriet, so I wandered off to find my own group of women. Surely absent Harriet's engaging personality, I could strike up a conversation. Nope. The travelers were polite, but as soon as we had traded a couple of sentences, they talked among themselves and offered me only indulgent smiles. When someone asked me if Harriet was coming over, I retreated to the back of the tent.

The program called for presentations by both Harriet and me. She spoke first to a happy crowd. As she conveyed her enthusiasm for travel and helping people, the crowd connected with her in a way I had never seen before. There was magic happening here, and I was clearly not part of it. Not wanting to spoil the mood, I slipped away before my presentation.

As I walked to our house, I remember thinking: I'm married to a rock star.

—*Alan Lewis*

In today's economy, businesses seem to think the road to success is through cost-cutting. Companies look at automatic teller machines, pay-at-the-pump gas islands, and self-checkout grocery stores and try to figure out the next service they can get customers to perform for themselves. Since wages are lower in Asia, they direct their customers' telephone calls to India and send their manufacturing plants to China. With the exception of Apple, it's nearly impossible to physically locate the company that built your personal computer. And just try to find help in a department store. You can wander around for five minutes looking for someone to unlock the dressing room and ring up your purchases.

American business is going "low-touch." It's a business strategy driven by bookkeepers, and it leads to a pretty cold and calculating appraisal of the customer's value to the company. In fact, many companies feel no need to build a relationship with their customers at all; a one-time customer is good enough. They believe price is the biggest factor influencing consumers' choices, so they cut, cut, cut their costs and pricing—all the way to the bone. They figure that investment in customers and customer service is a waste of money because when price is the driver, customers will go down the street for their next purchase anyway.

That business model doesn't make sense to us. We're not selling widgets, or hamburgers, or sacks of corn, so we don't think of our trips as "commodities" or even as "products." We think of them as *experiences*, exciting and unique adventures that have the power to make people's dreams come true. Our travelers become emotionally involved with our trips; the things they see in China and the people they meet in Egypt have the power to astonish them, teach them, infuriate them, and make them cry. Both the trips and the travelers require special handling.

At its best, travel is a people business, one that benefits from a close, two-way, "high-touch" relationship between a company and its customers. This is the kind of relationship we have built with our travelers, and it has become one of the foundations of our business. It not only guarantees repeat business for the company, it is also a source of personal satisfaction for both of us.

A Snapshot of Our Travelers

Almost all are over 50 … 65% are retired … Their average age is 70 … They come from all 50 states … 35% have a background in education … Two-thirds are women … 30% travel solo … 55% have traveled with us before.

Why We Love Our Returning Travelers

Most of our travelers take their first trip with Grand Circle because a friend has referred them and they like our low prices. But they return because of the value and the quality of the experience. They discover that we go to interesting destinations, employ great trip leaders, use centrally located hotels, visit local villages and schools, and include more meals and features than our competitors. We like to say we deliver a four-star trip at a three-star price. We miss occasionally, but when we do our travelers let us know, and we use that feedback to improve our trips.

Our business model depends on these returning travelers. Acquiring new customers is very expensive, especially in the travel business because trips are such big-ticket purchases. It requires a lot of marketing. We've found that the least expensive way to fill our trips is with people who have already traveled with us. Repeat travelers "know the ropes," share a certain camaraderie, and help make our trips more enjoyable for the first-timers. They also talk about their previous trips among themselves, and many decide where they will travel next based on these conversations. Happy travelers often return home and refer their friends to us, too. This is an added bonus; in fact, 80 percent of our profit from first-time travelers comes from these referrals.

When Alan and I bought Grand Circle, it was not solely to run a travel company. It was to run a company that was going to help make people's dreams come true and help make the world a better place. We've learned so much about those things from our travelers. They tell us about long-lost family members they've located in Europe. They share their diaries of places they never imagined visiting. They tell us about the close friendships they've made with fellow travelers. They applaud the accomplishments of schoolchildren in Costa Rica and contribute to our earthquake relief fund for Haiti. Our travelers are our partners in our great big adventure. That is what drives us and what drives everyone at Grand Circle.

—Harriet Lewis

Small conversations have the power to change the world. We don't want our travelers to return and say, "Let me tell you what I saw." We hope they return and say, "Let me tell you who I met and what I learned."

—Harriet Lewis

A Big Mistake

We have had an Inner Circle program for frequent travelers since the early 1990s, but we didn't always give it the attention that our most loyal travelers deserved. For most of that decade our main focus was on prospecting for *new* customers, which required a big investment in time and money, instead of investing in our *best* customers. Sure, we would send our repeat travelers a special newsletter, *The Insider*, and offer frequent traveler discounts, and give recognition on trips, but we didn't always communicate how really vital they are to our business, or differentiate between our occasional travelers and our really passionate travelers.

We learned the true value of our most frequent travelers after 9/11, when so many American travel companies went out of business. Our bookings fell off sharply in all categories except among our most frequent travelers. These folks are really determined to see the world—they are truly intrepid—and they just kept traveling. They saved our company. From that moment on, we kept our attention focused on our most loyal travelers, those who have traveled with us eight, ten, even 20 times.

—Alan Lewis

Here's what the model looks like: Repeat travelers keep our marketing costs down … which helps us keep our prices well below the competition … which in turn keeps our travelers coming back. It's a circle—and it drives both the company's profit and our travelers' satisfaction. Repeat business isn't the only thing that keeps our costs down, of course; our worldwide organization, our "buy direct" strategy, and our targeted marketing all play a part. Together, they create our "Unsurpassed Value." Our strategy is to pass our savings on to our travelers in the form of lower prices, and then to deliver surprising value once they depart on one of our trips.

Do we do this because we're nice people? Well, we think we're nice, but we do it because of the circular nature of the business model. Break

Grand Circle associates and Rebuilding Together Boston team up to renovate a house as a community service project in Dorchester, MA, 2010.

LEFT TOP: Donations from Grand Circle Foundation are helping children in this remote Nepalese mountain village lead happier, healthier lives.

LEFT BOTTOM: Charlotte, Alan, and Edward Lewis on a family vacation in Ireland, 1995.

RIGHT: Harriet Lewis speaks to a group of women travelers in Harriet's Corner, Boston, MA, 2010.

The Lewis family in Africa, 1998.

Grand Circle's Young Women Leaders dress as famous women travelers in history, Boston, MA, 2009.

TOP: Edward, Charlotte, and Harriet Lewis volunteer at a community service project at the Greater Boston Food Bank, Boston, MA, 2010.

BOTTOM LEFT: Executive Offsite, Camden, ME, 1993.

BOTTOM RIGHT: Associate Chris Pederson keeps a low profile on a LEAD Training Trip in Lapland, 1998.

TOP LEFT: Board of Directors meeting in Costa Rica, 1994.

TOP RIGHT: Eleonore and Gerald Young, 61-time travelers from Jacksonville, Florida, at the "Precious Moments" statue in Carthage, MO.

BOTTOM LEFT: Alan Lewis and Mark Frevert ski Antarctica, 1993.

BOTTOM RIGHT: Edward, Charlotte, and Alan Lewis on a zip line canopy tour, Barbados, 2009.

TOP: Bob Weiler, Roland Barth and Alan Lewis set off to bring the Foundation worldwide. Costa Rica, 1992.

BOTTOM: Harriet Lewis (second from right) rings the opening bell at the New York Stock Exchange in honor of Corporate Philanthropy Day, 2006.

Harriet and Alan Lewis with the worldwide regional leaders at BusinessWorks, Kensington, NH, 2005.

any piece and the model falls apart. We could jack up our prices and make a ton of money—for a short period of time. But then we would lose the volume from returning travelers and our marketing costs would escalate. Lower volume would also upset our vendors, who would start raising their prices to us. Our costs would rise, and pretty soon we'd be like every other travel company.

Our "Unsurpassed Value" model works exceptionally well. In good times, we grow in traveler volume and profits, and in tough times our loyal travelers keep the wolf away from the door. More than once, our travelers have kept traveling with us when other travel companies have seen their business stop cold. Everything depends on this win-win relationship with our travelers, and for that reason we put a lot of time, energy, and thought into it.

A Love Letter

Dear OAT,

In reference to your letter, "We want you back."

Well … you had us back on the very first day of our very first trip. We have loved each and every trip we have taken with you … the Pyramids in Cairo, floating down the Amazon, the Peking duck hanging in windows in Beijing, walking the Great Wall, loving every minute of Dickey Orphanage in Tibet, sleeping under the stars in Morocco, meeting long-lost family in Sicily … oh, and I could go on and on.

Believe me, dear OAT, you haven't lost us. This year, we decided to give back, and are planning to go back to Peru to volunteer for a month. We will be back, traveling with OAT, and looking forward to new and even more exciting vacations.

Sincerely,

Joyce Piazza
5-time traveler
Phillipsburg, New Jersey

Growing up traveling was awesome. I can't even begin to imagine how different my life would be without these mind-opening experiences. My Mum once told me that at age 4 or 5 the longest trip she took was to New Hampshire; when I was 4 years old, I went to Alaska!

I am grateful that my family schlepped us halfway across the world and back, occasionally pulled me out of school, encouraged me to try everything, gave me enough space to explore my curiosity but enough support that I still felt safe. I look back at the cultures we've experienced, the friends we've made, the food we've eaten, the lives we have been a part of or just glimpsed, and I say, "Thank you."

—Charlotte Lewis

How We Get Repeat Business

The relationship we have with travelers amazes us. They constantly tell us that Grand Circle is *their* travel company. Astonishingly, 55 percent of our travelers have traveled with us before, and more than 33,000 households have made seven or more trips with us. Gerald and Elenore Young of Jacksonville, Florida, have gone on 61 trips with us over the past 21 years.

The trips are the big draw, of course, and we work incessantly to deliver great value and unforgettable experiences. Ralph Moody, the Hall of Fame race-car driver and race-car builder, once said, "If you make something that's good, you're going to sell the hell out of it," and he's right. What's different about how we do it is that we give our travelers a big say in how we design and deliver our trips. We listen to every particle of advice they give us—in their letters, in the quality surveys, at cocktail parties, on the telephone, over the Internet, and at special gatherings—then *we act on it*. We truly believe that the travelers know best, and we strive to give them what they want. That's respect, one of the building blocks of our relationship with them.

Another building block is benefits. We run a number of discount and loyalty programs to recognize and encourage repeat business. We offer a five percent discount to frequent travelers, and $100 credit for every new traveler they refer to us (the new traveler gets $50 off that first trip as well). We also give recognition to frequent travelers before and during a trip and, whenever possible, we assign them to the best rooms and cabins. Combine unsurpassed value with good discounts and incentives, and our competition has a hard time attracting our travelers away from us.

Another building block is travel protection. We know that our travelers lead busy lives that sometimes entail last-minute changes in plans. We also know our travelers sometimes get sick or need to tend to family emergencies. These uncertainties often keep older people from traveling; they hesitate to make reservations, fearing they will lose their deposits or even the entire price of their trip. But not at Grand Circle. We understand that life sometimes throws curveballs. In 2001, after the terrorist attacks of 9/11, we became the first company in the industry to offer travel protection that gives a full refund in money or travel vouchers up to the moment of departure.

Unsurpassed value, good discounts, preferential treatment, and comprehensive travel protection make it easy and risk-free for our travelers to book another trip. That's good customer renewal practice, and a good deal for both the company and the traveler, but that's not really a *relationship*, is it? To build an honest relationship with customers takes another crucial element—interesting, consistent, and respectful two-way communication.

We Listen to Our Travelers

Travel is fun and travelers love to tell their relatives, friends, and neighbors all about their trips. They also tell us. When they get home, they find our post-trip questionnaire in their mailbox. Repeat travelers come to expect it, and many of them look forward to filling it out. We ask them about every aspect of the trip, and we ask them to be completely frank. We let them know we depend on their comments; their personal experience is absolutely the most important information we can get about our trips—better than sales figures, better than trip leader reports, better than our own best judgment.

Just as we say "Locals know best," we also say "Our travelers are always right." Our travelers are the experts on our trips, and we listen to every word they say, especially when they tell us how to improve our trips. Grand Circle travelers are a tight community, and even when they've already taken the trip, they want to help us make it better for the next travelers. They are not only our customers, but our partners, our eyes and ears on the ground, sending us priceless information every day.

Of course, information is worthless unless you act on it. We honor our travelers' efforts on our behalf by taking their suggestions seriously. We have invested millions of dollars in our quality control system, and we put a lot of time into analyzing the quality surveys and summarizing the data for the senior leadership and the product managers. Automated scanning allows our overseas associates and trip leaders to see the results, too. Whenever we have a meeting about a particular trip, the quality surveys are right there on the conference table. If a question arises, we ask, "What do our travelers say?" Soon, everyone in the room is searching through the traveler feedback for guidance. We tally scores and read the handwritten comments. We call travelers up if we need more information. Our travelers' feedback has never led us astray.

Travelers ask us if Harriet and I ever read the comments they write on their questionnaires. Yes, we do. Our computer system automatically scans them, and our quality people periodically assemble samples of them for us

The gathering of women travelers in New Hampshire began with a round of compliments on our trips. Our travelers are of a generation that values courtesy and encouragement, but we wanted constructive criticism, so Harriet said, "We know we do many things right, but tell us what to improve." That gave the audience permission to let go, and we got some great recommendations, particularly on solo travelers and our Vacation Ambassador (VA) referral program.

For example, we thought it would be a great idea to do home events for the VA program, sort of like Tupperware parties. Our travelers demurred, saying that kind of event is too staged for travel planning among friends. We also thought trips for women only would be great. They squelched that idea, too, saying they like having the men around. The women had many good laughs and many good ideas. There is no better way to build a great company than to listen to your customers.

—Martha Prybylo,
17-year associate
Executive Vice President,
Worldwide People and Culture

At 51, unexpectedly, I found myself a widow. One of the things that happens when you lose your spouse is you lose your plans. You find that you are going to travel in a different way. You're going to travel alone. But when you go with OAT your needs are taken care of. You don't have to be fearful; you know where you're going to eat; you know you have a great schedule; you know you have really great people to take care of you. That really changed everything because it reopened the world to me and it made me feel like all was not lost. I still have that adventure spirit, and it can be fulfilled by going with this group of gals and traveling this way. It opens up your life again. It really changes it.

—Nadine Berman,
   3-time traveler
   Boston, Massachusetts

to read at home. In the winter, we read them by the fire in the library on Beacon Street in Boston. In the summer, we read them on our screen porch at Beaver Dam in Kensington, New Hampshire. We love reading what our travelers have to say in their own words, and you'd be surprised at how many good ideas we've gleaned from these comments. When members of our leadership team in Boston go into the field, we always urge them to take 50 to 100 surveys with them; that way they can hit the ground running, knowing exactly what the local issues are.

We Hear You!

In the last year alone, we've made dozens of changes to our trips that came directly from travelers' suggestions. For example, we added a post-trip extension to Prague on one of our Danube River Cruises in Europe, and extended our post-trip stay in Japan from four days to seven on our popular Yangtze River trip. We doubled the time onboard a private charter ship in Russia from one week to two, added two more game-viewing drives to a pre-trip extension in South Africa, and included a tour of Bulgarian fortresses on an Eastern Europe trip. On one of our trips in Egypt, we included a visit to the Temple of Dendera, which had been optional, because travelers said it should not be missed. We also added more staff to our Call Center in Boston, so travelers wouldn't have to wait so long on the phone. We don't want our travelers to wait to speak to us; we want to hear every word they say!

Through Thick and Thin

By listening to our travelers, we've also received early warnings about things that have gone awry—not only with our trips, but also in our travelers' lives. For example, in 2008 we began to feel the pressure of the oncoming worldwide recession. So did our travelers. Many of them told us on their post-trip surveys that they still wanted to travel, but they needed some time to wait out the economic downturn. Others said they were holding their own financially but were reluctant to commit to a trip only to realize months later—when it would be too late—that their money would have been better put elsewhere.

What is remarkable is that our travelers told us all of these things. They didn't just turn their backs on us; they reached out to express their regret and their hope that they could travel again sometime soon. We understood our travelers' concerns and appreciated their confidences. And, of course, we wanted them to keep traveling, too.

So we changed a number of our policies to make it easier for our travelers to travel. We offered a temporary 30-day risk-free guarantee, free domestic air travel, and free single supplements on land trips and extensions. Every change was either the suggestion of one of our travelers, or was inspired by their feedback. Ours is a true partnership, for better and for worse, with effective two-way communication that allows us to keep traveling together. It may sound corny, but it is a secret of our success.

Our Travelers Give Us Advice

Quality surveys aren't our only source for traveler feedback. When we need help on a special project, we will send out a letter or an e-mail query, and we invariably get a tremendous response.

For example, in 2009 we decided to publish a book of tips for women traveling abroad; we would give it to our frequent travelers to thank them for traveling with us. It was actually our daughter Charlotte's idea. She had accompanied Harriet to a get-together with 200 frequent travelers on Long Island, in New York. At one point, Harriet and Charlotte joined a group of five women at a table. The women had been swapping stories and tips, as travelers usually do when they get together, and the wealth of information stunned Charlotte.

"Mom, between the five of them, these women have visited just about every country I've ever heard of," she said. "And they had such great information. If I had a tape recorder, I could've written a book!"

So that's what we did, and we asked our travelers for help. Most of the tips included in this popular publication, *101 Tips for Women Travelers*, came directly from our women travelers. We were surprised by the number of tips we received—more than 400—and by the many great ideas they offered us. One traveler taught us how to "concentrate" shampoo for travel; another advised solo travelers to wear a wedding ring—whether they are married or not. What didn't surprise us was that Grand Circle travelers are very knowledgeable and experienced. They know how to travel the world.

> During a gathering of travelers, I asked how many couples had been married for more than 50 years. Several hands went up. I pointed to one of the women and asked her what the secret of a long marriage was. "Him learning to say, 'Yes, dear,'" she answered without hesitation. Everybody laughed and more than a few wives' heads bobbed in agreement. After everyone quieted down, I asked the woman how long it took her husband to learn that lesson. Again, without hesitation, she answered, "Forty-nine years." Now it was the husbands' turn to bob their heads in agreement.
>
> —Alan Lewis

We also asked for our travelers' help when we were writing this book. Early on, we sent out surveys to 10,000 women travelers asking for their advice on topics and titles, and we brought other travelers in to the office to critique the design. Later, we sent chapters out for comment. Without our travelers, there would be no Grand Circle story, so we wanted to get it right.

Our Travelers Tell Us Where to Go

To a surprising extent, travel is a fashion business. "Hot" destinations come and go with world events, fluctuating currencies, popular fiction —even celebrity globe-trotting. In the 1990s Eastern Europe and then China were "hot"; today's hot destinations include India, Tunisia, Vietnam, Cambodia, Laos, and the Panama Canal. Many travel companies spend thousands of dollars each year trying to forecast trends. We have a better idea. We just ask our travelers where they want to go next.

And they tell us—in their post-trip surveys, in letters, via our website, and by e-mail. And of course they tell us every time they book a trip. More than 119,000 people will travel with us in 2010—that's a big database for spotting trends. Knowing our travelers' preferences helps us anticipate hot spots, build inventory in desirable locations, and offer trips we know our travelers want. Our travelers are our soothsayers, and we reward them by giving them unforgettable experiences in places they long to discover.

Targeted Catalogs

Because our travelers tell us where they want to go next, we can target our marketing, sending catalogs that will interest them when they want to receive them. This is a "high-touch" business practice, and it depends on having a relationship with our customers that is personal and information-based. It is the kind of relationship that most travelers want from us.

We didn't always do this. In the early days of the company, our marketing approach was to acquire a list of likely travelers and then bombard them with catalogs—sometimes more than a hundred a year—plus countless individual brochures and "personalized" letters. *"Eastern Europe! South America! Prices slashed! Don't wait, Mrs. Johnson. Book today!"*

This approach tended to polarize our customers. Some of them loved it. To them, every catalog was a catalog of dreams, and they pored over them, especially the Overseas Adventure Travel catalogs, which had big,

Another Big Mistake

Several years ago we were offering a trip to Israel, a popular destination for many travelers—Christian, Jewish, and Muslim alike. Unfortunately, the trip tanked in our travelers' quality surveys, garnering only a 46 percent "Excellent" rating. Our travelers let us have it. The guides were terrible, they told us, the hotels only so-so. What's more, the trip had no soul.

Our travelers are all about relationships: relationships with their families, relationships with their friends, relationships with their trip leaders, and relationships with each other. Ordinarily, we design our trips with relationships in mind, but this time we had failed. Our travelers wanted to have more personal and more familial experiences in Israel, so they could get behind the often tragic headlines and make a more human connection with the people of the country.

We listened carefully to their suggestions and made several important changes to the trip: terminating our ground operator and hiring local staff; hiring and training our own trip leaders; and including many more cross-cultural encounters, including a dinner within the Jewish Orthodox community, a discussion with the leader of a Bedouin women's society, a meeting with Jewish farmers, a talk with a Palestinian woman, and a home-hosted meal with a Druze family.

And what happened? Our "Excellent" scores rose from 46 percent to 82 percent. It's true: We often make mistakes, but our travelers are always right.

beautiful pictures, and lushly written itinerary descriptions. We even won a gold medal from the Direct Marketing Association for one of those catalogs in 1997, the one called "Doorway to Dreams."

But many of our customers *hated* all those mailings. We had thousands of complaints. "*Take me off your mailing list!*" "*Mr. Lewis, don't you dare send me another catalog.*" "*Think of all those trees!*" We had built a relationship with these customers, but it was not the kind of relationship we wanted. It took a while to understand that frequent, indiscriminate mass mailings were not the kind of "high-touch" relationship people wanted. They wanted to feel a personal relationship that responded to their own interests and desires. We're not there yet—we still get complaints about the volume of mail—but we get it now, and we're working on it. For example, we recently launched a quarterly mailing plan for travelers who prefer that schedule.

Give Us a Call Some Time

In our Call Center on Congress Street, associates answer 11,000 calls a week from our travelers—calls to ask questions, calls to book trips, calls to change an itinerary, and calls to complain. For most of our travelers, their most personal contact with the Boston office is with that friendly voice on the phone. When you call the main number, that voice belongs to Laverne Schaff, and it's live, not a recording. Laverne has been our phone and front desk receptionist for 15 years, and she brings a lot of energy, cachet, and encouragement to the building. She represents the spirit of personal connection that we strive for with every traveler.

We value that connection. When a traveler calls, we want our associates to have everything we know about the traveler and our trips at their fingertips, so they can jump right in and help. Over the years, we have spent millions of dollars on technology for the Call Center, to keep it up and humming. We also invest heavily in training, even sending our Call Center associates on trips periodically so they can talk about them from firsthand experience.

Business consultants always ask why we have our Call Center in downtown Boston. They tell us no cost-conscious company would put a call center in such a pricey place, and they invariably suggest that we move it offshore or to a low-wage region.

We're not fools; we've done the arithmetic. We know that outsourcing our Call Center would probably save us $3 million a year. But the consultants don't understand our business model. We are a high-touch company with a strong two-way relationship with our customers. We want the Call Center in our own building so we can personally ensure that our travelers get the best possible service on the phones. In fact, every member of the leadership team listens in on live calls occasionally—

it's called "double-jacking"—so they can maintain direct contact with our travelers. The head of our Call Center is a member of the Executive Team and he works with us daily and coordinates with the marketing department so our message is consistent in print, on our Web pages, and on the phones. We keep the Call Center in the building so we can stay in direct communication with our travelers.

Relationship-Building on the Web

We've said it before: Harriet and I are a little bit technologically challenged, and we were "late adopters" of Internet technologies. By the time we made it into cyberspace, many of our travelers were already there. That turned out to be a good thing, because once we targeted a big investment to our website, our traffic really took off. It was Edward and Charlotte who set us straight about the Internet (cross-generational feedback is one of the benefits of a family business). We now appreciate the immediacy of e-mail communication, the ability to create personal spaces on the website, and the ease of exploring our trips online made our communication with our travelers so much richer. And the interactive nature of the site fosters the kind of two-way communication we're after.

For example, travelers can now get trip information, find deals and discounts, and access their online accounts 24 hours a day. They can post reviews of trips they've taken online for the benefit of other travelers (the reviews now number in the thousands). They can send an e-mail to Harriet from a link in Harriet's Corner, a section of the website where Harriet and our travelers share stories and pictures from their travels. They can post a question, join a discussion forum, find a roommate for an upcoming trip, get a recipe, or sign up for an electronic newsletter— all with the click of a mouse. On our new Grand Circle Foundation website they can learn about all our Foundation projects; they can even make donations through the site. We love the way the Web makes our communication so easy, and we love the "virtual community" that gets bigger and better every day.

The Internet has also become very important to us in times of trouble, because it allows us to reach many travelers quickly through e-mail and through updates and announcements posted on our website.

Edward and I recently traveled to Sri Lanka and India together. On our return home we made a list of all the countries we've been to on our own and as a family. He is 28, I am 26, and we've been to roughly 40 countries. I still can't believe it.

Growing up traveling has made me less afraid, more understanding and respectful of cultures including my own. I thank my parents for that gift. The result is that I am not a xenophobe or a bigot. It's funny, I have a hard time understanding people who actively choose not to venture out, to leave their safe harbor, and to see the world beyond their hometown.

—Charlotte Lewis

On OAT's *Discover Thailand* trip some years ago, California travelers Loujean and Barry LaMalfa attended a puppet show put on by a group of children from one of the schools in the Chiang Mai district sponsored by Grand Circle Foundation. One of the children, a 10-year-old girl named Fair, caught Loujean's eye, and they struck up a friendship that has lasted eight years.

Working through OAT and with Fair's mother, the LaMalfas arranged to sponsor Fair's education at a prestigious girls' school, where she became a fine singer and president of the school. The LaMalfas now live half the year in Thailand and remain close with Fair and her family. As Loujean says, "Barry and I feel blessed to be able to be a part of her life—and if it wasn't for our first trip to Thailand with OAT, none of this would have been possible."

This is how we kept travelers current on the news when the volcanic eruption in Iceland closed airports all over Europe in the spring of 2010. Between the community-building and the emergency messaging, our investment in the Web has already paid off.

Friends for Life

Many of our travelers form special friendships with people they meet on our trips, and they often travel together again and again as "travel buddies." As every veteran traveler knows, there is something about travel that allows you to talk openly with relative strangers and discover new things about yourself, so these travel friendships can become pretty intense.

We recently heard from a group of women who met on one of our trips to India. It was a wonderful trip, and the women became quite close. One of the group, a woman named Adele, had recently been diagnosed with breast cancer, and she doubted she would be able to travel on any more trips. Imagine the group's surprise when, several months after their return from India, Adele wrote to the others saying she'd thought it over, and the one thing she wanted more than anything in the world was to take a last trip with her buddies—this time to Costa Rica. So off they went on that last trip, laughing and cherishing each and every day of the adventure. Friends for life—as long as that might be.

Sadly, Adele lost her battle with cancer just ten days after the group returned from Costa Rica. But her irrepressible spirit remains very much alive in the hearts of her "travel buddies" whether they are exploring exotic destinations together or staying closer to home.

—Harriet Lewis

Meeting Our Travelers Face to Face

Another way we foster our relationship with travelers is through special events, like the women's gathering in Kensington, and at get-togethers with our travelers when we are visiting our offices overseas. These events are a lot of fun, with lots of talk about travel. They are especially useful because they provide an opportunity for real-time, uncensored, two-way communication.

We're not big believers in professional focus groups. We believe a large audience and a traveling microphone give us better guidance than a few people sitting around a table talking to a marketing guy in a suit. We want more talkers and a more genuine exchange than a focus group can give. In troubled times, we hold get-togethers more often so our travelers can hear from us directly about our plans for dealing with the problems. After 9/11 and during the financial crisis of 2008 and 2009, it really buoyed us to meet with so many travelers who were still eager to travel. We gave each other the confidence to keep on going.

In an interesting about-face, the virtual Harriet's Corner on our website has inspired a real-life, physical space on the garden level of our building at 347 Congress Street. This cheerful room, which is also called Harriet's Corner, is open to visiting travelers and to our community partners, who meet periodically to collaborate on joint projects. We also use Harriet's Corner for get-togethers and special events. In fact, it was here that some of our travelers got their first peek at this book, when we asked them to come in and give us their thoughts on the design.

Of course, there is no better feedback than from travelers in the middle of a trip. They are excited and usually complimentary, but we're not there to get a pat on the back. As we circulate among the travelers, we always ask, "What *haven't* you liked about this trip?" Sometimes we wince at what we hear, but these conversations are important for us, because, like it or not, our travelers are always right.

The Foundation of a Good Relationship

We are deeply moved when our relationship with travelers extends beyond the excitement of a trip overseas to a mutual commitment to help change people's lives. This often happens when travelers become personally involved in our work with Grand Circle Foundation.

When our travelers visit one of our Foundation sites on a trip, they often make an emotional connection with the local people, especially with the children in the schools and orphanages we support. On their

Kites rise highest against the wind, not with it.

—*Winston Churchill*

return home, some of these travelers send donations, organize fundraising events, or sponsor scholarships to help the communities they visited. In 2010 alone, our travelers personally contributed nearly $650,000 to Grand Circle Foundation and to Foundation-supported sites.

We are honored and humbled by everyone who helps us carry on our mission of giving back to the communities we visit. We consider their benevolence a testament to the remarkable relationship we share.

Susan Rickert, Philanthropy Hero

Susan Rickert, 12-time traveler, San Francisco, California, visited Tanzania on her first trip with Overseas Adventure Travel. The itinerary included a stop at a school similar to the one she had taught at as a Peace Corps volunteer 35 years earlier, except a portion of this one's roof had been torn off by a storm, forcing 96 children into one classroom. Susan was appalled by the situation—how could the children learn? That afternoon, she gathered her fellow travelers under an acacia tree and raised $1,200 on the spot for a new roof. Since then, she has helped raise more than $100,000 for five schools in Tanzania and has found sponsors for 17 scholarships for students. In 2007, Susan earned the first Grand Circle Foundation Washburn Award, named for Brad and Barbara Washburn, in honor of that work. Since then she has shifted her focus to the village of Las Palmas in the Amazon basin of Peru. To date she has raised $2,700 for a short-wave radio, solar panels for the first aid clinic, and soccer equipment for the school there.

Going High-Touch in a Low-Touch World

We've always been a little contrarian, and rejecting the popular "low-touch" business strategy was an easy decision for us. We believe travel is an emotional experience and that travelers want a close relationship with their travel company, with their trip leader, with their fellow travelers, and with the people whose communities they visit. This philosophy requires us to listen to our travelers and to take action when they make good suggestions. Repeat travelers are crucial to our business model, so we believe we've made the right choice in adopting a "high-touch" strategy.

The result is a community of people—business leaders, associates, and travelers—all pursuing discovery and great value while helping to change people's lives. It's a wonderful adventure, and we're pleased to have our travelers along for the ride.

VOLUME 256 • NUMBER 124
72 pages
50 cents

The Boston Globe

THAT 60S SHOW
Today: Sunny, mid-60s
Tomorrow: Cloudy, rain, mid-60s
High tide: 5:15 a.m., 5:33 p.m.
Full report: Page B12

MONDAY, NOVEMBER 1, 1999

No SOS call, no survivors

217 on EgyptAir jet die in crash off Nantucket; broad probe launched

The EgyptAir Boeing 767-300ER that crashed yesterday.

By Matthew Brelis
and Mitchell Zuckoff
GLOBE STAFF

An EgyptAir jetliner en route from New York to Cairo with 217 people on board went into a terrifying dive, apparently broke apart, and crashed into the waters off Nantucket early yesterday.

There were no distress calls, no clear causes, and no survivors.

EgyptAir Flight 990 carried 129 Americans, according to Egyptian government officials, including a group of 54 tourists hoping to see the Pyramids and other treasures of antiquity. The tour was organized by a Boston-based company, but none of its participants were from Massachusetts.

The victims included residents of Connecticut, Vermont, Maine, New York, New Jersey, and several Western states, as well as citizens of Egypt, Sudan, Syria, and Chile, Egyptian and US officials said. Two infants reportedly were among the dead.

A massive, multinational investigation was launched to determine why the 10-year-old Boeing 767-300ER plunged into the Atlantic 60 miles south of Nantucket shortly after taking off from John F. Kennedy International Airport.

"There is no indication of any criminal activity at this time," said Barry Mawn, special agent in charge of the Boston office of the FBI, one of six US agencies working with the Egyptian government on the investigation.

President Clinton expressed his sympathies for the victims and their families and said there was no evidence of foul play.

"I think it's better if people draw no conclusions until we know something," said Clinton, who called President Hosni Mubarak of Egypt to offer condolences and pledge US assistance.

Coast Guard teams reported pulling one body from the 59-degree waters during a search-and-rescue mission that began 20 minutes after the plane disappeared from air traffic control radar screens. Also recovered were seats, seat parts, a wheel, passports, life jackets, and two partly inflated life rafts.

Coast Guard Rear Admiral Richard Larrabee said there were no burn marks on the life rafts, but cau-

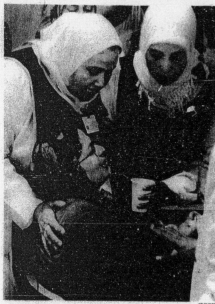

Workers at Cairo International Airport yesterday tried to comfort a relative of an EgyptAir Flight 990 passenger.

Despair in Cairo

Relatives greet news with tears, anguish

By Charles M. Sennott
GLOBE STAFF

CAIRO – Horror and chaos engulfed the makeshift information center at Cairo International Airport yesterday as scores of family members scanned a computer list of the 217 people aboard EgyptAir Flight 990.

From those who had confirmed loved ones were on board the downed plane, there were tears and cries of anguish. A man with gray hair was wailing, "My son. My son. His baby is 6 months old."

A middle-aged woman in a black veil grabbed the list from the EgyptAir officials, screaming, "I want to

know, I have to know."

She saw the list, and collapsed. A team of doctors and nurses attended to her, first with smelling salts, then with what appeared to be a tranquilizer. In one corner of the room, members of a family were weeping and joining in quiet prayers as they read from the Koran.

Hishem Mansour saw on the tattered computer list the name of his cousin, Wala Hanafi, 21, but demanded further, "Is she dead or is she lost?"

Some were too terrified even to check the list, not wanting to see what they feared.

Tariq Samek stood in the hallway
CAIRO, Page A12

Fatal flight

EgyptAir Flight 990, bound for Cairo, crashed off Nantucket half an hour after leaving New York yesterday morning, killing all 217 on board.

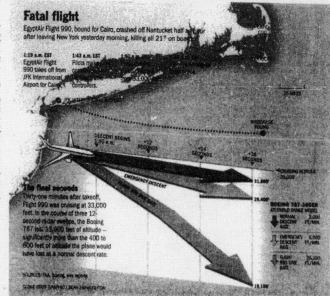

1:19 a.m. EST EgyptAir Flight 990 takes off from JFK International Airport for Cairo.

1:43 a.m. EST Pilots make contact with controllers.

DESCENT BEGINS 1:50 a.m.

The final seconds
Thirty-one minutes after takeoff, Flight 990 was cruising at 33,000 feet. In the course of three 12-second radar sweeps, the Boeing 767 lost 13,900 feet of altitude – significantly more than the 400 to 600 feet of altitude the plane would have lost at a normal descent rate.

SOURCES: FAA, Boeing, wire reports
GLOBE STAFF GRAPHIC / SEAN McNAUGHTON

July drama replayed

Searchers recall JFK Jr. crash

By Thomas Farragher and Joanna Weiss
GLOBE STAFF

NANTUCKET – Emergency crews scrambling before dawn. Flotsam on the Atlantic Ocean. Debris fields and death off the coast of Massachusetts.

For the second time in 15 weeks, that nightmarish tableau darkened a bright New England weekend morning, disturbing still-raw wounds of air disasters that have captured instant and urgent international attention.

"It seems like it never ended," said Coast Guard Petty Officer Todd Burgun. "We're right back into the same thing. And it's heartbreaking. There's a point when you know there's not going to be anybody alive out there."

Burgun was on call July 17 when the plane carrying John F. Kennedy Jr., his

Two hemispheres entwined in tragedy

No terrorism sign: Bomb-threat talk is dismissed. A10.
EgyptAir's record: The com-

Eerie echoes: Anxious relatives gather again. A15.
Local tie: Many cite loyalties

CHAPTER 9

Expect Trouble

The call came at four o'clock on a Sunday morning in late October. Alan and I were home in Boston, and the call woke us both from a sound sleep. It was Mark Frevert, calling to tell us that a plane had gone down 60 miles south of Nantucket.

It was an EgyptAir flight, flying from Los Angeles to Cairo. It had stopped in New York, as scheduled, to pick up passengers and refuel. It took off late from Kennedy Airport, but had flown uneventfully over Long Island and then over open water before suddenly, inexplicably, falling from the sky. There had been no SOS call, no radio communication at all with the tower, just a sudden steep plunge into the waters off Nantucket. The Coast Guard was heading to the scene. There was no word of survivors.

We had 54 Grand Circle travelers on that flight.

"Oh, my God," I said to Alan. I took a deep breath, and let it out slowly. Alan and I were planning to visit Egypt ourselves the next year. I had never been there. We were so excited, planning that trip. We would see the Pyramids, sail down the Nile, visit the Valley of the Kings. It would be the trip of a lifetime … But not for these travelers. I couldn't believe it. I sat by the phone, looking out the window into the dark night, imagining the moments of panic and horror and prayer as the plane nosed down into the cold Atlantic.

"Shake it off!" I told myself. "We have work to do."

And we did. We needed to contact the travelers' families to break the news. We needed to take care of our travelers on the ground in Egypt, and the ones scheduled to go later in the week. We needed to meet immediately with our partners at EgyptAir. Alan was already on his way to Congress Street; the phones would be ringing, and we couldn't let those anguished calls go unanswered. There was a lot to do, and I was grateful for it.

Dawn was just breaking when I started making calls to associates, asking if they could come in to the office to help on the phones. Grand Circle is not a 24-hour operation; this was Sunday, Halloween, and I didn't know if we could get enough people to staff the Call Center. I needn't have worried. When I got to the office, I found 80 associates had come in, many unasked, some in shock, some in tears. Many hadn't been on the phones in years. They were willing to take any assignment; they just wanted to help.

Crises bring out the best and the worst in people. On this occasion, we saw the best. Over a few short days we devoted our hearts and minds to consolation, while grieving ourselves. No previous world event had ever hit us this hard personally, and none has since. I will be forever grateful to our wonderful associates who stepped forward in those days. Their kindness and compassion got us through.

—Harriet Lewis

The crash of EgyptAir Flight 990 was definitely our darkest hour, the most emotional of the many crises we have faced personally and as a company. The terrorist attacks of 9/11 were a greater threat to our business, and so was the worldwide financial crisis of 2008–2010, but the loss of our 54 travelers is something we will never get over.

We had always known that the travel business is subject to crises. Our first year at Grand Circle was just one crisis after another: airport attacks, the hijacking of the *Achille Lauro*, the crash of Air India Flight 182, the U.S. airstrike on Libya, an earthquake in Mexico City, the meltdown at Chernobyl. It was like an omen, but we were too busy scrambling to keep the company afloat to see how essential it would be for us to become expert crisis managers. That realization evolved over many years and many crises; in fact, in the last 25 years we have come to see crises as "moments of truth," times that test our leadership and engage our vision and values in new and difficult ways. We have also come to see that in crisis there is always opportunity, somewhere.

In the following pages, we list just some of the crises that have afflicted the world during our time at Grand Circle. It is a true parade of horribles: accidents, natural disasters, an epidemic, wars, plane crashes, financial crises, riots, bombings, political demonstrations, and terrorist attacks. These are subjects that most travel companies don't want to talk about, but we know our travelers see the world realistically and they want to know the truth. The vast majority of our trips occur without incident, but in the rare case when a crisis does arise, we want our travelers to know what we'll do.

The Crash of EgyptAir Flight 990

It was 1999, and we were coming up on the new millennium riding a hot streak. Our River Cruises were booming, and we had just opened five new overseas offices—in Thailand, China, Portugal, Italy, and Tanzania. Sales had topped $315 million for the first time. Our biggest worry was that our computers would go haywire when the calendar rolled over to Y2K.

But the mood turned dark on that late October night when EgyptAir Flight 990 crashed off Nantucket, just 150 miles from our Boston head-quarters. We had 54 travelers on the plane: 42 for Grand Circle's *Ancient Egypt & the Nile River* CruiseTour; another 12 for OAT's *Cairo and the Eternal Nile* trip. Nothing like this had ever happened to us before.

There was a lot of confusion about the cause of the crash. Was it mechanical failure? Terrorism? A deranged pilot suicide? To this day we don't know for sure, and what became clear in the first several hours of the crisis was that it didn't really matter. Not to us, and not to what we had to do. The investigation into causes and motives was outside our control. Speculation was pointless. We had our own work to do.

Alan immediately sent members of the senior leadership to key crisis locations. Mark Frevert and Joe Kurosz went to Nantucket. Bob Dine and Joe Cali went to Kennedy Airport, where the families were gathering and the National Transportation Safety Board (NTSB) had established a response team. When Alan got to New York a little later, he found Bob and Joe in head-to-head discussion with the mayor, Rudy Giuliani. In Boston, dozens of associates sat at the phones in the Call Center, talking to family members and arranging flights for them to New York. Another team was on the phones to Egypt, where we had a hundred travelers already on trips, offering to book early passage home or to change air carriers if travelers wanted that (none did).

Our first priority was to take care of the families, and their shock and bewilderment was almost unbearable. For days our devastated associates listened to their stories, fighting back their own tears as sons and daughters and grandchildren poured out their grief and confusion over the phone. Our associates had no special training in this kind of crisis; they would often finish a call and break down sobbing themselves, then sit

The most emotional day for me at GCT was the last day of my sabbatical. It was Sunday, and I had set the alarm to wake up early to enjoy my last day off. The radio was announcing that an EgyptAir flight originating at LAX had gone down just past Long Island. I got a sick feeling in the pit of my stomach that something was wrong. Literally just minutes later, the phone rang. It was Harriet asking me to come into the office. I dropped everything and rushed in. I took calls from many concerned travelers who called just to express their condolences and support. It was a very thoughtful and sad time.

—Sally Booth,
17-year associate
Supervisor Help Group

A Chaplain's Story

For a two month period in 1999, I was on call with the Red Cross and the National Transportation Safety Board (NTSB) for airline emergencies. I was going about my regular routine as an Emergency Services Chaplain in Charleston, South Carolina, when normality was disrupted on October 31, 1999.

Within eight hours of being notified that EgyptAir 990 had crashed, I was in Newport, Rhode Island, where more than 700 family members from all over the world were waiting for any word about their relatives and friends who were on Flight 990. The Chairman of the NTSB and Rhode Island's Coroner held briefings for the families twice a day in the Family Assistance Center. Within 24 hours of our arrival, four places of worship had been set up and clergy assigned. The four faith groups were Christian, Jewish, Islamic, and Coptic. All of the rooms became a gathering place for prayer, worship, and seeking solace during the next week.

In the hallway I overheard Bob Dine and Alan Lewis quietly talking about what they could do for the relatives and friends of people traveling with Grand Circle. I offered my assistance, and from there an eternal relationship was forged. During the next week, and at the memorial service a year later, I had the blessed opportunity to spend time with Grand Circle families.

Six weeks after the crash, Bob and Alan flew me to Boston to speak at a Grand Circle holiday gathering. I spoke for several minutes and led a prayer for the passengers on the tragic flight. What I noticed was a group of wonderful associates who cared enormously for their travelers and their co-workers.

This was a very tragic time for the families of those who perished; it was also a difficult time for Grand Circle associates. I'm thankful that I could see how a great company approaches tragedy, and proud of the way the company took care of the families. Let us continue to pray for the families who lost so much during this ill-fated flight.

—Chaplain Rob Dewey, Coastal Crisis Chaplaincy

back down to call another family member. We assigned an associate to each family, to give some continuity of care as we arranged for the families to come to Newport, Rhode Island, where the plane wreckage was being taken. Over the course of a couple of days we spent more than $2 million to cover families' air travel and hotel costs.

More than 120 family members came to Rhode Island, 14 from one family alone. The NTSB was slow to make a decision about a memorial service, so we arranged a private service for the Grand Circle families in Newport, calling on the services of Chaplain Rob Dewey, of the Coastal Crisis Chaplaincy. Later in the week there was a public service for all the passengers with dozens of personal recollections of those who had died. A year later, hundreds of people came to an anniversary service, also in Newport. All of the family members walked down to the beach and put a flower into the water, then a Coast Guard helicopter released hampers of flowers over the crash site.

The memorial services were very moving, but to be honest, we never felt much "closure." There can never be closure on so terrible a tragedy. We remember it all the time. Harriet still tears up when she tells the story. But it did teach us that the best thing you can do in the face of death is keep going, lending a hand wherever you can.

The Terrorist Attacks of 9/11

9/11 was different. We didn't lose any travelers on that day, but the company took a big hit financially. In the wake of the attacks, international travel came to a standstill. In October, our bookings were down 90 percent; by November, cancellations were up 80 percent. We had to lay off 250 associates, 160 in Boston alone. Alan had forecast sales of $500 million earlier in the year; we wouldn't even come close.

We weren't alone, of course. After 9/11, fully a third of U.S. travel companies merged or went out of business entirely. Fortunately, we had plenty of cash reserves and a sound recovery plan. Other travel companies looked for new business—and failed. Our approach was different. Instead of seeking new trips and new customers, we retrenched. In what would become our signature response to a business crisis, we focused hard on the things we do best.

We cut our product line by 20 percent, focusing on the trips with the highest quality ratings. We promoted our River Cruises, the trips over which we had the most control, because we owned the ships. We retargeted our advertising, putting aside new prospects in favor of a list of 200,000 previous travelers, and we courted our loyal Inner Circle members. We renegotiated contracts with our overseas vendors so we could cut costs, then passed the savings on to our travelers. We called them the Five Key Strategies, and we knew them by heart.

On 9/11, a bunch of us were gathered in one of the offices. We saw the first tower go down on TV. When I saw those people running, I started to cry. I had this intense urge to run home and gather up my children. Maybe they didn't know. How would I tell them? Suddenly we noticed how quiet it got outside. Dead silence. Then we heard planes overhead—fighter planes. The hijacked airplanes had taken off from Boston; we were under our own emergency alert. Businesses shut down, traffic was snarled all over town, and horns were blaring. It was chilling.

—Karen Hansen,
25-year associate
Director, Corporate Marketing

Our 5 Key Strategies After 9/11

1. Cut underperforming trips to reduce product line by 20%

2. Focus on River Cruises and our own ships

3. Target marketing to our best travelers

4. Build stronger relationships with Inner Circle members

5. Seek 25% cost reductions from vendors, then pass all savings on to travelers

The Five Key Strategies weren't guidelines or suggestions—they were law. Each key strategy had its own goals, and we measured every action and every outcome against them. When someone proposed an action, anyone within earshot felt free to challenge whether it supported one or more of the Key Strategies. A radical new travel protection program passed the test; it allowed travelers to cancel a trip up to the moment of departure—something no other travel company had ever done before—which strengthened our relationship with our customers and gave them the confidence to book trips. Another radical suggestion, to cut all our All-Inclusive programs, also passed the test; though the trips brought in $50 million in sales a year, their quality scores were relatively low overall. In this way, the Five Key Strategies disciplined the organization and got everyone moving in the same direction.

9/11, One of the Worst Days of My Business Life

On 9/11, I was with Mark Frevert and some old outdoor leadership buddies climbing in the Cascade Mountains in Washington. My first reaction on hearing the news was disbelief … then horror. I needed to get back to Boston right away, but there was no air travel—none. I started to get apprehensive. When a crisis occurs, I need to take action, but I was stuck on the other side of the country. I called Harriet and asked her to meet with the Executive Team. That's when I learned that our Chief Operating Officer had completely lost it. He couldn't make a single decision. Eventually, Joe Cali stepped into the power vacuum, thank God, but for the time being we seemed to be leaderless.

Canada was still flying, so Mark and I rented a car and headed north. Mark drove, while I talked on my cell phone, sorting out traveler issues with Harriet and developing the Five Key Strategies with Wes DeVries, a longtime consultant and founder of DM Assistance, Inc. I stayed on the phone the whole way. By the time we got to Vancouver, Canada had shut down its airspace, too. We spent the night in Victoria, and were deeply moved when hundreds of Canadians turned out for a candlelight vigil on the waterfront. But as we headed back to Seattle the next day, my frustration returned. People depended on me, and I was still 2,500 miles from the office.

On that terrible day, I was stuck in a rental car racing up and down the highway between Seattle and Vancouver. For an outdoors, action-oriented person, this was a nightmare. On Thursday, when the air ban finally lifted, we took off from Boeing Field in a chartered prop plane. The heat didn't work and it would take nine and a half hours to get to Boston, but I was finally headed home to deal with the crisis firsthand.

— Alan Lewis

The entire week or two following 9/11 was extremely emotional, not only for the lives lost but also watching the associates struggle through. We were all emotionally drained, patience was tried, the uncertainty was unbearable. We supported one another here in Boston, and the outpouring of support from the regional offices was overwhelming.

—Lisa Norton,
20-year associate
Executive Vice President, Marketing

There is only one thing more painful than learning from experience and that is not learning from experience.

—Archibald MacLeish

It was a grinding climb back and we were often demoralized, especially after the layoffs, which came down in late September. It was Jim O'Brien who pulled us together that time. A West Point graduate and onetime Army Ranger instructor, Jim wasn't about to let us buckle under the strain. At the corporate meeting following the layoffs he gave a hell of a speech to the remaining associates. "There are no fair-weather fairies in this outfit," he told us. "We will go on. We will rebuild. We will keep traveling. If anyone has any doubts we can do it, call me over the weekend, and we will discuss it. Here is my home phone number. See you Monday."

We also got a lot of support from our travelers. Seven weeks after the attacks, we invited about a hundred travelers who had recently returned from Turkey, Egypt, and other hot spots in the Middle East to meet with us on Congress Street. The purpose was to get their advice on how to run the business in this new climate of terrorism. Like Jim O'Brien, they told us the best thing we could do is keep traveling. "Don't be afraid," they said. "Be the company that doesn't back down, the company that allows us to keep seeing the world."

We took heart from the words of one traveler in particular, eight-time traveler Quinn Matthewson, of El Cajon, California, who wrote: "I have no doubt at all this country will prevail and that GCT and OAT will remain viable. You may temporarily lose of few clients, of course, but I would hope most sincerely, and believe, you will do well in the months ahead, difficult as it may be from time to time. I, for one, will continue to recommend people travel and do so with you. The reasons are the itineraries, the price, the pacing, the attention one gets, and your caring ways. You do have a lot of allies out there. You don't need my advice, I know, but this will be a long struggle for you. Keep the chin up. We'll all come out OK, stronger than ever."

Our travelers had such faith in us, and they gave us so much encouragement. We have a relatively young workforce at Grand Circle, but our customers are all over 50—some of them well over 50. Their life experiences include the Great Depression, World War II, Korea, Vietnam, the Civil Rights and Women's Rights movements. Their strength, perspective, and resiliency are amazing. Our mission is to help change people's lives, but on this occasion, they changed ours by giving us confidence and hope. We dug in, and in time sales came back. Against all predictions, 2002 was a record year for the company.

The Financial Crisis of 2008–2010

The most recent crisis to shake us up was the worldwide financial crisis that hit in the fall of 2008. We had seen recessions come and go, but nothing like this. Home values collapsed, financial institutions went into bankruptcy, automakers went into bailout, stocks collapsed overnight, and cash investments earned next to nothing.

We had some alarming months in the fall of 2008 when our sales declined sharply; our travelers were nervously guarding their bank accounts. We immediately undertook an aggressive cost-cutting campaign, with a goal of cutting $52 million from our 2009 contracts— savings that were then passed on to travelers in the form of steeply discounted prices. At an offsite in South Carolina in 2009, we identified other ways to help our customers travel, instituting free domestic air travel, waiving most of the usual supplementary fees imposed on solo travelers, and extending our usual 14-day risk-free guarantee to 30 days. We put our best trip leaders on the maximum number of departures, replaced some low-performing trip leaders, launched Harriet's Corner to communicate better with our travelers, and offered a free matching service for solo travelers. Our mission was to leverage one of our Extreme Competitive Advantages—Unsurpassed Value and Excellence—and we did it. Once again we came back strong; 2009 was the third-best year in our company history, and our quality ratings were the highest ever.

Then, in April 2010, after an earthquake in Chile and mudslides in Peru, a volcano erupted in Iceland. It was almost comical. Would there be no end to our tribulations? Airports closed for six days all across Europe, stranding some of our travelers and keeping others from starting their trips on time. We got out of that mess, too, shortening some departures, allowing most travelers to travel at another time at no extra charge, covering the expenses of those who were stranded, and expediting our travelers' claims with the insurers. By the time the ash cleared and we could finally breathe a sigh of relief, there were brighter skies on the horizon: The dollar was at its highest point against the euro in four years, and our 2011 bookings were way ahead of projections.

Handling a World Crisis

Every crisis is different. But whether the crisis is a transportation failure, a terrorist attack, a financial collapse, a natural disaster, political unrest, or some other calamity we haven't yet imagined, we must be ready to handle it quickly. And we've handled many, many crises. A glance at the short list on the opposite page will give you an idea of the kinds of crises we have faced; a longer list appears at the back of the book, in the Appendix.

Over the years we have developed an approach to crisis management that gets us moving fast. We don't dwell on external events because those are things we can't control. Instead, we focus on our mission and values and on our Extreme Competitive Advantages, because these have carried us through crises in the past. Our crisis response varies somewhat with the circumstances, but it tends to follow the seven actions listed below. The important thing is to assess the situation, make a plan, and take action—quickly. If the fast plan doesn't work, we change course and try something else; we care less about the process than the results. An account of our key crises leadership points appears in the Appendix.

Mobilize the Worldwide Organization

The first thing we do in a crisis is get on the telephone to someone close to the problem in the field—a trip leader, a regional manager, a ship's captain, a vendor, or an experienced traveler. If no one is close, we get someone on an airplane immediately to conduct a firsthand assessment. The important thing is to communicate, communicate, communicate.

We are well positioned to do this because of our worldwide organization. With 38 offices in 31 countries, we have instant access to people on the ground who can tell us what is really happening. It's like having our own wire service; in fact, we have more international offices than most news organizations. While the rest of the world is glued to the TV, listening to rumors and second hand information, we are getting direct reports from our overseas associates, in English, along with an immediate analysis of what the crisis means for our travelers and our business.

The on-the-ground analysis is the important part. It's what gets us off the mark fast. And it's only possible because of our corporate culture.

Some Crises We Have Faced

1985	Hijacking of the *Achille Lauro* cruise ship and murder of an American tourist
1986	U.S. airstrike on Libya; major impact on travel abroad
1986	Chernobyl meltdown; 30 killed, 135,000 evacuated
1988	Pan Am Flight 103 bombed out of sky over Scotland; 270 killed
1989	Tiananmen Square protests; widespread condemnation halts tourism to China, five GCT China products reduced to one
1991	U. S. war with Iraq; 40% of U.S. tour operators go under
1997	60 tourists killed in Luxor, Egypt; our travelers choose to keep traveling in Egypt
1999	Kosovo/Bosnia conflict, Danube River closed to Black Sea; Grand Circle ships rerouted
1999	EgyptAir Flight 990 crash, 54 GCC travelers killed
2000	"Flood of the Century" halts River Cruises on Danube
2001	9/11 terrorist attack on the United States, we suffer large layoffs and losses
2003	SARS epidemic curtails tourism in Asia
2004	Tsunami devastates South Asia
2005	Terrorist bombings in London; 52 killed, 700 wounded
2006	Train bombings in Mumbai, India, kill 200 people
2008	Worldwide financial crisis; markets plunge around the world, curtailing travel for many Americans
2010	Volcano in Iceland disrupts air travel across Europe

During the SARS epidemic, in 2003, one of our associates in China sent me an e-mail, strongly recommending that we suspend our China trips until after the epidemic subsided. This was not what we wanted to hear, as China was a big money-maker for us. It turns out the associate had good on-the-spot information, and we followed his advice. Our associate took a big risk that day. He had no special relationship with me, and his immediate supervisor disagreed with his recommendation. But he believed in our value of open and courageous communication. I was grateful for his honesty.

—Alan Lewis

The Grand Circle Crisis Response

1. Mobilize the worldwide organization

2. Focus on actions that can make a difference

3. Take care of travelers

4. Create a plan, take fast action, then reassess

5. Reduce costs and pass all savings on to travelers

6. Promote trips away from the crisis region

7. Keep traveling

We believe that locals know best, so over the years we have turned over a great deal of responsibility to our regional offices, empowering them to contract with hotels, manage our ships, design itineraries, hire program directors, keep accounts, and deliver our unforgettable experiences.

Our overseas offices do not *represent* Grand Circle; they *are* Grand Circle. So when a crisis arises, we look to them for leadership and information. In fact, in an emergency we will give them direct authority to make decisions that involve our travelers. For example, in 2010 political demonstrations in Bangkok erupted into violence and rioting. Bangkok is home to our largest overseas office, and Southeast Asia is one of our biggest markets. Our regional manager, Rung Chatchaloemuut, was trapped inside a hotel for ten days, but we gave her full authority to decide how to manage the itineraries of our travelers in Bangkok. She was, after all, in the thick of things, and she had a much better idea how to keep the travelers out of harm's way than we did in Boston.

Here is another important thing: In a crisis, we do not retreat from our philanthropic involvement in the region. We continue to fund the schools, orphanages, museums, archaeological sites, and other initiatives that we support through Grand Circle Foundation. For example, when terrorists bombed the U.S. embassies in Tanzania and Kenya in 1998, we continued to support our schools in those countries. These projects are part of our business strategy—our travelers visit many of the sites—

but they are also our friends and our partners. Supporting them is not a luxury of good times, but a part of who we are.

Focus on Actions That Can Make a Difference

It's easy to get distracted during a crisis. Crazy things are happening. Without focus, people tend to flail around or retreat into unimportant details. This is true of almost everyone, including our own associates. We all need direction, fast, so we can take effective action. We know from long experience that we cannot control a crisis, we can only control our response to it; we also know that in a crisis, we must leverage the things we do best. In other words, effective crisis management requires a sharp focus on the few things that can *actually make a difference to the outcome.*

We focus the company's attention by gathering the senior leadership and department heads around our Extreme Competitive Advantages. Then we ask them to identify the top five issues using our leadership model, which focuses on top people, top vendors, and top products. Then we identify the top five actions to resolve those issues. These lists are put in rank order, so we know what's most important and can deploy the top resources to the top issues. Keeping the leadership focused on our Extreme Competitive Advantages and business and leadership models is essential for achieving quick and decisive action in times of crisis.

With this fast flip-chart analysis, we have everyone's attention and the beginning of a plan. It is an application of the "80/20 Rule," the management principle that tells us that 80 percent of our results will come from the top 20 percent of our resources and actions. We have never known it to fail. Later, this quick assessment will become a strategic plan.

Take Care of Travelers

Our first priority in every crisis is always to take care of our travelers and associates in the regions affected. This might mean establishing direct communication with their trip leaders; rerouting their itineraries; arranging for hospital care, security, or embassy protection; or booking flights to bring them back to the United States early. It also includes communicating with the designated relatives back home.

In any moment of decision the best thing you can do is the right thing, the next best thing is the wrong thing, and the worst thing you can do is nothing.

—Theodore Roosevelt

When a Holland America bus crashed in Alaska in 1987, associates flew in from Boston to be with our hospitalized travelers. When an OAT van hit a horse-drawn cart in Tunisia in 1998, we mobilized our associates in the country to stay with the injured travelers; the same year, when fires in Borneo closed airports in Malaysia, associates helped revise our OAT travelers' itineraries. The list goes on and on. We are experienced crisis interventionists; we know what to do for our travelers on the road.

The next priority is to provide as much information as we can gather to travelers scheduled to depart on upcoming trips to the regions. This includes news about current developments, safety information, and a list of options available if travelers choose to not take their scheduled departure. Of course, if a "hot spot" develops in a region that threatens our travelers, we will suspend trips to that area until the danger passes. We did this after 9/11, for example, curtailing development of several very promising trips to India and Nepal because of their proximity to suspected terrorist camps in Afghanistan. Though we were confident that these trips would be hugely popular in the future (as, in fact, they are today), we kept them off our books for almost three years.

Letting Our Travelers Decide

Our travelers are adults with a lot of life experience. In a crisis, we believe we honor them best by explaining the situation and letting them decide for themselves what to do. For example, in 1997, 60 tourists were killed in a terrorist attack at the ruins in Luxor. We had 158 travelers in Egypt at that time, and 113 of them were scheduled to visit Luxor the next day. We gave those travelers a choice: Skip the visit to the ruins, continue as planned, or return home. In the morning, 111 of the travelers went to Luxor as planned. Of our 158 travelers in Egypt, only two went home, and that was at their children's insistence. Our travelers trusted us, and they wouldn't allow terrorists to deny them the experience of a lifetime.

—Mark Frevert, Executive Vice President/Chief Architect

Create a Plan, Take Fast Action, Then Reassess

Once provisions are made for the travelers, the senior leaders immediately put together a strategic response from the "Top Fives." The plan identifies goals, assigns roles, and determines the best process for getting the job done. We call this our "road map," and it is based in the G.R.P.I. model for team effectiveness described in the Appendix. It is not a detailed map—more like a bird's-eye view of how to get from where we are to where we want to be. Once the route is established, many hands will contribute to the details of planning and execution.

Most companies wait a week or more for the dust to settle, but we move fast and meet often: every two hours at the beginning, then at least daily until the crisis is resolved. To move quickly, we use what we call "directional information." Directional information is not all there is to know about a subject, but it's enough to set a direction. It's the information at hand, and every travel company has it. What is unique about Grand Circle is that we are not afraid to act on it. We don't dither. We don't wait for a committee report. We go full-speed ahead toward the goal we have identified. We can do this without fear because we have no compunction about changing direction if the plan doesn't work. We say, "Act early. Act aggressively. Act often. Make mistakes. Reassess. Reassess. Reassess." We call this impulse for an immediate, focused response "clarity over certainty," and we consider it a key to good leadership.

Another unique feature of our crisis response is that we don't lock leaders up in a room by themselves and we don't hire outside crisis consultants. We go directly to the people in the organization who can help. Just as we call on our overseas associates to get a clear picture of what is going on in the region, we call in every Boston associate who has firsthand experience with the current problem, or who has prior experience handling similar crises. We will also tap people who we know will aggressively apply our values, especially open and courageous communication, risk taking, and speed. No matter their title, position, leadership experience, or length of service, they will be there in the conference room, helping the leadership achieve clarity and direct the response. It is in times of crisis that our principle of "Leadership from Anywhere" really pays off.

Back in 1995, there were rumors that Regency Cruise Line would go bankrupt at any moment. We had 150 travelers with them at the time, and no information about what was going on. We couldn't even get through on the phone. I was told to pick up my papers and fly to New York—*at that very moment*. My mission was to get the name and number of someone at Regency's headquarters so we would have inside information to help get our travelers home. When I got there, the door to the office was closed. The president and everyone had all quit! But I found my way to the mailroom, and there was this one guy all by himself, trying to field all the phone calls. Mission accomplished!

I had been with Grand Circle only three months when this happened. It was my crash course in crisis management. That was the day I really understood the importance of speed and risk-taking as corporate values.

—Ginny Stokes,
15-year associate
Senior Vice President,
Ocean Cruises

Time is one resource that none of us can ever get back. In ordinary times, it is the greatest business cost. During a crisis it can be your worst enemy. You have to confront every crisis with the greatest possible speed. We do that by making hard decisions about the tough issues first. This is often about *people*, especially top people. We've found that the organization moves fastest in crisis when the naysayers and the fearful are relegated to the sidelines. So that's where we put them.

—Alan Lewis

A Big Mistake

After 9/11, we made a commitment to keep traveling. We never believed the government would shut down the airlines, at least not for more than a day. We were wrong. The government shut down all air traffic into and out of the country for four days. While most of our air operations team worked to get our stranded passengers home, we also kept rebooking departures on the assumption that we would be flying again the next day, and the next. We finally got it all sorted out, but we exhausted some great people along the way.

—Bob Dine, Executive Vice President

Reduce Costs and Pass All Savings on to Travelers

Many people stop traveling during a crisis. This has serious consequences for our business, so we immediately lower our prices—often drastically. We can do this because as demand slackens or collapses, our vendors will offer us cost reductions; we simply pass these savings on to our travelers. We've experienced this so many times that we actually cut our prices *before* getting concessions from our vendors. We trust them to help us, not only because we have built long-term relationships with them but because we can help *them*. They've worked with us long enough to know that our travelers will keep traveling, especially if the price is right, so we can help fill their empty rooms, motor coaches, and restaurants.

Travelers tell us over and over again that their most memorable trips are when everyone else stays home. Major tourist attractions are uncrowded, and travelers can make wonderful connections with local people. At the same time, people in troubled destinations are grateful for visitors who help support the local economy, and go to great lengths to make them feel welcome. It's a win-win situation: Our travelers get an unforgettable experience, and local people get our business and our compassionate presence.

My Lesson in Crisis Leadership

In 1999, when I had been with Grand Circle for only a few months, NATO began bombing bridges in Yugoslavia. A year earlier, Grand Circle had invested heavily in ships on the Rhine, Main, and Danube rivers; now wreckage blocked the rivers and more than a thousand aircraft were flying overhead. It was March, prime selling season for summer travel, and bookings had slowed to a trickle.

Alan and Mark called me to a meeting. "This will end soon, but we can't wait," Alan said. "Travelers book months in advance. Every day that goes by increases the risk that our ships will run empty during the high season and our travelers won't get the trip they want."

What could improve the situation? Alan didn't hesitate. "Let's develop a promotional catalog, cut prices by 50 percent, and get it mailed by Friday."

Was he serious? Who was going to book these trips—at *any* price? Besides, it takes three to four *weeks* to get a catalog out, not three days!

I thought, "This is never going to work," but, sure enough, a catalog was designed, printed, and mailed in three days.

Travelers started booking trips. By June 11, the bombings had ceased, and our ships sailed peacefully at 90 percent capacity. More than 20,000 travelers joined us that summer for the river trips of their dreams.

—Joe Cali, Executive Vice President, Analysis

Promote Trips Away from the Crisis Region

Since travel usually declines in troubled areas, we look for other destinations that will appeal to our travelers, then offer great values on these alternative trips as well. This strategy provides our committed travelers with high-value alternatives, while attracting new bookings. For example, when war broke out in Yugoslavia in 1991, we promoted our trips in Costa Rica; during the SARS epidemic in Asia, we promoted new trips to Canada and later, when SARS turned up in Canada as well, to South America. We can do this because we offer trips all around the world and have a worldwide operation that can accommodate sudden changes in demand.

On the other hand, we almost never leave a trouble spot. We may suspend some departures or reroute some itineraries, but we keep our offices open and stand ready to accommodate any travelers who are willing to go. For example, we were the only U.S. tour operator to stay in Zimbabwe after killings there in 2000. That same year, 7,000 of our travelers visited Fiji despite a coup and rising racial tensions in the islands. After 9/11 we continued to travel to both Egypt and Turkey. Crisis in Israel? We stayed. Hoof and mouth disease in the U.K? We stayed.

Troubles come and go, and we want to be positioned to take lots of travelers to fascinating destinations when the crisis situation has passed. By continuing operations in a troubled region—or at least keeping our offices open—we maintain the trust and loyalty of our vendors, Foundation partners, government agencies, and our own associates in the region. Those relationships will pay big dividends over time.

Above All, Keep Traveling

A big part of our philosophy is to "Keep Traveling"—even if there are only a handful of travelers booked for a given departure. We want to be the travel company for those intrepid souls who will travel even when times are tough, even in times of crisis. We know that these people are our best customers. We learned that lesson after 9/11, when our most frequent travelers kept traveling and helped us weather the storm. We are so grateful to them—and we want to keep them as our loyal customers.

Passionate travelers will always find a way to go where they want to go. If they don't go with us, they will go with some other company—and we don't want that to happen. As we execute our crisis plan, we always have our eyes on the future, and that future requires that we keep traveling today.

Never Leave a Trouble Spot

On 9/11, I was by myself for a moment in our Boston office, walking between floors, when I had a sudden thought: What will happen to the people in Egypt? What about Farid, who was our guide when we finally took that trip to Egypt in 2000? His family had been in the tourism industry for five generations. Egypt depends on tourism, and they have always been fantastic hosts for our travelers. I was afraid Americans might now be reluctant to visit Egypt, a Muslim country, but if people quit traveling, how would these good people feed their families? My whole way of thinking about the crisis was changed by my recent travels in Egypt.

Alan and I wanted to help build goodwill between our countries, so we decided that Grand Circle would continue promoting travel to Egypt. In fact, on September 14, 2001, we sent our new ship, the *M/S River Anuket*, down the Nile. It was the first American-owned ship in Egypt, and it sailed only half full. But we persevered. In 2002, our Egyptian bookings were still down, but the travelers who went had truly unforgettable experiences. Our relationship with the Egyptian tourism industry, already strong because of our support of EgyptAir after its crash two years earlier, soon grew even stronger, to the benefit of our travelers and associates, and we now have three ships on the Nile.

—Harriet Lewis

Every Crisis Disguises Opportunity

After the EgyptAir Flight 990 crashed, it would have been easy to abandon the airline as our competitors did. After all, the cause of the crash was unclear. But we work hard to establish our long-term vendor relationships. We knew the leadership of the airline personally, and we know the value of loyalty. Just as we don't leave a country when there's a problem, we don't abandon a vendor unless its agents do something dishonest or their quality no longer meets our standards. We continued to contract with EgyptAir at a time when they greatly needed our busi-

When you get into a tight place and everything goes against you, till it seems as though you could not hang on a minute longer, never give up then, for that is just the place and time that the tide will turn.

—Harriet Beecher Stowe

Courage is being scared to death and saddling up anyway.

—John Wayne

ness and our loyalty has been repaid many times over the years in excellent air pricing, preferential flight availability, and concessions when we've needed them. We foresaw that opportunity and have profited from it.

A similar thing happened after 9/11. As bookings plummeted, our competitors cancelled vendor contracts all over the world—flights, hotel rooms, ship berths, meals. We moved into the vacuum, securing discounted long-term contracts with properties and services our competitors had previously locked up. When travel resumed, our competitors had to settle for second-tier properties at a higher cost. We emerged as the dominant player in several new regions, including South America and the Mediterranean.

Many opportunities occur because competitors freeze or panic. We know they won't slow down for very long, so we move quickly to take advantage of their missteps. If we're fast enough, we can seize the opportunity while our competitors are still trying to come up with a plan, and in doing so, we come up with a long-term advantage. Nailing opportunities requires nerve, speed, risk-taking, and a long memory. We've dealt with many crises since that first terrible year. We know what to do. In fact, we now feel that if the company does not emerge from a crisis stronger than it was when we went in, then we have merely survived, not succeeded. Our goal for every crisis is to hang tough, leverage our Extreme Competitive Advantages, and emerge with a stronger leadership position.

Leaders Can Emerge from Crisis

Some people rise to the occasion during a crisis; others shrink into the knee-well of their desk. It has been heartwarming for us to see unexpected leaders emerge from troubled times, not only because they have given us hope and direction in the moment, but because they affirm our long-held belief that people can lead from anywhere.

In fact, nothing elevates leaders like crisis. We have seen it countless times. It seems that crisis can serve as a kind of leadership incubator, a place where personal growth emerges from the very act of facing adversity. People seldom feel comfortable taking the reins in time of crisis if they aren't also expected to lead in ordinary times. Crises can make leaders, but rarely outside of a corporate culture that empowers leadership every day and believes that people can lead from anywhere.

Not everyone can handle the stress of a crisis, however, not even designated leaders. The sad truth is that some people leave midway through the crisis or soon after. On 9/11, for example, our Chief Operating Officer became completely paralyzed by indecision and had to be taken home. He left the company three weeks later. We realized in hindsight that while this individual had a wonderful resume, he had never fully embraced our values of open and courageous communication, speed, risk taking, and thriving in change—values that are critical to crisis management.

Crises Are Emotional

There is one more aspect of crisis that we want to discuss. Crises are emotional events. We all have feelings. Nobody is superhuman, certainly neither of us. We try to mentally prepare ourselves for dealing with tough situations—both inside the company and in the greater world. In troubling times we support each other. We make a habit of assessing each other's reserves of courage and resilience. When one of us gets worn down, we see it as our job to remind our partner to get a break with plenty of rest. No one can run full-tilt every waking moment. We don't ask it of ourselves and we don't expect it from our associates.

We also remind each other to take care of our associates, and never take them for granted. Crises drain everyone emotionally, and we try to cushion the impact. We organize breaks and downtime. We find out whether family or friends have been directly affected by the crisis. And we send people home for rest when they seem to be at the breaking point.

When the crisis is finally over, we celebrate! We organize some crazy stuff so people can have fun. Everyone has earned it. Then, after a couple days, we do an after-action report assessing what we did right and what we did wrong. As a company, and as individuals, we've always learned more from our mistakes than from our successes. We especially assess the performance of our top people and ourselves. A crisis forces everyone to live in vivid Technicolor, so we take some notes while everything is fresh in our minds, knowing that the next crisis is just around the corner.

Alan is always telling people about his girlfriend SARA. He even has a doll with her name in his office. SARA stands for Shock, Anger, Rejection, Acceptance—the sequence of emotions that psychologists say most people go through in times of crisis. We've been down this emotional path many times. It seems that different people go through the sequence at different speeds, and sometimes they bounce back and forth among the stages. We've found that simply acknowledging the stages is a big help in getting through a crisis and back to more even ground.

—Harriet Lewis

Lillian Stoff, a 14-time traveler from Mamaroneck, New York, prepares for her first ostrich derby in Oudtshoorn, South Africa.

CHAPTER 10

Never Quit on Your Dream

We often use the picture at left in our catalogs and it always makes me smile— not only because riding an ostrich is such a preposterous thing to do, but because the woman in the photo is so obviously amazed to be doing it. She's not young, either. She's one of our travelers, a woman well past "a certain age" and certainly "old enough to know better," but a woman who is not about to let age slow her down—at least not while she's riding that ostrich!

Many of our travelers have similar pictures in their travel albums—pictures of people doing unexpected things, like making tortillas at a home-hosted dinner in Costa Rica, or doing the hokey pokey with first graders in Peru. I see a lot of these pictures because travelers send them to me to publish in Harriet's Corner. In the pictures, the travelers are having a ball. They make me think how lucky we are to be in a business that makes people happy. How many people get to say that?

Twenty-five years ago, when Alan and I decided to buy Grand Circle Travel, we thought we knew something about the future. We were in our mid–30s and we had a big dream. We would build a great travel company, and it would change people's lives. We thought it would be easy. After all, travel is so amazing—so eye-opening, so exciting. How could it not *change you?*

Well, some of it has been easy and some of it has been hard. We've told you about many of the ups and downs in this book. What we didn't foresee was how far and how deep the changes would go. What began as a simple desire to help people see the world soon became a mission to help our associates become leaders, then to give back to our local community, then to create a worldwide philanthropic foundation, then to support social entrepreneurship here and abroad. It seems incredible that the decision we made on the beach on Captiva Island all those years ago could have had such a big effect.

We can't take all the credit—or even most of it. We've had help from many, many people along the way. Also, the more I travel, the more I see that travel really does have an extraordinary power all its own. It gives you big ideas, and at the same time makes you humble. That's a great recipe for making connections and getting things done.

A couple of years ago I took a group of ten teenagers from inner-city Boston on a leadership trip to Tanzania. They were bright, determined, college-bound youngsters, leaders in their schools and active in community projects, and yet some of them had never been outside their neighborhoods, never mind out of the country. They bloomed in Tanzania. They were like sponges—so interested in everything going on around them, so eager to meet people, so incredibly open to new ideas. And they were fearless. They traveled 7,000 miles to a country they had only read about; they taught playground games to Tanzanian children; and they sat down with village elders and talked about their dreams.

For these young people, it was a whole new world. For me, it was familiar. These young people were junior versions of our "mature" travelers: thoughtful, curious, excited, ready to take on the world. Travel had worked its magic on them, just as it does on every trip we offer at Grand Circle. If we'd brought in some ostriches, these kids would have climbed right on board.

—Harriet Lewis

The future is always unknown, but we know that our future is bright. We'll have troubles, of course, but we're in the greatest business on earth. We have a strong company with tremendous depth in leadership and experience. We have great trips and wonderful travelers who are always eager to explore the world with us. What could be better?

We're optimists by nature and we tend to avoid doom-and-gloom-sayers, including the popular media, which seems to be always screaming about some horrible thing that's happening or about to happen. Life is too short to carry around all that baggage. Besides, we've made it through many changes and crises; we know we'll get through the next difficulty and just keep growing. We've found the trick is to get up, shake off any negative thoughts, and get back on the course we want to be traveling.

Extreme Competitive Advantages

We are confident about the future because we have six Extreme Competitive Advantages, six areas of dominance so strong and so far advanced that we know it would take our competitors at least three years to replicate them. That is, if we stood still … and we never stand still. We constantly work to enlarge our Extreme Competitive Advantages, in good times and in bad, because we believe that excellent companies do a few things exceptionally well. Here they are:

Grand Circle's Extreme Competitive Advantages

1. People Are Number 1—Worldwide Organization

2. Unsurpassed Value and Excellence

3. Strong Traveler Loyalty

4. Women Travelers

5. Small Group Travel

6. Small Ship Cruises

People Are Number 1—Worldwide Organization

Over the last 15 years we have built the most extensive worldwide organization in the travel business. We now have 38 offices in 31 countries, and employ 220 overseas associates and 1,500 local Trip Leaders, crew members, and Program Directors. Our overseas associates design, buy, and deliver our trips in ways we never could from Boston, and our local trip leaders immerse our travelers in cultural experiences that are truly up-close and personal. Our travelers have been telling us for years that local guides are best. It took us a while to make the change from American guides, but once we did, we never looked back.

Our worldwide organization also helps us in times of crisis. Our overseas associates are our eyes and ears when trouble emerges in their area, and because they understand our corporate culture, they are ready to lead us out of difficulty from wherever they are. We are a company of champions, a truly global enterprise operating in all corners of the world. No other American company has anything remotely similar. They can't, because they don't have the local people on the ground. It's not the bricks-and-mortar offices that matter so much as the people; that's why we say "People Are Number 1."

Harriet and I are both very competitive. We want to be the best and we want to stay at the head of the pack. From our earliest days at Grand Circle, we've strived to build advantages that would knock out the competition. If your competitor can easily replicate your advantage, it's not really an advantage, is it? It's just a fleeting benefit. Blink and the rest of the pack has passed you by. No way is that going to happen to us.

—Alan Lewis

Unsurpassed Value and Excellence

Travelers know Grand Circle as the company that delivers wonderful trips at a great price. This is our second Extreme Competitive Advantage, the one we call Unsurpassed Value and Excellence. Over the years we have found many different ways to keep our prices down. We buy direct wherever we can, bypassing local ground operators. We also market direct, eliminating travel agents and their commissions. Instead of prospecting for new customers, which is expensive, we cultivate our repeat travelers and their referral business. We own and operate our own ships; we keep our load factors sky high; we negotiate favorable contracts with vendors who want our high volume, year-round business; and we scoop up inventory when our competitors dump it in a crisis-induced panic.

As for "Excellence," it is our travelers who keep us honest. They let us know how we're doing—through the 200 post-trip surveys that we receive every day. "Quality" is one of our six core values, and we track it assiduously: chasing down every lapse, following every lead for improvement, and canceling entire programs if our travelers tell us we are on the wrong track. When some prospective investors jokingly called us "Maniacs on excellence," we sent them packing, because *they just didn't get it*. Trips are a dime a dozen, but great *experiences* take constant tending. More importantly, great trips ensure repeat business, the engine driving our business.

Our Excellence Scores in 2009

Overseas Adventure Travel — 83%

Overseas Adventure Travel Small Ship — 79%

Grand Circle Travel — 80%

Grand Circle Small Ship Cruises — 80%

Overall: 81%

Strong Traveler Loyalty

Our travelers love us, and they travel with us again and again. On a typical trip, more than half the travelers have traveled with us before. Many take several trips a year with us, and 33,000 households have traveled with us more than half a dozen times. Our travelers are so pleased with their trips that they refer between 30,000 and 40,000 new travelers to us every year. It's a mutual admiration society of the very best kind, and we honor it by paying keen attention to the customers we already have.

Other travel companies prefer the "cast a wide net" approach, always looking for new customers in the widening pool of retiring Baby Boomers. We went down that road for a long time. But we've found that our more personal approach, while more time- and labor-intensive, is more profitable—and more satisfying. We feel we are building a company of active, like-minded travelers, people who believe, as we do, that travel is a joy and a privilege, and an opportunity to grow and help make people's dreams come true—maybe even change their lives.

Women Travelers

Two-thirds of our travelers are women. They often travel as singles or with friends, and when they travel with their husbands, they usually make the travel decisions. It took us a while to understand how powerfully these women shape our trips; in fact, it wasn't until one year ago that we added women travelers to our list of Extreme Competitive Advantages. At that point we began asking them the eternal question: What do women want? And they told us—four things in particular: up-close cultural experiences, involvement with Grand Circle Foundation, discounts for solo travelers, and help finding compatible travel partners.

We have done our best to deliver in all of these areas. We have increased the personal interaction in our *a Day in the Life* and *Invest in a Village* programs, and we are searching our itineraries for new Foundation sites with whom to partner. We've worked with our vendors to offer some free single supplements on most of our trips, and we've launched a companion matching service, on our website. Being conscious and supportive of women travelers is rare in the travel business, but we pursue it wholeheartedly. This is Harriet and Charlotte's doing, and we are embarrassed it took so long to really hear them. And we thank them, because now we have a big edge.

So often, when I meet the women who travel with OAT, I've feel like we know one another—though in fact we are strangers. It makes sense, really, because the motives that compel us to explore the world are the same. At our stage in life, we've played many roles that have required us to give of ourselves or take care of others—we've been wives, partners, mothers, and parents to our parents. We've shared joy and sorrow, our hearts and our souls. Now, we've reached a stage when it's our time, *our* turn. Our financial portfolios may be down, but we'd rather build portfolios of memories, photographs, and belly laughs. So we're packing our bags and hitting the road.

—Harriet Lewis

Never mind that I have spent my children's inheritance with you. I have walked the Great Wall, viewed the Taj Mahal, and ridden a camel to the Pyramids. You are my company.

—Charlotte Gates,
Inner Circle traveler
Atlanta, Georgia

Another Love Letter to OAT

Dear OAT,

I leave for Nepal with OAT next month. It will be my 14th OAT trip. Ten years ago, I was recovering from the unexpected loss of a 36-year marriage. I had been traded for a girl my daughter's age. My response was to roll up in a ball. At a bridge game, a gentleman had just come back from an OAT trip to Turkey. I perked up at his enthusiasm, and the next week he brought me a brochure.

I had always loved to travel, but off-the-beaten-path travel never appealed to me. I didn't want to go anywhere you couldn't plug in your hair-dryer. I was fascinated by the exotic sound of a trip to Nepal and I told myself only seasoned travelers would choose that remote place. I knew I needed a jump-start, so jump-start I did. I jumped right into magical Kathmandu.

I could not believe the beautiful sights and sounds that surrounded me. Our guide was a retired Gorkha—quiet, dignified, funny, and very knowledgeable. He made me eager to learn about the world. I joined a group of 10 travelers and OAT provided me with a roommate—with whom I am still friends. And that was just the beginning of some wonderful adventures. I have been on seven continents with you. I have stood, mouth agape, in multiple places and said to myself, *"Mary Lou, you're where?"*

Since 2002, I have taken many of those trips with the guy now in my life and he has enjoyed the trips enormously. He keeps telling me how much he has learned about the world and about life. And now next month, I'm going back to where it all began—Nepal.

Thank you. You have found us magic places and knowledgeable guides to teach us about them. You have opened the doors to hospitable folks everywhere and the understanding that we all want pretty much the same thing no matter what our differences may be.

—Mary Lou D'Altorio,
  14-time traveler, Pittsburgh, Pennsylvania

Small Group Travel

Overseas Adventure Travel is the undisputed leader in small group travel—on land and on water. This is an enviable place to be because small group travel is the fastest growing segment of the travel industry. We are adventure travelers ourselves, and we understand the allure of out-of-the-way places, intimate perspectives, and close companionship on a trip. We also know that a successful small group trip is not a big-group trip cut down to size; it is a whole other experience. We have spent 16 years developing itineraries that really take advantage of small-group size (no more than 16 travelers on OAT land trips, and no more than 25 on OAT ships), and OAT's small ships are now ranked among the best in the world.

We believe small group travel is the wave of the future. As the world gets smaller, travelers will want to take a closer look at places that are off the beaten path, where they can engage personally with fellow travelers and with local people going about their daily lives. Our curious, convivial, independent-minded OAT travelers are already traveling that road—more than 50,000 of them a year. We salute them!

Small Ship Cruises

When we first started out, we would never have predicted that we would make a name for ourselves in small ship cruises. Harriet has never been a big fan of boats, and Alan's prior experience with water was chiefly from the seat of a lifeguard's chair. But today Grand Circle dominates the small ship cruise market; it is our sixth Extreme Competitive Advantage.

We didn't quite know what we were getting into when we bought—and then built—our first ships in the late 1990s. But we learned fast, and we now own and operate a fleet of 60 small ships all over the world and we completely dominate the river cruise business. Our advantage comes from two hard-won achievements: complete control over the ships' operations—outfitting, staffing, provisioning and service—and the integration of our signature land tours. It's a win-win for our travelers—and a bargain, too, because we can price our cruises $1,000 to $1,500 less than our competitors.

Why Our Competitors Don't Really Worry Us

We don't worry about competitors sneaking a peek at this book and trying to copy our Extreme Competitive Advantages. In fact, they try to copy

My wife and I have many wonderful memories of our trips on the *River Adagio* and Grand Circle's other river ships fleet. One of these special moments occurred during our very first trip with Grand Circle, in 1998. When we arrived at our ship docked in Amsterdam, many crew members were there to help carry our luggage on board. An older officer with stripes on his sleeves took our two bags and cheerfully carried them aboard. Later, I asked the hotel manager who had carried our luggage onto the ship. He told us with a smile, "That was Captain Liemberg. He always likes to help us."

Where else would you find the captain of a ship lugging a passenger's bags up the gangway?

—Hugh Foster,
18-time traveler
Reston, Virginia

I can't say enough about Grand Circle and what they have contributed to our lives. I feel emotional about it, and as an older person I can appreciate these things. I never in my whole life dreamed that we would ever encounter these places. We are so grateful.

—Mary Ann Trumko,
31-time traveler
Cudahy, Wisconsin

them all the time. We don't worry because we know how long it took us to consolidate these advantages, and we know it would be very difficult to implement them outside of our unique corporate culture. If our competitors make a concerted effort, they could maybe replicate what we've done in five years. By then, we'll be way down the road.

A Grand Future

Five years ago, on the occasion of Grand Circle's 20th anniversary, we asked our associates to take out their crystal balls and tell us what they saw in our future. It was a playful question and the responses were wonderful. They foresaw trips to Cuba, to the moon, and to other planets. They imagined a Grand Circle airline and a Grand Circle hotel chain. One associate predicted Harriet would go head-to-head with Martha Stewart, publishing a magazine for aging Baby Boomers called *Living Grandly*. Another said we'd be branded as pirates—because we kept stealing everybody else's ship business. One fearless soul predicted we'd be a billion-dollar company by 2015. That's still possible: though we took a big hit during the recent worldwide recession, our sales for 2010 are back up to $600 million. We are back in a big way. But though we are proud of our growth, we are more proud of the relationships we have forged with our travelers. If we had to choose between big and personal, we would choose personal every time.

As for us, we foresee several travel trends. We believe small group travel and small ship travel will surpass larger coach-based tours in popularity, at least among our travelers. In fact, that may happen within the next couple of years, as OAT travelers currently account for 43 percent of our total travelers and close to half our sales.

We also think travelers across the industry will be looking for more experiential, hands-on travel programs that will allow them to engage more directly with overseas destinations, perhaps even assisting local communities in local work and service projects. Homestays, work vacations, and "voluntourism" are already popular travel styles in the youth and young adult markets; we're watching closely to see whether there will be a demand for similar programs in our market. Certainly our travelers are already very committed to the notion of giving back to the communities we visit, through donations and fundraising for various Grand Circle Foundation projects. We expect that trend to continue and increase as Americans come to feel more and more a part of the global village.

Over the past 25 years we've observed that travelers come in many sizes and shapes. They come from many different walks of life, and hold different political and religious views. But they have certain things in common. They are curious and seek out information. They are tolerant of differences, open-minded, and compassionate. They see themselves as lifelong learners. They travel the world because it is endlessly interesting and because with each trip they learn something new about themselves and feel a deeper connection with some essential planetary and human condition.

We believe that in the coming years, as the world becomes smaller and more interconnected through economic and financial markets, transportation, and communication, our travelers will play important new roles. Never merely tourists, our travelers will now act as ambassadors, representing American ideas and values in more and more communities abroad, and bringing back information and true-life stories to counter ignorance at home. They will become fact-finders and teachers themselves. As Mark Twain said, "Travel is fatal to prejudice." In the same way, we believe our travelers will help heal the world, one unforgettable experience at a time.

Keeping It Real

The future will not all be smooth sailing. We'll encounter problems and disappointments. One of our big challenges will be to keep our corporate culture as urgent, fresh, and compelling in the coming years as it was at the beginning of the company. Corporate culture is not a collection of slogans on the wall; it is a living entity and it needs tending—especially *our* culture, which is youthful, antiauthoritarian, risk-taking, and sometimes chaotic. We are no longer a young company, and we need to resist the kind of complacency and routine that often settle on companies in their middle years. We have to keep it lively. We need to keep it real.

This means protecting and defending the culture every day, living the values, and keeping the vision and mission in front of both the leadership and the associates at all times. It also means remembering that Grand Circle is truly The Great Company, filled with extraordinary people who have the courage to lead. We go to sleep at night confident that the company is in good hands. We're not perfect, that's for sure. We've tried to be honest about our many mistakes—some of them pretty big and expensive. Despite our missteps, we're incredibly proud of how far we've come.

Listen to the mustn'ts child,
Listen to the don'ts,
Listen to the shouldn'ts,
The impossible, the won'ts
Listen to the never haves
Then listen close to me—
Anything can happen, child,
Anything can be.
—Shel Silverstein

What "Changing People's Lives" *Really* Means

Alan and I have always had this idea of "helping change people's lives," but the idea has changed over the years. At first it was mostly about opening the door to travel, and then letting travel do the work. I remember my first trip abroad, when I was 21. I went to Europe and Turkey, and it was so eye-opening. Everything was so fascinating and so much fun. I stood in a bazaar on the Bosphorus, transfixed, and thought, "This is amazing. Everything looks and smells and tastes so different. The people are interested in me—I can tell—and I want to meet every one of them."

I wanted our travelers to feel that way, too. At the same time we had the idea that Grand Circle would be a different kind of company—so different that it would change our *associates'* lives, too, by challenging them to do more than they thought possible, and by demanding leadership from everyone.

Over time, the idea just got bigger and bigger. We began our personal practice of giving back to our community in Boston and later we encouraged our associates to do the same. Then, in 1992, we set up Grand Circle Foundation to help change the lives of people living in the places we visited. This wasn't so much an act of charity as an act of gratitude, because Grand Circle would never be so successful without the partnership of the people in our destinations: our overseas associates, our vendors, our Foundation partners, and the people who have welcomed our travelers and taught us so much.

In the last ten years or so we have set our sights even higher—not just opening people's eyes and helping out with donations to targeted projects, but partnering with whole communities to create sustainable change, and even to promote peace and global understanding.

This is the creative energy of a truly powerful vision. It can create ever widening circles of influence, and can achieve ever greater things.

—Harriet Lewis

We began this book by sharing our dream. We wanted to build a great travel company, but a *different* kind of company than we had seen in corporate America. We wanted to build a company where associates looked forward to coming to work, where people could grow and become leaders in the business and also in their personal lives. We wanted to deliver unforgettable experiences to our travelers at incredible values. And we wanted to help change people's lives in our company, in our community, and in the world.

Are we there yet? Not quite, but we've come close, and fully realizing our dream will remain our life's work.

The View from Here

Over the years, we have often envisioned ourselves in our 80s, rocking away on our porch at Beaver Dam in New Hampshire. We see ourselves talking to our grandchildren, telling them about our lives. We want to tell them that we've had a life well lived, we've taken every chance we had, we've laughed a lot and we've loved a lot, and we've made a difference.

We're now in our early 60s, and we find ourselves reflecting more deeply about our remaining years. Our planning has also become more purposeful. Writing this book has been important to us not only because it has become a repository of memories, but because we feel a responsibility to share, to teach, and to tell the story of a great company.

Telling the story of Grand Circle has reminded us of advice we continue to follow to this day: *Find and follow your passion … Be part of something bigger than yourself … Do something excellent … Dare to lead from wherever you are … Make mistakes … Make a difference.*

But if there is a single inspiration we'd like readers to take away from this book, it is this: *Dream big, gather a group of brave people around you, and then set out to change the world.*

It can be done.

Never doubt that a small group of thoughtful, committed citizens can change the world. Indeed, it is the only thing that ever has.

—Margaret Mead

The Lewis family in the barn at
Beaver Dam, N.H. November 2009.

Appendix

Company Profile

When we bought Grand Circle Travel in 1985, the company had 120 employees, 16,000 customers, and $27 million in sales. It was losing $2 million a year, but we knew it had potential.

Over the next 25 years, with the help of a cadre of amazing coaches and colleagues, we built Grand Circle into one of the most respected travel businesses in the industry. In 2010, we will serve more than 119,000 travelers, employ more than 2,200 people around the world, reach sales of $600 million, show a profit of $60 million, and have pledged or donated more than $50 million in philanthropy through our Grand Circle Foundation.

During the time we've owned the company, more than a third of U.S. travel providers have either merged with other companies or gone out of business. This book chronicles Grand Circle's remarkable growth and success through stories that explain our unique corporate culture, our business and leadership models, and our philosophy of incorporating philanthropy into our strategic plan for the company.

Business schools like Harvard and Babson have done case studies on our businesses to examine how we did it. The answer is simple—we have the best people in the industry. Here are some facts and figures that profile our success.

Company Sales

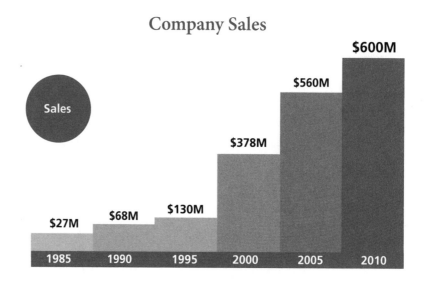

Travelers and Excellence

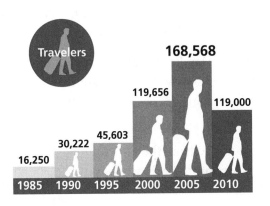

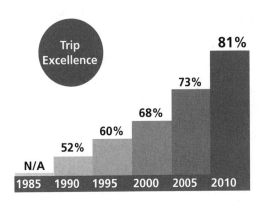

Associates and Foundation

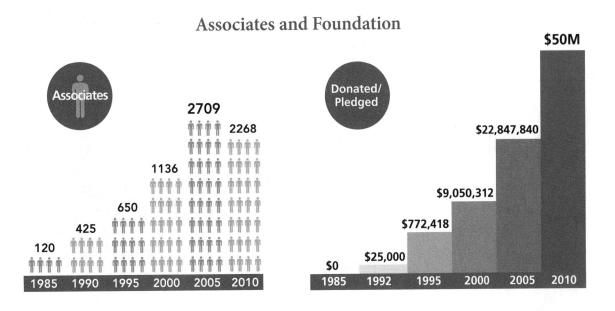

A Tradition of Excellence in Giving Back

Corporate Leadership

2007 • 2006 September — Cited as one of top 15 "Largest Corporate Charitable Contributors" in Greater Boston during the *Boston Business Journal's* annual Corporate Philanthropy Summit. Grand Circle also was ranked third in per-employee contributions at $4,578 in 2006 and was the only privately held corporation to place in the top 15 ranked companies.

2006 June — Grand Circle CEO Alan Lewis named Ernst & Young New England "Social Entrepreneur of the Year," recognized for leadership and innovation in philanthropy that includes more than $30 million in giving since 1992.

2006 February — Excellence Award from the Committee to Encourage Corporate Philanthropy (CECP). Founded by Paul Newman (Newman's Own) and Ken Derr (formerly of Chevron), CECP recognizes companies that demonstrate outstanding CEO commitment, dedication to measurement, and innovation in corporate philanthropy. Previous winners include: GE, Novartis, and Arch Chemicals (2004); Pfizer and Hasbro (2003); Target and Whole Foods (2002) and Timberland (2001); and Merck (2000).

Alan Lewis accepting the CECP Excellence Award.

2006 June — "25 Best Medium-Sized Companies to Work for in America" Awarded by Great Place to Work® Institute, Inc and Society for Human Resource Management. Recognized for unique corporate culture and innovative management strategies that create a successful organization with a highly productive and satisfied workforce.

As part of CECP's National Corporate Philanthropy Day festivities, Harriet Lewis (second from right), joined an impressive roster of CEOs for the ringing of the New York Stock Exchange's opening bell.

2005 June — *Boston Business Journal* "Best Places to Work." Top 20 in large company division.

Philanthropy

Grand Circle Foundation

2009 — West End House Boys & Girls Club Passport to Belonging Tribute, April 2009.

2006 — Citizenship Award Presented to Harriet Lewis by City on a Hill Public Charter School.

2004 — Neurofibromatosis Cornerstone Award In recognition of stalwart support of Neurofibromatosis, Inc., for more than two decades.

2004 —The New England Women's Leadership Award (NEWLA), "Circle of Giving" Award presented to Harriet Lewis In honor of women who have not only risen to positions of respect and influence, but have also given back to their communities.

2004 — Thompson Island Outward Bound North Star Award In recognition of extraordinary service to Boston youth, and for helping promote Thompson Island's mission.

2003 — UNESCO World Heritage Centre *Partners in Conservation* Program Grand Circle Foundation was chosen as UNESCO's first corporate partner in the Partners in Conservation Program.

2002 — AIDS Action Corporate Partner Award In recognition of courage, compassion, care, and longtime commitment to ending the AIDS epidemic.

2001 — Big Sister Association Achievement Award Presented in recognition of commitment to community service that helps others reach their dreams. Grand Circle Foundation was cited as a role model for corporate social responsibility.

2001 — Shelter, Inc., Recognition Award In recognition of longtime support of homeless families in Boston.

2000 — Hero of Philanthropy Award Given by the New England Chapter National Society of Fund Raising Executives in recognition of Corporate Philanthropy.

1998 — Thompson Island Founders' Award For dedication and leadership that has enriched the lives and improved the education of youth in need.

1996 — Save the Harbor/Save the Bay Founders' Award For environmental leadership.

Excellence in Travel

Grand Circle Small Ship Cruises

2008 December — World Travel Awards
Awarded World's Leading River Cruise Operator

2010, 2009, 2008, 2007, 2006 January—*Condé Nast Traveler* Gold List Grand Circle Small Ship Cruises—included in Gold List of "World's Best Cruise Lines."

2010, 2009, 2008, 2007, 2006 February — *Condé Nast Traveler* Cruise Poll (Individual Small Ship category)
2010: 10 ships rank in Top 50
2009, 2008 #1 Small Cruise Ship in the World: M/S *Bizet*
2009: 12 ships rank in Top 50
2008: 7 ships rank in Top 30

Grand Circle's worldwide fleet exclusively serves American travelers, and has been recognized for the meticulous service of its dedicated, English-speaking crews.

2009, 2008, 2007, 2006, 2005 November — Condé Nast Traveler Readers' Choice Awards—Grand Circle Small Ship Cruises rated among the Top 5 Small Ship Cruise Lines in the world.

2007 March — *Travel + Leisure* readers rank Grand Circle Small Ship Cruises #1 "Best Value Cruise Line."

2007 June — *Travel + Leisure* readers rate Grand Circle Small Ship Cruises in respective listings for "World's Best Service."

2009, 2008, 2007, 2006 July — *Travel + Leisure*'s World's Best Awards readers' survey ranks Grand Circle Small Ship Cruises in list of "Top 10 Best small ship Cruise Lines."

OAT's 50-passenger small ships, the M/V *Athena* (above), *Artemis* and *Arethusa*, have set a new standard of excellence for cruising the Mediterranean and the Red Sea.

Overseas Adventure Travel

2007 March — *Travel + Leisure* names OAT among the Top 3 "Best Value Tour Operator/Safari Outfitter."

2002-2006, 2008-2010 — *Travel + Leisure* **"World's Best Awards"** in the "Tour Operators and Safari Outfitters" category.

2006 May — **Humanitarian Award**, Presented by the Tanzanian Tourist Board to OAT for its support of rural schools in Tanzania. Through Grand Circle Foundation and OAT travelers, close to $100,000 has been donated toward local education efforts at five schools. Foundation support comes through the *World Classroom* initiative.

Our Honorary Directors

LEADERS WHO INSPIRE AND GUIDE US

Grand Circle Foundation's Honorary Directors have traveled the globe, summited the world's tallest mountains, led museums and universities, and received top honors in their fields. We are honored to benefit from the great example of leadership set by these exceptional men and women.

GRAND CIRCLE FOUNDATION HONORARY DIRECTORS

Angeles Arrien
Cultural Anthropologist, Author, Educator; President, Foundation for Cross-Cultural Education and Research

Through her diverse roles as an anthropologist, author, educator, and business consultant, Angeles Arrien maintains that certain values and beliefs transcend cultural barriers and encompass all of humanity. Her work has been embraced by medical professionals, academics, and corporations.

Willy Chambulo
Owner and Managing Director, Kibo Guides, Tanzania

An unforgettable character with a passion for his homeland and Maasai heritage, Willy Chambulo is a shining example of an entrepreneur who chose generosity over greed. He staffs his operations with local community members to help stimulate the economy, so his beloved country reaps the benefits of his success.

Lady June Hillary
Humanitarian; Chairman, The Himalayan Trust

Lady June Hillary shared her late husband Sir Edmund's passion for aiding the Sherpa people of the Himalayas. Since his passing in 2008, Lady June has assumed the role of Chairman of the Himalayan Trust, continuing the legacy of humanitarianism in Nepal that her husband began in the 1960s.

Dr. Robert Muller
*Former Assistant Secretary-General, United Nations; Recipient,
Albert Schweitzer International Prize for the Humanities, 1993*

Over his 40-year career at the United Nations, Dr. Muller focused his energies
on bringing peace to the world. He is the recipient of the Albert Schweitzer
International Prize for the Humanities, which is awarded to those who have made
extraordinary humanitarian contributions.

Ree Sheck
*Writer and Conservationist; Former Information Director, Monteverde
Conservation League*

Ree Sheck moved from New Mexico to Costa Rica in 1990 in order to work
full-time in rain forest conservation. She served as Information Director for the
Monteverde Conservation League, an internationally recognized grassroots
organization, and runs a foundation that supports schools in 15 communities.

Kazimierz Smolen
*Polish Resistance Fighter and Holocaust Survivor; Former Director, State
Museum at Auschwitz-Birkenau*

Poland's Auschwitz-Birkenau camp saw the deaths of an estimated four million
Jews—and among those who survived its horrors was Kazimierz Smolen. As part
of his life's work to educate future generations about the Holocaust, he returned to
the camp to serve as director of the State Museum there.

Lech Walesa
President of Poland, 1990-1995; Recipient, Nobel Peace Prize, 1993

Lech Walesa was the founder of the Solidarity movement that led Poland out of
Communism and inspired other revolutions in Central Europe in 1978. He later
served as President of Poland and was named one of the most influential people
of the 20th century by *Time* magazine.

Barbara Washburn
Mountaineer and Explorer; First Woman to Summit Mount McKinley

Barbara Washburn joined her late husband, Bradford Washburn, in mapping
and photographic expeditions that included Mount McKinley, the Grand Canyon,
Mount Everest, and the Matterhorn. A former teacher, she is member of many
charitable and educational groups dedicated to children.

In Memoriam
OUR FORMER HONORARY DIRECTORS

Dr. Rodrigo Carazo (1926–2009)

A lifelong advocate of peace and literacy in his home country and around the world, Dr. Rodrigo Carazo—former President of Costa Rica and one of the founding Honorary Directors of Grand Circle Foundation—passed away on December 9, 2009. "We have lost a dear friend, a great leader, and a rare individual who not only dared to dream of peace—but dared to take action towards his dream," say Alan and Harriet.

During a turbulent period in his country's history, Dr. Carazo founded the University for Peace, where he taught students from around the world about peaceful resolution to conflict and the preservation of our natural resources. Over the years, the Foundation has supported the University with donations totaling $100,000.

We honor the memory of Dr. Rodrigo Carazo through our ongoing commitment to education—both in his beloved Costa Rica, and at every *World Classroom* school around the world.

Bradford Washburn (1910–2007)

Bradford Washburn, a longtime friend of Grand Circle and one of Grand Circle's Founding Honorary Directors, passed away on January 10, 2007, at the age of 96.

Brad was a lifelong explorer with an amazing spirit of adventure. He dramatically advanced our understanding of the world's great mountain ranges. He led pioneering mapping and photographic expeditions from Mount McKinley to the Grand Canyon, Mount Everest to the Matterhorn. In keeping with the Foundation's mission, he was long dedicated to education: He was Director of Boston's Museum of Science for more than 40 years.

"Since the Foundation's creation in 1992, Brad and Barbara have helped guide us in our giving back," say Alan and Harriet. "We feel honored to have known such a passionate, adventurous man."

Sir Edmund Hillary (1919–2008)

Sir Edmund Hillary, who passed away on January 11, 2008, was the ultimate model of the values espoused by Grand Circle, with special emphasis on thriving in change and risk-taking. Sir Edmund often said of himself: "I really am an ordinary person with a few abilities which I've tried to use in the best way I can." He was among the first notables to grace Grand Circle Foundation Honorary Board when the Foundation was created in 1992.

For many, Sir Edmund is best known as the first to summit Mount Everest with Tenzing Norgay in 1953. While he is recognized as the first man to go up the mountain, Sir Edmund is admired for returning again and again to Nepal for his commitment to the Sherpa people, and for his leadership in environmental responsibility. He was responsible for the opening of 20 schools, four hospitals, and more than 10 clinics in the area. The Foundation has supported Sir Edmund's commitment to the Nepalese people and his Himalayan Trust.

"Sir Edmund has always been a great friend to us," say Alan and Harriet. "He was a true inspiration. He said that he was never satisfied with what he had accomplished; he felt that he could always do more. He was always looking for the next challenge. We both believe this as well."

Henry M. Morgan (1926–2002)

Before becoming Honorary Chair of Grand Circle Foundation, Henry Morgan served as Dean of the Boston University School of Management and as an executive with several companies—including Polaroid Corporation, where he established one of the first corporate diversity training programs in the U.S. He also served on the Board of Directors of as Ben & Jerry's Homemade Inc.

"Henry's life was so incredibly full," remember Alan and Harriet. "We will always admire him for the way he committed himself so fully to helping others. And while he was doing all these great things, he always seemed to be having fun. He was a real lover of life." This was evident in the halls of Grand Circle, where he always sported a jaunty bow tie and a smile. Those who were privileged to know Henry will never forget his warmth, energy, and commitment to making the world a better place—through his large vision, and in the small acts of kindness he bestowed on so many.

Lars-Eric Lindblad (1927–1994)

Lars-Eric Lindblad was a Swedish-American entrepreneur and explorer, who pioneered tourism to many remote and exotic parts of the world. He led the first tourist expedition to Antarctica in 1966 in a chartered Chilean navy ship, and for many years operated his own vessel, the M/S *Lindblad Explorer*, in the region. Observers point to the *Lindblad Explorer*'s 1969 expeditionary cruise to Antarctica as the forerunner to today's sea-based tourism there.

Nancy Anderson

Nancy Anderson was a passionate community advocate and ardent environmental activist. She served as an officer in the WAVES (Women Accepted for Volunteer Emergency Service) from 1944-1946. From 1975 to 1993 she played key leadership roles in various environmental programs associated with the Lincoln Filene Center at Tufts University. In 1979 she founded and later directed the New England Environmental Network, (NEEN). A decade after launching the NEEN, Nancy lent her expertise, voice and passion overseas where she founded the Eastern Africa Environmental Network.

Giving Back to the World We Travel

Region	Foundation Site	Country
Africa	Irkirit Primary School	Kenya
	Association for Handicap Peoples in Tingher	Morocco
	Dar ET-Taleb, Education Center	Morocco
	Jacob Basson Primary School	Namibia
	Esitjeni Primary School	Swaziland
	Banjika Secondary School	Tanzania
	Bashay Primary School	Tanzania
	Njia Panda Primary School	Tanzania
	Kambi Ya Nyoka Primary School	Tanzania
	Ngamo School	Zimbabwe
	Ziga School	Zimbabwe
Asia	Huo Kou Primary School	China
	De Ji Orphanage	China
	Shao Ping Dian Primary School	China
	Guang Ming Primary School	China
	LP Public School	India
	Adarsh Bal Vidhya Mandir	India
	Saini Adarsh Vidhya Mandir	India
	Laxmi Primary School	Nepal
	Baan Boonyapark Early Childhood Center	Thailand
	Machachulalongkorn Buddhist University	Thailand
	Mahamakut Buddhist University	Thailand
	Krorvan Primary School/Krorvan Village	Thailand
	Dien Phu Primary school	Vietnam
	Minh Tuorphage/Duc Son Pagoda	Vietnam
Australia	Sigatoka District School	Australia
	Yipirinya School	Australia
	Kaitao Middle School	New Zealand
Europe	Antun Masle Elementary School	Croatia
	Kinderdijk Windmills	Holland

Region	Foundation Site	Country
Europe	Chianciano Etruscan Museum	Italy
	Pompeii—World Monuments Fund Site Josefa Ortiz de Dominguez	Italy
	State Museum of Auschwitz-Birkenau	Poland
	Ataturk Primary School	Turkey
	Cumhuriyet Primary School	Turkey
	Ephesus	Turkey
	Hacibektas High School	Turkey
Middle East	Al Awada School	Israel
	Al Bayrouni School	Israel
	El Shohadaa School	Egypt
	Abu Bakr Experimental School	Egypt
	Wadi El Malekat School	Egypt
	Al Taref School	Egypt
	Saad Zaghlool School	Egypt
	Valley of the Kings—World Monuments Fund Site	Egypt
North America	Josefa Ortiz de Dominguez School	Mexico
Central America	San Josecito de Cutris School	Costa Rica
	San Francisco School	Costa Rica
	San Luis Pueblo Nuevo Primary School	Guatemala
	General Manuel Benigno Higuero Guardia School	Panama
	San Carlos Primary School	Panama
South America	La Concepcion School	Argentina
	Sinamune Disabled Children's Orchestra	Ecuador
	Pachar School	Peru
	Pucruto School	Peru
	Villa Marcelo Primary School	Peru
	Virgen de Fatima School	Peru
	Yanamono Clinic	Peru

A Summary of Crises We Have Faced

1985 Athens airport attacks, Jordanian airliner shot at during takeoff and TWA flight hijacked

1985 Hijacking of *Achille Lauro* cruise ship and murder of an American tourist on deck

1985 Air India Flight 182 crash; 329 killed in bombing over the Atlantic on flight between Canada and U.K.

1985 Earthquake in Mexico City; 10,000 killed, 250,000 homeless

1985 Rome and Vienna airport attacks; 19 killed, including 5 Americans

1986 U.S. air strike on Libya; major impact on U.S. travel abroad

1986 Chernobyl meltdown; 30 killed, 135,000 evacuated

1988 Pan Am Flight 103 bombed out of sky over Scotland; 270 killed

1989 Tiananmen Square protests; widespread condemnation halts tourism to China, five Grand Circle China products reduced to one

1991 War erupts in Yugoslavia; Grand Circle's top 1990 product wiped out as Slovenia and Croatia split from Serbia

1991 Iraq invades Kuwait

1992 U.S. war with Iraq; 40% of U.S. tour operators go under

1994 Rwanda genocide; top two OAT trips affected

1996 TWA Flight 800 crash out of JFK, 230 killed; widespread speculation on terrorism and safety of old aircraft

1997 60 tourists killed in Luxor, Egypt; our travelers choose to keep traveling in Egypt

1998 Bombing of U.S. embassies in Kenya and Tanzania

1998 Swiss Air Flight 111 down in suspicious circumstances off Nova Scotia

1998   OAT van accident, Scotland; several travelers hospitalized

1999   Kosovo/Bosnia conflict, Danube River closed to Black Sea; Grand Circle ships rerouted

1999   Bombing of Chinese embassy in Belgrade; diplomatic tensions rise

1999   Earthquakes in Turkey; travelers question safety in Istanbul

1999   EgyptAir Flight 990 crash, 54 GCC travelers killed

2000   Killings in Zimbabwe; we are the only U.S. operator to stay

2000   GCC traveler drowns off Great Barrier Reef

2000   World Cruise bankruptcy, GCT travelers abandoned in South Pacific; we fly travelers home and issue refunds

2000   "Flood of the Century" halts River Cruises on Danube

2000   Debussy ship accident, Lyon; 24 GCT passengers and 2 Program Directors hospitalized

2000   Coup in Fiji, racial tensions escalate; tourism declines but 7,000 GCT travelers continue to travel

2000   Crisis in Israel; we are the only U.S. operator to stay

2001   Hoof and mouth disease in U.K.; OAT programs continue to run

2001   Flooding on Rhone and Soane rivers; 2 Grand Circle river ships stuck in south of France

2001   9/11 terrorist attack on the United States, U.S. bombing of Afghanistan, anthrax scare; we suffer large layoffs and losses

2002   Bombing in Bali tourist district kills 202 people

2003   U.S. invasion of Iraq

2003   SARS epidemic curtails tourism in Asia

2004   Terrorist attacks in Spain

2004   Chechen terrorists take 1,200 schoolchildren and other hostages in Beslan, Russia; 340 people die

2004   Tsunami devastates South Asia

2005 Terrorist bombings in London; 52 killed, 700 wounded

2005 Earthquake in India kills more than 8,000 people

2006 Train bombings in Mumbai, India, kill 200 people

2006 North Korea fires test missiles over Sea of Japan, fueling fear in Asia

2007 Tribal violence in Kenya

2007 Coordinated bomb attacks in Thailand

2008 Worldwide financial crisis; markets plunge around the world curtailing travel for many Americans

2008 Terrorist attacks in India

2008 Earthquake in China kills 67,000 people

2009 Continued world economic crisis

2009 Air France Flight 447 disappears off Brazil with 228 passengers aboard

2009 Train bombing in Russia kills 26 people

2009 Attempted terrorist attack aboard NW Airlines Flight 253 by Nigerian man claiming to be with Al Qaeda

2010 Devastating earthquake in Haiti; 230,000 people killed

2010 Earthquake in Chile, mudslides in Peru

2010 Volcano in Iceland disrupts air travel across Europe

2010 Political unrest in Thailand

2010 Financial crisis in Greece, fall of euro

Keys To Leadership in a Crisis

1. **A Crisis is a Gift**
   - Moment of Truth
   - In Times of Difficulty—There is Always Opportunity

2. **Your Best Preparation is Your Culture**
   - Culture of Leadership
   - Values—Open and Courageous Communication, Risk Taking

3. **If You Do Not Emerge Stronger You Have Only Survived Not Succeeded**
   - You Missed the Opportunity

4. **Moments of Truth are the Best Leadership Test You Will Ever Get**
   - Some Leaders Will Fail—Move Them Out or Out of the Way
   - Some Leaders Will Excel—Recognize and Promote Fast
   - New Leaders Will Emerge—Move Them up Fast

5. **Act—Be On Your Toes vs. Your Heels**
   - Act Early
   - Act Aggressively
   - Act Often—Make Mistakes

6. **Get a Plan**
   - Fast
   - Focused
   - Get Alignment
   - Stay True to Core Business—Don't Scattershoot

7. **Secure Your Leadership Postion— Think 3–5 Years Ahead**
   - Extreme Competitive Advantages
   - Seize the Opportunity
   - The Window of Change is Only Open for a Short Time

8. **Overcommunicate**
   - The Facts
   - The Plan
   - The Results
   - The Mistakes

9. **Stop What Doesn't Work and Go Like Hell at What Does**
   - Measure your Results
   - Get Everyone on Same Page
   - Reassess and Change Course if Needed Based on Results
   - Celebrate Small Victories and Big Wins

10. **Know Your Lessons for Next Time**
    - There Will Be a Next Time

G.R.P.I. Process Model

Description and Use

This model provides a framework for diagnosing and improving team effectiveness. The model is hierarchical: start with goals; then allocate work/roles; then identify team processes; and finally, deal with personalities, style and cultural differences to minimize process loss by systematically working through each layer of team development.

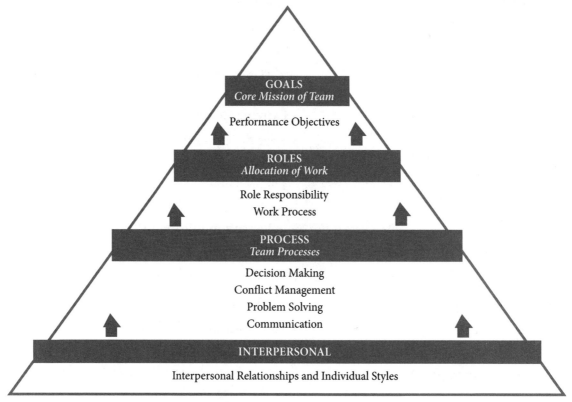

GOALS
Core Mission of Team

Performance Objectives

ROLES
Allocation of Work

Role Responsibility
Work Process

PROCESS
Team Processes

Decision Making
Conflict Management
Problem Solving
Communication

INTERPERSONAL

Interpersonal Relationships and Individual Styles

GOALS

1. Goals are clear and people are committed to them.   1 2 4 5

ROLES & RESPONSIBILITIES

2. The work is organized in a way which clearly leads to accomplishing the team's goals.   1 2 4 5

3. There is maximum use of the different resources of individuals on the team.   1 2 4 5

4. Everybody is clear on their responsibilities and jobs.   1 2 4 5

5. The leadership is shared.   1 2 4 5

Rate your team: 1 = Too little or to no extent
                  5 = To a great extent

PROCESS

6. Decisions are based on who has the expertise and best information, not on hierarchy or authority.   1 2 4 5

7. Conflict on the team is confronted openly and constructively.   1 2 4 5

INTERPERSONAL RELATIONSHIPS

8. There is trust and openness in communication and relationships.   1 2 4 5

9. Time is taken to examine our process (how we relate to each other, communicate, handle conflict, etc.) to improve the way we work.   1 2 4 5

10. Flexibility, sensitivity to the needs of others, creativity is encouraged.   1 2 4 5

GRPI Process Tool

The GRPI model can be used effectively as an assessment tool or as a planning model. Use the GRPI model sequentially, but consider the following ideas to probe the team's thinking and to add depth to the facilitation process.

Goals

- Where they defined, verbalized, and was there buy-in on goals?
- Clarity on goals vs. tasks
- Was the goal clear to all members? How did you know?
- Did the goals change? Why?
- Were goals from previous activities incorporated into these goals?
- Are you a learning team?

Roles

- List all roles (e.g. facilitator/coordinator/leader, timekeeper, process observer, ethics/quality reviewer, etc.)
- Did those roles have clear definition? Did they change? Why?
- Were members satisfied and comfortable in their roles?
- Were strengths and interests recognized and utilized in role acquisition?
- How was leadership being exerted?

Process

- Was there a process time-flow? Rate the balance of planning vs. implementation time.
- How were decisions made? What were the decision-making models? Was it a deliberate choice?
- Were schedule and agendas used effectively?
- Were multiple alternatives generated before action took place?
- Were adjustments made as the task progressed? Why? How?
- Did the team pause regularly to assess its progress and quality?

Interpersonal

- Were all skill sets recognized?
- Was the climate conducive to freedom to express opinions? Did anyone have anything left unsaid at the end? How does the team know?
- Is the team stronger as a team after the task?
- Was there effective listening? Give examples.

Editorials and Articles

USA TODAY

Destinations & Diversions

By Jayne Clark, April 5, 2002

CAIRO — She had defied her adult children and ignored the protestations of friends, endured a 22-hour journey and the bone-crushing weariness of crossing 10 time zones. And now, sitting here at a table laden with crisp falafel and roasted lamb on a boat in the Nile, she had no regrets.

"I told my son that if anything happens, just write on my tombstone, 'Died Happy in Egypt,'" said Barbara Windt of Culver City, Calif.

Windt's 113 travel companions on a two-week guided tour of the tombs and treasures of ancient Egypt were of like mind, even as reports of suicide bombers and anti-American attacks elsewhere in the Middle East became fodder for nightly dinner conversation. Indeed, the group's very presence in a region that post-9/11 sensibilities—rightly or wrongly—deem a potential hot spot, signal that, gradually, American travelers are overcoming the fears that kept them grounded in the months following the terrorist attacks on New York and Washington.

And so-called senior travelers appear to be leading the charge. At Grand Circle Travel (the former travel arm of the AARP), which caters to the over-50 market, the greatest growth in business since September is among those 65 and older. After laying off 160 of 500 Boston-based staffers during the post-Sept. 11 slump, when business dropped 40%, the phones began ringing again in mid-December. In the first quarter of 2002, bookings ran 30% ahead of last year. And not just to domestic havens, either. Exotic, far-flung locales such as India, Morocco and Egypt are suddenly back in demand, company officials say.

Perched on the top deck of a Nile River cruise ship, retired university professor Don Ray had no trouble explaining his decision to visit Israel and Egypt last month.

"I'm old enough to know better, but young enough not to resist," said the 67-year-old Tucson, Ariz., resident.

Indeed, tour operators who cater to older travelers report that not only is business returning to normal levels, but elders are venturing to some unexpected places.

"It's surprising," said Karl Kannstadter of the Toronto-based adventure travel company ElderTreks. "Part of it is pent-up demand, but six months have gone by (since Sept. 11) and people are starting to feel comfortable again."

Operators ranging from the non-profit, education-oriented Elderhostel to upscale Abercrombie & Kent echo the sentiment.

Grand Circle continued its Egypt itinerary throughout the fall and winter (it expects to send 2,200 travelers there by year's end), although departures were cut from four to two per month. The company also has sent 185 clients to Israel since September. Other companies have taken a more conservative stance on so-called hot spots, however. Elderhostel has suspended trips to Egypt, Jordan and Israel for the foreseeable future. ElderTreks canceled its spring tour to Nepal because of a lack of bookings and also dropped trips to Indonesia and a Silk Road itinerary, which was to depart from Pakistan. But other exotic and sometimes troubled spots such as Peru and India remain popular.

Grand Circle chairman Alan Lewis credits the willingness to travel in uncertain times to the broader perspective of many older travelers.

"These are people with tremendous resilience. They've been through a ton— World War II, the Korean War, the Gulf War. They want to follow their dreams, and they're not going to let anyone stop them from doing what they want to do."

Discounts and liberalized cancellation policies are helping to fuel the rebound. But so, too, is the willingness of intrepid seniors to set off for the unknown. Their children are grown, they have more time and money at their disposal and they're willing to accept risks.

The American group of mostly sixty- and seventysomethings that embarked on a mid-March sweep through Cairo and up the Nile with Grand Circle, supports the notion. They traveled mostly in pairs and sported solidly American names— Beck, Collins, Craft. They came from solidly American places—Peoria, Duluth, Buffalo.

Some were seasoned travelers. Others were not. At the orientation in a conference room at Cairo's Ramses Hilton, program director Tarek El Saadi delivered the usual admonitions. Don't drink the water. Negotiate the fare before getting in the cab. When using an ATM, the money will come out in Egyptian pounds, not U.S. dollars.

"You're in Egypt," he reminded, dryly.

Downplaying safety concerns

Earlier, over breakfast, Ted Esteves, 71, and his wife, Connie, 69, downplayed safety concerns.

"Anything can happen. Even at home," Connie Esteves said, indicating the angry gash under her eye, where she caught a line drive on the golf course before leaving her Boca Raton, Fla., home.

Added her husband, "At our age, we've got to start taking some risks if we want to see the world. There's trouble all over."

Outside the restaurant, two tourist police relaxed curbside, leaning against their automatic weapons as casually as if they were umbrellas. The police presence in and around Egyptian tourist haunts is as ever present as the dry, desert winds. They stand sentry outside hotels, museums, Pharaonic temples and pyramids, where passing through metal detectors is now part of the price of admission. Plainclothes tourist police take the front seat on tour buses, the butts of their automatic weapons poking against the backs of their suit coats like some horrific growth.

The government-issued escorts, strapping young Egyptians in natty (and unseasonably warm) suits, accompanied the Grand Circle clients at a discreet distance as they toured Cairo's gritty streets and the nearby pyramids at Giza. They boarded the river ship that carried the tourists farther south as they worked their way up the Nile to the Valley of the Kings at Luxor and beyond.

Their presence had some travelers considering unanticipated points of etiquette: Do you invite your personal tourist cop to join you for breakfast? Is tipping advised? Is casual chitchat OK?

The Egyptian government beefed up security after 58 foreign tourists were killed in a 1997 attack by Islamic militants at Queen Hatshepsut's Temple in Luxor. The "accident," as Egyptians refer to it, decimated tourism for a time. But by 2000, revenues hit a record $4.3 billion, making tourism the No. 1 source of foreign currency. Though 2001 totals fell after 9/11, the government is determined to protect this lucrative industry.

The heavy security presence is meant to quell visitors' anxieties in a country already dogged by its proximity to Middle Eastern turmoil and travelers' sometimes-shaky grasp of geography, said Egypt's Tourism Minister Mamdouh El Beltagui. (After all, many don't know Giza from Gaza, he said with a laugh.) However, key security measures are invisible to tourists, he added.

Either way, Americans seem unperturbed by the hired guns, particularly since Sept. 11, said Nabil Labib, an Egyptologist who escorts American tourists. "They appreciate it. They know it's not (to protect them) from street crime, but from terrorists."

Many layers of history

In fact, Cairo's most ominous threat to the uninitiated is the traffic.

"Driving over here isn't like anywhere else," explained program director Ihab Kamel, as passengers on his tour bus flinched and winced at the dangerous dance of dodge 'em playing outside against a backdrop of graceful mosques and soulless concrete apartment blocks lining the road into central Cairo. "You'll find it strange and amusing."

More like bewildering and terrifying. Cars dart over the asphalt to the beat of screeching rubber and blaring horns. Lane markers in this manic city of 15 million are purely decorative. Tour members wouldn't be driving, of course. Few, in fact, would even be walking, at least in Cairo, where crossing the street requires an act of faith.

"Can you imagine escorting 114 people over there?" asked Labib, motioning to the Egyptian Museum, within clear view of the group's hotel. "It would take hours!"

Indeed, one of the advantages of group-tour travel is that it reduces the hassles endemic to going it solo. Participants were relieved of chores such as hefting luggage, negotiating fares and navigating streets. The days progressed according to schedule as they paraded from one monolithic and unfathomably ancient marvel to the next. Moving in tandem from the Sphinx at Giza to the forestlike columns at Karnak to the Nubian temples of Abu Simbel, knowledgeable and affable Egyptian guides breathed life into 4,000-year-old antiquities.

But by necessity, group tours diminish spontaneity. And being squired by guides who focus on the extraordinary can obscure the wonder of the ordinary.

On Day 7, after the river ship docked in Aswan, at least one passenger ducked out of the evening's Egyptian theme party in the ship's lounge and struck out along the broad, white corniche leading into the city. Weary of group dynamics, Marillyn Morningstar, a free-spirited artist from Lake Havasu City, Ariz., (and probably the only passenger sporting seven tattoos) headed for the grand Moorish- style Old Cataract Hotel where Agatha Christie wrote part of *Death on the Nile*. Granted entrance after assuring several guards she was only stopping in for a drink and a look around ("How long will you be?" "Where are you from?" they grilled), she was invited to leave the hotel's lovely (and empty) Nile-side terrace after declining to spend a minimum tab.

"First time I've been kicked out of a hotel when I wasn't even drinking," quipped the 75-year-old.

Morningstar found a more collegial greeting behind the curtained entrance of a beauty shop tucked amid the narrow alleyways of Aswan's bustling souk. There, proprietor Shady El Saher (Drawing Hena Making a TATTO—Best Wishes, reads his card) deftly free-handed a temporary henna design on her arm, produced fresh cucumber pulp to treat a black eye suffered earlier in the trip and demonstrated the amazing art of Middle Eastern hair removal, using a simple loop of thread.

Past is present

A dinner arranged in private homes, a standard feature on the Grand Circle tour, allowed visitors some commercial-free interaction with well-off Cairo residents. At one such dinner in the gilded and tufted apartment of a Cairo physician, his wife and three children, the parents laid out a fabulous feast of home-cooked specialties while the kids mingled. One son, Shady El Sherif, 24, has attended enough of these affairs to anticipate Americans' questions.

"They ask, 'Do you have a microwave?' Then, 'Do you have a dishwasher?' And I want to say, 'Did you ride in on a camel or something?' "

But past is present in much of rural Egypt. Farmers consult the ancient Egyptian calendar to sow their crops. In Luxor, archaeological detritus lies half buried along the remains of a 4,000-year-old avenue that linked Luxor Temple to the Karnak complex two miles away.

It was near Luxor at the Colossi of Memnon, two six-story sandstone statues, that Donna West, 56, of Baltimore, shook Egyptian President Hosni Mubarak's hand in a chance encounter. The presidential motorcade paused, and Mubarak emerged to congratulate workers on recently completed restorative work on the 3,400-year-old behemoths. Someone in the crowd cried, "USA," and the president thrust his hand forward, grasping West's, among others.

"It was better than the camel ride," she declared.

Days later, back in Cairo in the lobby of the Ramses Hilton, a newly arrived tour group wore the dazed look of the jet-lagged.

Yes, their friends and families had reservations about the trip. No, they never considered canceling. And yes, they said, they did believe they'd have a fine time in Egypt.

TRAVEL WEEKLY

Philanthropy works
Op-Ed Submitted to Travel Weekly, March 13, 2006

I applaud *Travel Weekly* for it recent coverage of philanthropy in the travel industry. With the exception of this publication and a couple of consumer travel magazines, there's been very little coverage about our industry's efforts—and obligation—to give back to the countries we explore. This is unfortunate because many in our industry, such as Micato Safaris, Lindblad Expeditions, International Expeditions, and others have "given back," whether through charitable organizations or conservation efforts.

There is much more we can all do, but few travel leaders understand how their companies can actually benefit by making philanthropy a core part of their business.

I had the privilege of discussing some of these ideas to Encourage Corporate Philanthropy. From our industry, Marilyn Carlson Nelson, of the Carlson Cos., serves on the CECP's board of directors.

These days, with our media blaring stories about Enron greed, Capitol Hill influence peddling, and cruise ships literally losing passengers overboard, it's no wonder that corporate America sorely needs to redeem itself in the eyes of the public. America needs inspired thinking and funding to impact social issues we care about. We in the travel industry with our global reach, are in a unique position to lead the charge. To travel executives who think corporate philanthropy is just a nice APR gesture to be addressed only after the bottom line has been served, I say that philanthropy is not just about good works. It's good business.

My own experience with Boston-based Grand Circle Corp. is proof that when you make corporate giving a core part of your business strategy, profitability will follow.

When my wife, Harriet and I acquired Grand Circle in 1985, we made philanthropy and community service part of our corporate culture. We attracted associate who were motivated not just by their compensation but also by the desire to be part of something greater than themselves. We engaged everyone in the company (from top to bottom) plus our suppliers and community partners in programs in which we all had a personal stake. Last year, 94% of our associates in Boston and scores of associate around the world involved themselves in one or more of our philanthropic activities.

I believe that making philanthropy a core part of our business has been crucial to our success. Guess what? We've grown from a company with 10 associates and $27 million in sales to an international corporation with projected 2006 sales of $700 million and 3,000 associates in 45 offices.

Our philanthropic efforts greatly influence our ability to attract and retain some of the most talented associates in the industry as well as the most loyal customers. The competitive edge has enabled us to thrive for 29 years. In fact, I am convinced it is what allowed us to achieve a record year in the volatile post-9/11 period, a time when so many of our industry either suffered great losses, were forced to merge or went out of business.

Grand Circle's humble origins attest to the fact that you needn't be a Fortune 500 company to have your philanthropic efforts succeed. You just need to approach it strategically. We established the nonprofit Grand Circle Foundation in 1992 to manage all of our philanthropic programs, and we apply metrics to it just as we do with any of our travel operations.

Our overseas staffs establish partnerships with communities in the paths of our travelers, developing programs that give something back to those communities.

So I ask you, what communities does your company visit? What is your company doing to support those places? How are you engaging your associates? How are you serving the causes your customers care about?

Once you start asking yourself those questions, you will reinvigorate your business and begin to view corporate philanthropy not as an added cost but as the privilege of success. We can help change people's lives for the better and truly bring this world a little closer. In fact, it should be our first order of business.

Alan Lewis is chairman of Grand Circle Corp., which was recently honored with the CECP's Excellence Award for corporate philanthropy.

Boston Business Journal

Lesson Learned from Haiti: Partner With Customers To Make a Difference
Op-Ed Submitted to the Boston Business Journal, *February 18, 2010*

Human response to the recent earthquake in Haiti offers a critical lesson to U.S. companies in social entrepreneurship and philanthropy: make it easy and attractive for customers to give, and they will respond. The ability of people to make five-dollar donations through text messaging on their cell phones raised more than $25 million for the Red Cross in less than ten days. At our own travel company, we e-mailed our customers pledging to match their donations to the Red Cross and received $47,000 in the first three hours and a total of $395,453 during a two-week campaign. Most of the 4,282 people who gave are retirees and donated small amounts of $10 or $20, but their contributions, boosted by a match, can make a difference.

Despite the economy, humans continue to be generous beings, especially during times of crisis. We give what we can. But we are busy and much more likely to respond when we're presented with opportunities that make it easy and attractive to take out our checkbooks or fire up our PCs to give online.

We believe that business leaders have an opportunity to respond to human generosity by implementing programs that facilitate customers' inclination to help. These might include offering full or partial donation matches, creating collaborative volunteer activities, or establishing channels through which they can donate. The programs that businesses put in place should avoid creating another layer of bureaucracy to the donation process and be free of overhead or administrative fees. Our experience has taught us that an incentive to give, such as a matching program, may entice a customer to give in the first place and may even motivate him to give more than he had originally considered. After all, we all want to stretch the value of our dollar these days and for our donations to be as impactful as possible.

With thousands of businesses in New England and the ability to use technology and the web to donate quickly, we believe that we have a great opportunity to increase the philanthropic donations that we as a region make at home, nationwide, and around the world. Companies with a loyal customer base of people who trust and connect with them can offer simple ways to give back—immediately, during times of crisis, or more strategically when dealing with long-term social issues at home or abroad. The giving doesn't have to happen on a major level; families and businesses are feeling the pinch these days, but those $10 donations quickly add up, especially when matched by companies, and we can achieve much more together than we can by going it alone.

The philosopher Lao Tzu said, "The journey of a thousand miles begins with one step." Even a few small steps taken by a few more business leaders here in New England can make a difference to people in need. All we have to do is set the wheels in motion: we can always count on human generosity to move us forward.

Social Entrepreneurs Will Lead the Way
September 11–17, 2009 Volume 29, Number 33

There are two quotes that resonate with us during these challenging times. They come from two men who couldn't be more different. The first is from renowned physicist Albert Einstein who stated, "In the middle of difficulty there is always opportunity." The second is from Alan's dad, a WWII veteran and lifelong fighter for the underdog who became an "unconventional" businessman. It was he who advised Alan that "the window of opportunity is only open a short time, so you need to push as much change through it as fast as you can. And don't blow it."

These messages are particularly relevant to us today because we believe that our generation is in the midst of a rare opportunity. The world economic downturn has fundamentally changed all of our landscapes—political, social, and economic, and presented us with an exciting challenge: how do we go forward?

Few leaders can rise above times of turmoil in order to recognize opportunity. In the past, it has typically been one sector—either business, government or nonprofit, that has emerged to lead us during times of social or economic transformation. Today, none of these institutions can dominate. Each is too slow to handle the challenges we face and too resistant to fundamental change.

We believe it will be social entrepreneurs, a new breed of leaders, who will guide us. Here at home, they'll be the ones to provide the jobs, the vision and the blueprint to make Massachusetts better, including effecting critical improvements in our inner cities.

Who are social entrepreneurs? They are mavericks, leaders from all sectors. They take more risks and make more mistakes than most. They combine sensible business practices with out-of-the-box thinking to solve significant social problems. They differ from philanthropists in that they commit their leadership and expertise to causes, not just their money.

Massachusetts can claim social entrepreneurs from all sectors. We honor progressive CEOs through our Lewis Family CEO Social Leadership Award, including this year's recipient Joel Lamstein, co-founder and president of John Snow, Inc., and we respect such other strong social entrepreneurs as Len Schlesinger of Babson College, Robert Lewis of StreetSafe, Susan Rodgerson of Artists for Humanity, and this newspaper's publisher, whose annual CEO Corporate Philanthropy Summit has inspired scores of CEOs to get involved.

Many business leaders we've met with recently believe it's just a matter of time before things go back to the way they were. Most nonprofit leaders today, however well intended, operate with outdated models that are inefficient and ineffective. And government trudges along, often wasteful and without the ability or opportunity to think collaboratively.

We have to change—there's no way around it. In this new era, it will be social entrepreneurs who will lead the way, if we help them. Let's partner with them to find solutions to critical social problems. Let's work together to push as much change as we can through the window while it's open. This is our moment in history. Let's not blow it.

—Alan and Harriet Lewis

Entrepreneurs need mentoring in philanthropy
December 1–7, 2000 Volume 20, Number 43

A recent report by Catalogue of Philanthropy puts Massachusetts taxpayers at the very bottom in terms of individual giving.

While our corporations do better—ranking 14th nationally, according to the foundation Center in Washington, D.C.—critics have pointed out that in a state with the third highest per-capita income, individuals and businesses a like are falling far short of what they should be doing.

Much of the criticism targets entrepreneurial companies and the so-called "dotcom millionaire." In my opinion, philanthropy should be part of the entrepreneur's vision from the beginning, but the commitment needs to grow as the company does.

One of the most philanthropic things a company can do in its first five years is to grow and thrive. It should get established and create jobs. Once a company has sturdy underpinnings, then more limited philanthropic efforts should become a comprehensive, long-term strategy that makes giving back an integral part of the business enterprise.

This move from individual vision to corporate reality can be difficult. I have seen many young companies struggle while earnest in their desire to be philanthropic. This is where more mature companies can and should play an invaluable role. We can demonstrate by both advice and example how young companies can develop an authentic giving program that is more than mere marketing.

To be most effective, philanthropy needs to be strategic. This means your charitable contributions should serve the long-term best interests of your company. How you define those interests, of course, is key. Many companies feel that by contributing to an organization that serves their target markets, they may project a more favorable image to current or prospective customers and improve financial performance. I would argue that such "cause marketing" is quite different from true philanthropy.

I believe that a company's philanthropic commitment should focus on causes that hold genuine meaning for the company and its employees and express the values that spring from the heart and should of your enterprise. Supporting organizations and programs that intrinsically mean something to you will encourage you to stick with them over the long haul and, thereby, have the best shot at doing the most good.

The overall notion of philanthropy needs to become part of a company's corporate culture. An effective way to do that, we've found, is not only to encourage employees to volunteer their time to the organizations we support, but also to tell us what causes they want us to support in the first place. By doing this, all are involved with a mission much larger than the business enterprise. This kind of philanthropic commitment helps attract and retain good employees, which is especially important in today's tight labor market.

I also believe it is wise to extend your philanthropy into every corner that your business touches, not just your home base. As a travel company, we support organizations in the destinations where we take our customers. It helps make us more welcome in the communities we visit, and seeing these projects enriches our travelers.

Perhaps most important is to understand when you and the organizations you support understand each other. Bringing representatives from your beneficiaries together withy you in a community advisory group or similar forum will help your company learn how to apply philanthropy most effectively, while helping your philanthropic partners secure the most useful resources. Such a forum also encourages nonprofits to learn from one another. And it enables you to provide advice and skill sets that nonprofits may need as badly as funding.

There are countless organizations and programs that are worthy of support. But simply writing a check is not the answer. Companies need to make philanthropy a part of their day-to-day business. They need to ensure that their contributions resonate with their employees. And they need to learn how best to serve as a supportive partner in what should become a longterm relationship.

The corporations and entrepreneurs that have established successful philanthropic programs owe it to their younger counterparts to share the lessons we have learned. Just as we help the deserving nonprofit, so we must offer leadership and support to fellow businesses seeking to get fledgling philanthropic programs off the ground. Going beyond marketing to true philanthropy has only one prerequisite, and that, beginning at the top and extending through all levels of your organization, is the willingness and the commitment to try.

Alan Lewis is chief executive officer and owner of Grand Circle Corp., a provider of international discovery and adventure travel for Americans over the age of 50.

BOSTON Herald

ERNST & YOUNG ENTREPENEUR OF THE YEAR; NEW ENGLAND 2006; SOCIAL ENTREPRENEUR Award recipient; Lewis sees giving as 'a core strategy'

By Fran Golden, June 16, 2006

Alan E. Lewis, chairman and chief executive of Boston-based Grand Circle Corp., has a message for corporate America: "Make giving a core strategy."

Why?

"It's good for business," Lewis said.

Most CEOs are confused about charitable contributions, said Lewis, 57. "They're not sure why they're giving; who they're serving first."

According to Lewis, the key reason to give is not just to make a company look good to its customers and stockholders but to cultivate a work force that wants to make a difference in the world. And can.

Lewis and his wife and vice chairwoman, Harriet, acquired Grand Circle in 1985. At the time, it was a $23 million firm serving members of the AARP (American Association of Retired Persons).

The Lewises have expanded Grand Circle into the world's leader in international travel for those age 50-plus.

In 1993, they expanded with the acquisition of Overseas Adventure Travel and by launching a small ships division—now with a fleet of 50 small ships.

Grand Circle's revenues in 2006 are expected to top $700 million. The company does nearly all its business through direct marketing. It has some 3,000 employees in 45 offices around the world.

In 1992, the Lewises formed the Grand Circle Foundation, donating 5 percent of GCC's after-tax revenues. Some $35 million in charitable giving has resulted.

In an interview at the company's Congress Street headquarters—where the entranceway is papered with postcards from around the world—Lewis said charitable giving has been an important factor in Grand Circle's success and growth, including allowing the firm to attract a certain type of employee.

"They really feel this is an organization that is trying to make the world a better place," Lewis said.

Money from the foundation goes to support humanitarian, cultural and environmental causes in communities where Grand Circle has offices and sends travelers—from Boston to Botswana.

Grand Circle employees are involved in the foundation's giving choices.

"It's not Alan and Harriet choosing the projects," Lewis said.

Big beneficiaries have included the Himalayan Trust, the Museum of Auschwitz-Birkenau in Poland, Thompson Island Outward Bound and Artists for Humanity in Boston.

Since 1992, GCC employees, too, have caught the giving bug and contributed more than 28,000 hours of volunteer service to local and international causes.

Lewis himself supports employee efforts. At the time of our interview he was complaining of feeling the effects of participating in a 92-mile Best Buddy bike ride.

"Being an entrepreneur is nothing. I've been an entrepreneur my whole life," Lewis said. "I don't get excited about that. Give me someone who's socially responsible and I get excited, because they can really make a difference."

The foundation's honorary board of directors includes Sir Edmund Hillary, the international explorer; Dr. Rodrigo Carazo, the former president of Costa Rica; and Nobel Peace Prize winner and former president of Poland, Lech Walesa.

Lewis said he believes there is "confusion" in corporate America on how to give back, "yet many in corporate America do really want to give."

And he said one important thing he's learned from his efforts is how important it is to teach people to be charitable. "It's so rewarding for them," he said.

"My real passion is I'd like to help change corporate America, and I do think the great leaders of this century will not be in politics, they will be in business."

He said successful leaders will get their worldwide work force involved in giving, not as something just off to the side. "It will be a core strategy and it really will make a difference around the world."

Fran Golden is the Herald's *travel editor.*

Glossary

To the uninitiated, the language of Grand Circle can seem to be a quagmire of jargon and slang. Here are some helpful translations:

AARP – American Association of Retired Persons. A nonprofit membership organization for people over the age of 50, founded by Grand Circle's founder, Ethel Andrus.

A Day in the Life – An initiative of Grand Circle Foundation, the *Day in the Life* experience for our travelers links school visits with authentic, hands-on cultural exchanges with the local community. The *Day in the Life* occurs on most OAT itineraries and includes a school visit, a walking tour of the village or town, an in-home meal with the students' families, a visit to a local entrepreneur, and a visit to a community center or senior center.

Associate – Term used for the people who work for Grand Circle Corporation.

BND – Booked Not Departed. Travelers who have booked a trip but have not yet departed.

Boston Excellence – Also known as Pre-Trip Excellence. A score given to us by our travelers on their post-trip surveys; it reflects the quality of their experience with Traveler Support, Telesales, and the Web, as well as the speed of delivery and quality of the information they receive from the Pre-Trip department (itineraries, airline tickets, etc.).

Brand – The company offers its trips within two primary brands: Overseas Adventure Travel (OAT) & Grand Circle Travel (GCT). Within those brands are five types of vacations: OAT Land, OAT Small Ship, GCT Land, GCCL River Cruises.

BusinessWorks® – Renamed in 1995, our annual BusinessWorks program reflects and supports our "lead from anywhere" management philosophy. BusinessWorks involves a series of physical and intellectual challenges designed to improve business and organizational literacy, identify and develop leadership ability, build teamwork and trust, and creatively connect our core values to business results.

Call Center – Located on the third and fourth floors of our Boston headquarters, the Call Center is where our Travel Counselors take telephone calls from our travelers to help them book their next vacation.

Call Pathing – The ability to automatically direct certain types of calls to specific associates.

Charlie Ritter Award – This award is presented to the Boston associate who best exemplifies support of our worldwide offices and regional associates. Award is presented annually with nominations coming from our regions.

Customer Renewal – The rate at which previous travelers rebook with GCC. Also known as "loyalty," customer renewal is at the heart of GCC's success.

Daily Bookings Report – Our daily report of the traveler count, including new bookings, cancellations, and revenue, broken down by program and segment.

Departure – The date when a trip begins.

Dom Air – Domestic Air Travel. Internal flight from a traveler's hometown to GCC's "gateway city" of departure.

Drop Date – The day a promotional mailing enters the mail stream of the U.S. Postal Service.

Enhancements – Elements of the travel package that "enhance" the experience, such as exclusive discovery series events, cocktail parties, and destination guides.

Excellence in Service Award – Given monthly, this award honors associates who demonstrate outstanding performance, exemplify our values, and show great commitment to our travelers and colleagues.

Executive Team – The senior management team that guides the company. Includes the CEO, CFO, Executive Vice President's of Marketing, Worldwide Operations, and People and Culture.

Extreme Competitive Advantages – Six core strategies, usually developed in response to company Moments of Truth that are designed to keep the organization clearly focused on goals and strategies in times of great change.

FT – Former Traveler. Someone who has traveled with GCC before (rather than a Prospect) but who does not have enough trips to quality as an Inner Circle member.

Feedback – Constructive comments, both strengths and areas to improve, given from one person to another in the interest of developing better communication and performance.

Final Docs – All tickets, passes, and final itinerary information a traveler receives before leaving on one of our programs.

Four Product Pillars – The four foundations around which all GCC trips are designed: Value, Choice, Pacing, and Discovery.

GBD – Our Good Buy Plan. GBD guarantees a traveler's trip price and saves the traveler up to 10 percent of the cost of the trip. The earlier a traveler pays in full, the greater the savings. No other travel company in the business guarantees the trip price and offers savings up to 10 percent when the traveler pays early.

GCCL – Grand Circle Cruise Lines, known formally as the Grand Circle Small Ship Cruise Lines.

GCF – Grand Circle Foundation. Established by Harriet and Alan Lewis in 1992, Grand Circle Foundation is dedicated to supporting the education of young people and the preservation of cultural treasures and traditions all over the world. Since its inception, the Foundation has pledged or donated more than $50 million worldwide.

GERT – The electronic brains (actually a computer program) behind our booking operation. GERT contains information about our travelers' trip history, booked trips, and contact information. The acronym stands for Grand Circle Enters Revolutionary Technology. She was named through an associate contest.

GRPI – A rating and team-development model used at the beginning and end of meetings to provide a framework for diagnosing and improving team effectiveness. The method starts with Goals, then moves on to Roles, Process, and finally, Interpersonal. Questions are answered based on a finger shoot from 1 to 5, with 1 being the lowest. In keeping with the company's philosophy of Open and Courageous Communication, no 3s are allowed— there is no "medium" or "average" response to any issue or condition.

Gateway City – A city that serves as a departure or arrival point for international flights.

Grand Circle LLC – The umbrella organization that comprises GCT, OAT, and GCCL.

Ground – Any portion of a trip that takes place on land, as opposed to air or water.

Group Leaders – Travelers who bring groups of 15 or more fellow travelers with them on our trips. As the 16th member of the group, Group Leaders travel free.

Gutsy Leader – Because true leadership can come form anywhere, a Gutsy Leader is a traveler, community leader, associate, Trip Leader, honorary director, or village member who humbles us with acts of generosity. It takes guts to change the world, and our leaders are helping to do so, each in their own unique way.

Harriet's Corner – A special place on Grand Circle's website where Harriet Lewis shares her favorite travel experiences and where travelers get to share theirs, too. Harriet makes regular updates to her journal, and presents videos, news, and views from and about our travelers.

Harriet's Corner 3D – Located in our Boston headquarters, this spacious and comfortable meeting room provides space for our travelers to gather for meetings with our associates, as well as for presentations, department meetings, and social gatherings. The room is brightly decorated with memorabilia from Harriet's lifetime of worldwide travel.

Hold the Pole – To be responsible for sticking to a strategy or a key business decision.

Home City – Where a traveler will depart from to go to the Gateway City for an international flight. A traveler whose Home City is Providence may have a Gateway City of Boston for a flight to Rome.

Honey Streit-Reyes Award – Named for our own living legend, who has worked tirelessly to create unforgettable experiences for our travelers, this award is given annually to an outstanding Regional Associate whose passion and commitment to create unforgettable experiences and learning opportunities has truly helped change our travelers' lives.

Hot Issue – An issue that acts as a barrier affecting the ability to move or advance the business. A Hot Issue typically involves Top People, Top Product, or a Top Vendor. Hot Issues affect our ability to deliver the highest quality product to our travelers.

Inner Circle (IC) Club Member – A frequent traveler who has completed three or more Grand Circle trips in a lifetime.

Invest in a Village – Building upon the foundation laid by the *World Classroom* and *A Day in the Life*, the *Invest in a Village* program is supported by Grand Circle Foundation, which works closely with village leaders to make meaningful, sustainable changes in their communities. To date, the Foundation has focused much of its giving on schools, which are typically at the heart of a village. Now, it is broadening its efforts to have a bigger impact on the village as a whole.

KRAs – Key Result Areas. The primary components of a job in which associates are accountable for specific, measurable results.

LEA – Leadership Effectiveness Assessment. A diagnostic tool for describing how a person is likely to perform in leadership situations. LEAs are used in our hiring and training processes.

LEAD Trip – A training trip designed for company leaders which allows them to experience GCC's culture through small-team overseas travel experiences. Trips are designed to evaluate and develop leadership skills and potential, as well as the opportunity to practice and develop a leader's ability to live the Company values.

Leadership Model – Top People, Top Products, Top Vendors improves excellence and profitability.

Lewis Moment of Truth Award – Heroes are defined by Moments of Truth. Recipients of this award, given four times since 2000, have displayed extraordinary leadership and unrivalled commitment, helping GCC thrive during times of great crisis.

The List – The database we maintain that holds information about our most valuable travelers.

Load Factor – The positive affect that filling our coaches and hotel allotments has on our profitability.

Maverick – An independent individual who helps break our frame of thinking and challenges us to find new ways to achieve our goals.

Moment of Truth – That dramatic moment when an individual must either step up or get out of the way so someone else can take the lead.

Net Sales – Total sales dollars less cancellations.

OAT – Overseas Adventure Travel. A company owned by Grand Circle Corporation which packages, as you might imagine, adventurous travel overseas. Generally these programs appeal to a younger audience than GCT does.

Offsite – Any meeting or event that takes place somewhere other than our Boston or regional offices.

On or Off the Bus – A term used to determine whether an individual fully supports a strategic direction or decision that has been made.

On Your Toes – Being in control of your own destiny, being aggressive, and looking forward. "I'd rather go out on my toes than on my heels."

Overall Excellence – The score given to us by our passengers on their post-trip survey. The score reflects the quality of their whole experience from pre-departure to their return home.

P & C – People & Culture. The GCC department that preserves corporate culture as well as provides traditional Human Resource support to associates—hiring, training, benefits and compensation, etc.

Program Director – The GCT associate who leads programs for us on location. Called Trip Leader for OAT programs. For simplicity, we have used the term "trip leader" when both Trip Leaders and Program Directors are included in the discussion.

PTT – Product Training Trip. A training opportunity for associates that enables them to experience a trip, gain product knowledge, make recommendations for improvements, and interact with fellow associates and passengers.

Pax – An industry abbreviation for passengers. We view our passengers as travelers because that is the essence of their experience with us.

Pinnacle Leadership Center – The site in Kensington, New Hampshire, owned by the Lewis family where groups go to hold meetings and participate in training. Also the site of our annual BusinessWorks.

Pres & Posts – The Pre-Trip and Post-Trip Extensions offered on our vacations.

Prospect – A person likely to take one of our programs but who has not traveled with GCC in the past.

Ropes Course (High Y, Pamper Pole, Dangling Duo, Multi-Vine Traverse, High V, Spiders Web, Trust Fall, etc.) – Names of events that associates participate in during BusinessWorks offsite, most of which require participants to be up off the ground. These are intended to help Associates better understand and appreciate risk taking and teamwork.

S.A.R.A. – An acronym that expresses the stages of dealing with change: Shock, Anger, Rejection, and Acceptance.

Sabbatical – A benefit that enables an associate to earn a 4-week sabbatical after 5 years of employment, and an 8-week sabbatical after 10 years of employment.

Sir Edmund Hillary (SEH) Team Member – A passenger who has completed at least three OAT trips in a lifetime.

TPP – Our Travel Protection Plan. By purchasing TPP, a traveler can cancel a vacation at any time—up to the day of departure and for any reason—and retain the full value of the trip, including deposit. TPP includes many other benefits, too.

Takeaways – Also known as "Learnings." Something learned from an experience, a conclusion or lesson that can to be taken away and subsequently used to best advantage.

Teamwork Award – Given quarterly, the Teamwork Award is presented by the management team in recognition of high-performing associates who exemplify our most important values in working together toward shared goals.

Ted Nathan Memorial Award – Established in July 1993 and given in memory of Ted Nathan, this award honors associates for their courage, conviction, and commitment to high ideals, exemplifying GCC's values in the pursuit of excellence. Ted Nathan was a Program Director from 1983-93, who brilliantly illuminated the travel experience for our passengers worldwide.

347 – What we call our Boston headquarters. It's our address on Congress Street.

Top People, Top Product, Top Vendor – GCC's leadership model. Focus on the big stuff.

Transformation Team – A group of associates carefully chosen for their specific skills and leadership abilities who join together to fix what's broken.

Trip Leader – The OAT associate who leads programs for us on location. For simplicity, we have used the term "trip leader" when both Trip Leaders and Program Directors are included in the discussion.

UFEs – Also known as "Unforgettable Experiences." A term coined to convey the idea that certain events in GCT programs should be truly unforgettable for our travelers, and that we should design and operate trips to encourage these experiences.

Ugly Straw Dog – Also known as an "Ugly Straw Puppy." A very rough draft of a plan to be presented for critical analysis before it is finalized and implemented.

VA – Vacation Ambassadors. Travelers who refer new travelers to our company through our Vacation Ambassador Referral Program.

Values – Grand Circle has six core values: Open and Courageous Communication, Risk Taking, Teamwork, Thriving in Change, Speed, and Quality. All associates must embody these core values and demonstrate them at all times.

World Classroom – Begun in 2005, the *World Classroom* initiative is a Grand Circle Foundation program devoted to helping local schools in the villages and towns our travelers visit on Grand Circle and OAT trips. *World Classroom* fosters the education of young people, but it also goes beyond the classrooms by strengthening the surrounding community and preserving indigenous arts and traditions. The Foundation's contributions help pay for new construction, renovation, equipment, and more.

How to Contact Us

Grand Circle Travel

347 Congress Street
Boston, MA 02210

Sales: 800-221-2610
Service: 800-321-2835
General: 617-350-7500
www.gct.com

Overseas Adventure Travel

One Mifflin Place, Suite 400
Cambridge, MA 02138

Sales: 800-955-1925
Service: 800-221-0814
General: 617-350-7500
www.oattravel.com

Overseas Adventure Travel

Grand Circle Foundation

347 Congress Street
Boston, MA 02210

800-859-0852
E-mail: foundation@oattravel.com
www.grandcirclefoundation.org

Grand Circle Leadership

Pinnacle Leadership Center
199 South Road
Kensington, NH 03833

617-790-3911
E-mail: grandcircleleadership@gct.com
www.grandcircleleadership.com